TALKS ON THE PATH OF OCCULTISM

TALKS ON THE PATH OF OCCULTISM

The Voice of the Silence

BY
ANNIE BESANT

GYAN

ISBN: 978-81-212-1912-9 Set (HB)
ISBN: 978-81-212-1936-5 Vol.1 (HB)
First Published, 1930
Published, 2018
Published by

Gyan Publishing House
5, Ansari Road
Daryaganj, New Delhi-110002
Phone: 011-47034999, 9811692060
www.gyanbooks.com
E-mail: books@gyanbooks.com

Printed at: G. Print Process, Delhi.

FOREWORD

THIS book is merely a record of talks by Mr. C. W. Leadbeater—now Bishop Leadbeater—and myself on three famous books—books small in size but great in contents. We both hope that they will prove useful to aspirants, and even to those above that stage, since the talkers were older than the listeners, and had more experience in the life of discipleship.

The talks were not given at one place only; we chatted to our friends at different times and places, chiefly at Adyar, London and Sydney. A vast quantity of notes were taken by the listeners. All that were available of these were collected and arranged. They were then condensed, and repetitions were eliminated.

Unhappily there were found to be very few notes on *The Voice of the Silence,* Fragment I, so we have utilized notes made at a class held by our good colleague, Mr. Ernest Wood, in Sydney, and incorporated these into Bishop Leadbeater's talks in that section. No notes of my own talks on this book were available; though I have spoken much upon it, those talks are not recoverable.

None of these talks have been published before, except some of Bishop Leadbeater's addresses to selected students on *At the Feet of the Master.* A book entitled *Talks on "At the Feet of the Master"* was published a few years ago, containing imperfect reports of some of these talks of his. That book will not be reprinted; the essential material in it finds its place here, carefully condensed and edited.

May this book help some of our younger brothers to understand more of these priceless teachings. The more they are studied *and lived*, the more will be found in them.

ANNIE BESANT

CONTENTS

CHAP.

PART 1

INTRODUCTORY

CHAPTER 1

THE OCCULT PATH AND THE INTERESTS OF THE WORLD

C.W.L.—*At the Feet of the Master* is one of three books—the other two being *The Voice of the Silence* and *Light on the Path*—especially intended to help people to set their feet upon the Path. It is most valuable for us, at the moment, because of its extreme simplicity, and because it bears especially the stamp and approval of the World-Teacher, who is so soon to come. It consists of teaching given by his Master to the young disciple J. Krishnamurti (called Alcyone in the series of his past lives recently published)[1] in the year 1909, when he was a boy of thirteen. His knowledge of English was not then perfect, and since the instruction was given in that tongue, both the teaching and the language had to be made especially clear. The Master Kūthūmi, with His marvellous power of adaptability, therefore put all that was necessary for the attaiment of the First Initiation into that wonderfully simple style which is one of the great recommendations of this little book.

The Light on the Path appeared in 1885, and *The Voice of the Silence* in 1889. Each of these books of

[1] *The Lives of Alcyone*, T. P. H., Adyar, 1924.

ethics has its own characteristics. Both the older ones are more poetical than *At the Feet of the Master*, although in it also there are some very beautiful expressions; it could not be otherwise, since it comes from the Master Kūthūmi. *Light on the Path*, we were told by Swami T. Subba Row, has several depths of meaning, one behind another, the most profound relating to the Initiation at the Mahāchohan level, a stage beyond where even our Masters now stand. *The Voice of the Silence* carries us as far as the Arhat Initiation. *At the Feet of the Master* applies especially to the First Initiation, so we will comment upon it first.

We have all heard often about the qualifications for the Path, but we shall continue to hear of them until we have succeeded in putting into practice everything that is written in such books as this. There is no difficulty in knowing exactly what ought to be done, and there is no obstacle in our path which is not of our own making, yet comparatively few people succeed in following these directions, because they have personalities which often get in the way. What is written in these books must be definitely applied by each person to himself. The teacher can explain and illustrate what ought to be done in various ways, but every one must tread the Path for himself. It is like training for a race or taking up physical culture: there may be a trainer who can give careful directions, but the candidate must exercise his own muscles; *nobody else can by any possibility do that for him.*

Millions of people around us are supposed to be living according to the precepts of their respective religions, but very few actually do so. Even those who live good and holy lives do not usually strictly follow all the precepts laid down for them. In some cases the teachings of exoteric religions are unessential or inappropriate, but in occultism no unnecessary precept is given; an exact adherence to all of them is required. This does not mean that we must have all of these qualifications in absolute perfection before we can be received by a Master—that would be the attainment of Adeptship; but they must be possessed to a reasonable extent, and they must be real, not merely polite fictions. When a professor of chemistry tells us that if we compound certain chemicals in a specified way we shall obtain certain results, we know that those results will follow, and that if the proportions are altered we shall not get what we expect, but something else. In religious matters people seem to think that a sort of vague approximation to the instructions given is quite sufficient, but in occultism that will not do at all; it must be taken as a science; and although we have heard so often about these qualifications, it is to be hoped that by going through them carefully and endeavouring to understand and follow with scientific precision exactly what is required, many who have not yet succeeded may be able to set their feet upon the Path.

These inner things are not far away and uncertain. Up to a few years ago they seemed more remote, because so few whom we knew had come into direct touch with the Masters, and a student might have thought to himself: "Yes, two or three men specially gifted, or in some way specially fortunate, have succeeded, but it does not seem to be for ordinary people." But now that a number have come into direct touch with Them, one may reasonably say to himself: "If these others have reached this, why not I?" The cause for non-success *must* be in ourselves, not in anything outside. It is certainly not the fault of the Masters, who are always there when the pupil is ready. In some there is one defect that bars; in others it may be only a general lack of development; but if there were not some deficiency we should all have succeeded. It is worth while to make a definite effort to find out what is the matter—what is lacking—and to remedy the defect.

There is a real inner world which surpasses in importance all this outer world, which is so incessant in its pressure upon us. Everywhere there are people who think themselves so busy and so wise in following their respective lines, and yet the truth is that all of them are working in the unreal and the outer, and few have realized that there is an inner and spiritual world which is of enormously more importance in every way than that which is external.

On the Path we have to play our parts in the world, but we do so only because of the true life inside. An actor plays on a stage because he has another life to live —a life which is consecutive and coherent. He may take various parts at different times, just as we come back in other incarnations and wear other kinds of bodies; but all the time the actor has his real life as a man and as an artist as well, and because there is that real life he wants to play his part well in the temporary life of the stage. Similarly, we wish to do well in our temporary physical life here, because of the great reality behind, of which it is but a very small part. If that is clear we shall see what is the relative importance of this outer life; that its only value to us is that we shall play our part well, whatever that part may be; what kind of part it is, and what happens to us in this mimic existence—these things matter little. It may be an actor's business to go through all sorts of pretended sorrows and difficulties; but these do not trouble him in the least. He may have, for example, to be killed every night in a duel; what does the feigned death matter to him? The only thing that concerns him is that he should acquit himself well.

It should not be hard to realize that the world about us is a mimic world, and that it really does not matter what experiences may come to us. All the things that happen to people from the outside are the result of their karma. The causes were set going long ago in other lives, and cannot now be altered. Therefore it is useless to worry about the things that happen. They come as the result of the past, and should be borne philosophically. Many people bear them foolishly and allow them to cause a vast amount of pain, suffering and worry. The right attitude is always to try to learn the lesson that they bring, and then to put them out of the mind as far as possible—like the bee and the flower, as our Indian brothers say. The way in which these things are borne moulds our character for the future, which is the only *important thing. One should use karma to develop* courage, endurance and various other good qualities, and then dismiss it from the mind.

This outlook is hard to reach because we are surrounded by thousands of people who are all taking the play as serious—as the only real life. What they say and do to us hinders to some extent, but a far greater obstacle in our way (though we never think of it) is the immense and incessant pressure of public opinion. That is simply stupendous, for there are many thousands who are ignorant to each one who knows the truth. They are thinking: "We must make haste to gain possessions and riches; what other people think of us is everything in life."

A great deal of thought is also poured out by those who want to gain positions and honours, to obtain invitations to certain dinners and balls, to get a duke or an earl on their visiting list, and so on. In religious matters too, there is a vast sea of delusion beating around us, for there are few who are liberal and millions who are not. Social delusions also abound, as for instance the prudery of England, where it is considered improper ever to speak of the sex side of things, so that for want of some small fragments of simple knowledge the young grow up in peril and sometimes fall into unexpected disaster, for there is a river of vice always running, into which it is easy for the ignorant to fall. People look upon the manners of the classical times of Greece and Rome as in many ways indecent, but from memory of those times I am bound to say that they were far less impure in thought than Europe is to-day.

We who understand more of the inner side of things have to stand against these really tremendous odds, and say to ourselves: "No, this is not so, all this is unreal, and we pray to be led from the unreal to the real." The real is the underlying life, the life which persists, the life which, as the Scripture puts it, is "hid with Christ in God". To live in that realization all the time and to regard the outer as not of essential importance is not easy, but that is exactly what has to be done. One of our Masters has said: "He who wishes to follow us must come out of your world into ours." This does not mean that one must give up one's daily life and live as a hermit—it implies that even more than before we perform heartily all the duties that are ours in this strange play of life—but it does mean that the aspirant must abandon his ordinary attitude and adopt that of the Masters.

Those who succeed in these efforts will some day find themselves accepted pupils of one or other of the Masters. When the man's thought becomes part of that of his Teacher the pupil can test his own thought by that of the Master, which is never affected by the crowd, and can see exactly what He thinks on any subject. Then he will soon get into the way of that and will understand His point of view; though at first he will be constantly meeting with unexpected shocks. Things that seemed of vast importance before do not now matter at all, and other things which he had passed by as comparatively unimportant, stand out as of great significance, because in some way, great or small, they affect our usefulness, and whatever affects our usefulness is important, because there we touch upon the real thing.

The pressure that comes upon the mind from all around in the mental and astral planes is not from on high at all. The ears must be closed to that, and open only to the sound from above, to the voice and thought of the Master. It is little wonder that in older days in India and other countries, whenever men set themselves to live the spiritual life, the first thing they did was to get out of ordinary life and go away and camp in a cave or jungle by themselves. They gained the advantage of escape from this pressure of ignorant opinion, and were freer then to follow their own way. Many of the Christian Saints also retired from the active world and became hermits and monks or associated themselves with people who were thinking on the same lines.

This advantage of retirement is still further increased for those who have the privilege of being in the aura of the Master or of one of His more advanced pupils. The vibrations of that aura are constantly acting upon the bodies of the pupil, tuning them up, shaking out unsuitable grades of matter and feeding them with what is required. The pupil should be always trying to develop some virtue—let us say love, for example. If left to himself he does so intermittently, for he constantly forgets about it; but the aura of his superior holds him to the higher standard of thought and feeling that he wants to establish permanently in himself. The effect is not unlike that aimed at in the treatment of the malformed limb of a child, when it is put into splints until it grows into proper shape. While in the aura of the Master the pupil feels that he could not think a wrong thought, even if he wanted to, which then seems to him impossible. In that position, we look smilingly down at our thoughts of yesterday, and say: "I never can have that feeling again; it has vanished like a dream." But to-morrow, when we are away from the Master, we may find ourselves struggling hard to maintain the higher attitude, which we thought so easy when in His presence.

At the present time those who are reaching towards the Path must try to achieve the same condition while they remain in active life, because it is intended that they shall help the world, not by meditation and thought alone—as no doubt the hermit and the monk did—but by mingling in its various activities. It is a very beautiful idea and a great privilege, but it is hard, very hard, to do.

The result of that difficulty has been that few have really achieved. Most have been content to take the Theosophical teaching much as the average Christian takes his religion: regarding it as very nice to talk about on Sunday, but not at all the thing to carry out every day and all day long. The earnest student of the inner life cannot be thus unreal; he must be consistent and practical, and must apply his ideals constantly to everyday life. To attain this constancy is difficult. It is not that people are unwilling to make some great effort for the Theosophical idea. If they could help a Master, could do some piece of work directly for Him, they would do it, though it cost them life itself. Remember what S. Augustine said: "Many there are who will die for Christ, but few there are who will live for Him." To become a martyr sounds magnificent, heroic; it is a great deed. But the martyr who does it has the feeling that he is making a mighty effort, and the consciousness of that bears him up and supports him through pain and suffering. He is keyed up for the moment to this great act of heroism. What has to be done now is much harder than that. It is not possible to keep oneself always strung to that pitch of heroism, amid the little daily troubles that are perpetually coming up. It is very difficult to keep the same equanimity of mind when dealing day after day with the same wearisome people, who will not do the things one thinks they should do. Living for Christ in all the small things—that is hard to do; and it is just because these things seem comparatively small that there is so much difficulty in following the Path.

Let us take these three books, let us follow their instructions, and see how far it is possible to apply them. Others have done it, and have succeeded in reaching the Path; why should not we? Success means the conquest of the self; it means that we take ourselves in hand and face the facts and, where there are weeds, pull them up. It does not matter how deeply they are rooted, or how much suffering it entails; up with them! Hard work, indeed; but those who have already entered on some of the higher stages tell us that it is very well worth while, infinitely worth while, to make any effort, great or small, whether it be once for all or many times.

CHAPTER 2

INITIATION AND THE APPROACH THERETO

C.W.L.—The name of this book was chosen by our President, out of thirty or forty which were suggested, and she is also responsible for the dedication

To Those Who Knock

the symbolism of which is obvious: "Knock and it shall be opened unto you; seek and ye shall find." In her preface Dr. Besant says:

> The privilege is given to me, as an elder, to pen a word of introduction to this little book, the first written by a younger Brother; young in body verily, but not in Soul.

Here is a point of great importance. In ordinary life, thinking only of this world and this one incarnation, we judge a person's age by the physical body; but in occult progress we consider the age of the ego, of the soul within. One must beware of judging by externals only, though almost everyone in the world does it. The soul grows steadily, and when it is highly developed it often begins to exhibit signs of its advancement in intelligence, emotion and occult power, even while the physical body is still young. Alcyone certainly showed this to be so in his case by the extreme rapidity of his progress. He responded to the teaching so fully that he was able to attain in a few months what would usually take many years, because for most it would mean a fundamental change in character.

Cases of this kind will be increasingly numerous in these days, because of the near approach of the World-Teacher. His principal disciples must be people in the prime of life and strength, most of them probably not much older than Himself in the physical body, and since He is to come soon those who are to be in that position then must be young now. It is exceedingly probable that some of those who are children now among us may in the future be prominent in the work, for it is likely that many of those who are destined for such good fortune will be born where they can have the teaching that will fit them for it, that is, in Theosophical families.

We should, therefore, watch for such possibilities, and see that any children that come in our way are told about the advent of the World-Teacher, so that they may know the possibility which is open to them. It must be left to them *to grasp the opportunity, but at least it* should be given. It would be very sad if any parent should hear from his son or daughter the reproach: "If you had told me about these things when I was young, I might have taken the opportunity, but you let me grow up without knowing anything about them; you let me grow into the worldly life, and therefore, when the opportunity offered, I did not take it." We must give the opportunity, but when we have done that, our duty is over, because it is not for us to try to force anyone into any line, or even to map out a future and expect these other and possibly greater souls to adhere to it.

The teachings contained in it were given to him by his Master in preparing him for Initiation.

The word Initiation has often been used in a very general way; but here it has a definite technical significance. Madame Blavatsky herself in the earlier days employed it somewhat loosely, but as our terminology has become more settled, the meaning of the word ought to be confined to the great Initiations, the five steps on the Path Proper, to use the old term. In the older writings we spoke of the Probationary Path, the Path Proper, and the Official Period as three stages in the advanced development of man. The Probationary Path means the period of probation for Initiation, the Path Proper is the Path of Holiness which begins with the first of the great Initiations (that in which a man "enters upon the stream") and ends with the attainment of Adeptship. Forty years ago we used to talk about "initiation into the Theosophical Society," and the word is used in connection with Masonic and other ceremonies; we must take care not to confuse those ideas with the great Initiations of the occult Path.

The period of probation for Initiation was in the early days spoken of as being divided into stages, which correspond to the four qualifications which are given in this book: discrimination, desirelessness, good conduct and love.

It is not correct to call these stages, or to speak of initiations between them. These qualifications are not at all necessarily taken up in the order given. They are written down in that order in the old Oriental books, but we are probably engaged in acquiring all of them simultaneously. We do what we can with all of them, and to some of us one qualification may be much easier than the others.

Discrimination has its position as the first qualification, because it enables a man to decide to enter upon the Path at all. The Buddhist name for it is *manodvāra-vajjana,* "the opening of the doors of the mind," which means that the man's mind is open for the first time to see that the spiritual things are the only real things, and that the ordinary worldly life is a waste of time. The Hindus name it *viveka,* which means discrimination. The Christian calls this realization 'conversion,' which is also a very expressive word, because conversion means turning and coming together with; it is derived from the supine of *verto,* to turn, and *con,* together with.

It means that the man having previously gone his own way, having thought nothing about the Divine Will, has now realized the direction in which that Divine Will wishes the evolutionary current to flow, and has turned himself into line with it. With many Christian sects it has degenerated to mean a sort of spasmodic, hysterical condition, but even that contains the idea of turning about and going along with the Divine Will. It is very much what was expressed by the apostle when he said, "Set your affection on things above, and not on things of the earth."

As there are steps on the Path, so there are other definite steps which mark the degrees of the pupil's personal relationship to the Master who prepares him for the Initiations. Initiations are given by the Great White Brotherhood, in the name of the One Initiator who is its Head—and by His order alone. But the pupil's relationship with his Master is his own affair. One may be, first, a probationer, or, secondly, an accepted pupil; or, thirdly, what is called a son of the Master; these are private relationships and must not be confused with the Initiations which are given by the Great Hierarchy itself.

The First Initiation is that step which makes a man a member of the Great White Brotherhood. Before that he is not really on the Path at all, but is training himself in preparation for it. It is not conferred arbitrarily, but in recognition of his attainment of a certain stage of evolution—what used to be called the union of the higher and lower self, the joining of the ego and the personality. A man who wishes to put himself forward as a candidate for the First Great Initiation must acquire the qualifications described in this book, and make his personality an expression of the ego; there must be no lower personality left to thrust itself forward, and to have desires of its own in opposition to those of the reincarnating self.

The change that then takes place is shown in the illustrations given in *Man Visible and Invisible.* The astral body of the savage is full of colours which indicate all sorts of lower passions, and is irregular in outline, because the man has no control over it; and the causal and mental bodies show no relation to one another. The causal is apparently blank; the mental has a little development, but it has not much connection with the astral body. In the astral body of the savage there are all sorts of emotions and passions that have nothing to do with the mind. He does not think about them; he does not know how to think; they are simply there, and they run away with him.

In the advanced man, however, all those vehicles are closely linked. The causal body is full instead of being empty; all the different colours expressive of the higher virtues are developed in it, and it is already beginning to pour itself out in various directions for the helping of others. The mental body contains the same colours, somewhat denser, but still the finest of their kind, and they represent the causal body on the lower level. The astral body is in turn a mirror of the mental—there are the same colours, only just a little darker and denser, because a plane lower.

The self in the savage expresses itself in all kinds of different emotions and passions of which the ego could not possibly approve, but in the developed man there are no emotions but such as he chooses to have. Instead of being swayed by his emotions and carried off his feet, he simply selects them. He says: "Love is a good thing, I will allow myself to feel love; devotion is a good thing, I will allow myself to feel devotion; sympathy—that is beautiful, I will allow myself to feel sympathy." And he does this with his eyes open, intentionally. The emotions are thus under the dominion of the mind, and that mind is an expression of the causal body, so we are coming very near to the condition of complete unity of the higher and lower self.

It should not be imagined that there are two entities in man. There never is any lower self as a separate being, but the ego puts down a tiny fragment of himself into the personality in order to experience the vibrations of the lower planes. The personality then becomes much more vividly alive than the ego, because it is at a stage where it can respond to those vibrations; consequently it forgets that it belongs to the ego, and sets up in the business of life on its own account, and tries to go as it would rather than as the ego would. In the course of many incarnations, however, the ego grows strong, and then the man can recognize that the personality is nothing but an expression of himself, the reincarnating ego, and that whenever it tries to be master instead of servant it is going wrong and needs to be controlled. It is our business so to order the personality that it shall express the ego, and nothing else. That is what Mr. Sinnett called giving allegiance to the higher self. In *The Voice of the Silence* we are told that the disciple should slay the lunar form. This refers to the astral body. It does not mean that you should commit an astral murder; it means that your astral body should have no existence but as an expression of the higher, that instead of having its own passions and emotions it shall reflect only what the ego chooses.

This condition must be attained before one can be presented for the First Initiation. The man must have control of his physical, astral and mental bodies. All these must be servants of the ego. To gain that mastery would mean a very great deal of work for the ordinary person, and many people would say: "I cannot do that; it is no use talking about it." It is altogether too high an ideal to set before them all at once, but it ought not to be so serious a demand to make upon those who have been meditating and thinking on these matters for many years. Truly it is not easy to tread down one by one all sort of passions and desires, to curb the astral and mental bodies; these things are hard, but they are splendidly well worth doing, and the result attained thereby is quite out of all proportion to even the great efforts required. The thought of making ourselves capable of greater usefulness to the World-Teacher is an additional incentive and encouragement in this arduous undertaking. Those who take these Initiations do not do it for themselves, in order to escape from the sorrow and the suffering of the world, but that they may be of use in the mighty plan.

There are certain definite changes which outweigh all others in a man's existence. The first of these is when he individualizes and enters the human kingdom—when he comes forth from the animal stage and begins his career as an ego. His attainment of Adeptship at the Fifth Initiation is another; it marks his departure from the human kingdom, because then he enters a superhuman state. That is the goal which is set before all humanity; it is the point which we are to endeavour to attain in this chain of worlds. At the end of this period the man who has done what God has willed for mankind, who has carried out to the utmost the divine design for himself, will thus pass out of the human kingdom; and many of us may do it long before the end.

In between these two comes another point of quite as great importance, the definite "entry on the stream" at the first great Initiation. The words used in admitting the candidate to the Brotherhood include this statement: "You are now safe for ever; you have entered upon the stream; may you soon reach the further shore." The Christian calls him the man who is 'saved' or 'safe.' That means that he is quite sure to go on in this present stream of evolution, that he is certain not to drop out at the day of judgment in the next round, like a child in school who is too backward to go on with the rest of his class.

The Initiate has to pass the Second, Third and Fourth Initiations before he reaches Adeptship, which is the Fifth, but when he gains that stage he unites the monad and the ego just as before he had united the ego and the personality. When the man has achieved the union of the higher and the lower self, his personality no longer exists except as an expression of the ego; he has now to begin that process over again, as it were, and make that ego an expression of the monad. Whether beyond that there lies another stage of the same kind we do not know, but it is at least certain that when we attain Adeptship we shall find opening before us a still more glorious vista of progress.

People often ask what will be the end of this evolution which we see outstretched before us. I personally do not know whether there is any end or not. A great philosopher once said, "It is equally inconceivable that there should be an end or that there should be no end; yet one of those two must be true." Some speak of absorption into the Supreme; but of that we know nothing. We know that our consciousness continues to widen; that before it lies grade after grade above and beyond our own. We know that it is possible to touch the buddhic level, and thus attain an enormous expansion of consciousness, so that besides being oneself one is also other and greater people.

In this we do not feel that we have lost individuality at all, but that we have so widened it that we are able to feel through others as well as through ourselves. All who can do this in meditation should continue the practice, and expand until more and more is included in the consciousness—not only those far above, but those below as well, although those above come first because they are so much stronger, so much more tremendous in their power. Such expansion takes place gradually and one wins one's way through subplane after subplane of buddhic consciousness, until presently he learns to develop a buddhic vehicle—a body which he can use at that stupendous height where all the spheres seem as one, and he can traverse space without actually passing through it in our sense of the word at all.

Now, since that is in the experience of a number of us, we are justified in assuming that the further extensions of that consciousness will be somewhat of the same kind. We have attained that unity without losing our sense of individuality in the very least, without feeling ourselves merged in a shining sea, as the poet puts it, but feeling instead that the shining sea has been poured into the drop.

Paradoxical as it may sound, that is the sensation; the consciousness of the drop widens into the consciousness of the sea. That being so, so far as we know it, we are surely justified in assuming that there will not be any sudden change in the method. We cannot conceive of being merged into something else and losing that consciousness which we have taken so long to develop. I believe it will widen so that we may become one with God, but only in the sense in which Christ put it when He said: "Ye are gods; ye are all the children of the Most High."

We can look far back in evolution and can also see far forward. We can be sure of a future extending over millions of years of useful activity, on splendid levels whose glory and power and love and development are inconceivable down here; but what lies beyond that we do not know. If we consider the matter from a common-sense point of view, we can hardly expect to know. If the final end of it were something that we could now understand, it would be a very poor kind of ending, altogether out of proportion to all the stages which lead up to it.

Our intellect is a narrow thing—how limited no man realizes until he comes into touch with its higher developments, when he begins to see that the intellect about which we have boasted so much is in reality a poor affair, a beginning only, a seed of a future tree. In comparison to that of the future, men have now only a child intellect, though it is that of a hopeful child, for it has done much already, and shows promise of more. But compared with the intellect of the Great Ones it is still that of a very little child. Therefore it cannot yet reach great heights and depths, and we cannot expect to understand either the beginning or the end. I, at least, am more than willing to admit quite frankly that I do not know what goal the Supreme has in His mind ; I do not know anything about the Supreme, except that He is.

The metaphysician and the philosopher speculate on these things, and gain from the effort considerable development of the mind and the causal body. Those who love such imaginations do no harm in indulging in them, but I think they should clearly understand that they are imaginations. The philosopher should not develop his theories into a system and expect us to accept it, for he is quite likely to be leaving out of account some of the most important factors. For myself, I do not speculate. I feel that the splendour and glory that unquestionably lie ahead of us are far more than sufficient to satisfy all our aspirations. "Eye hath not seen, nor ear heard, neither hath it entered into the heart of man to conceive the things which God hath prepared for them that love Him." That is true now, as it was two thousand years ago.

CHAPTER 3

HOW THE BOOK CAME TO BE WRITTEN

C.W.L.—Dr. Besant's Preface (which is dated December, 1910) then goes on to explain how Alcyone wrote the book.

> And were written down by him from memory—slowly and laboriously, for his English last year was far less fluent than it is now. The greater part is a reproduction of the Master's own words; that which is not such a verbal reproduction is the Master's thought clothed in His pupil's words. Two omitted sentences were supplied by the Master. In two other cases an omitted word has been added. Beyond this, it is entirely Alcyone's own, his first gift to the world.

The following is my own account of what happened, as given in *The Masters and the Path*:

> The story of how this little book came to be written is comparatively simple. Every night I had to take this boy in his astral body to the house of the Master, that instruction might be given him. The Master devoted perhaps fifteen minutes each night to talking to him, but at the end of each talk He always gathered up the main points of what He had said into a single sentence, or a few sentences, thus making an easy little summary which was repeated to the boy, so that he learnt it by heart. He remembered that summary in the morning and wrote it down.

The book consists of these sentences, of the epitome of the Master's teaching, made by Himself, and in His words. The boy wrote them down somewhat laboriously, because his English was not then very good. He knew all these things by heart and did not trouble particularly about the notes that he had made. A little later he went up to Benares with our President. While there he wrote to me, I being down at Adyar, and asked me to collect and send to him all the notes that he had made of what the Master had said. I arranged his notes as well as I could, and typed them all out.

Then it seemed to me that as these were mainly the Master's words I had better make sure that there was no mistake in recording them. Therefore I took the type-written copy which I had made to the Master Kūthūmi and asked Him to be so kind as to read it over. He read it, altered a word or two here and there, added some connecting and explanatory notes and a few other sentences which I remembered having heard Him speak to Mr. Krishnamurti. Then He said "Yes, that seems correct; that will do"; but He added, "Let us show it to the Lord Maitreya." And so we went together, He taking the manuscript, and it was shown to the World-Teacher Himself, who read it and approved. It was He who said: "You should make a nice little book of this to introduce Alcyone to the world." We had not meant to introduce him to the world; we had not considered it desirable that a mass of thought should be concentrated on a boy of thirteen, who still had his education before him. But in the occult world we do what we are told, and so this book was put into the printer's hands as soon as possible.

All the inconveniences which we expected from premature publicity came about; but still the Lord Maitreya was right and we were wrong; for the good that has been done by that book far outweighs the trouble it brought to us. Numbers of people, literally thousands, have written to say how their whole lives have been changed by it, how everything has become different to them because they have read it. It has been translated into twenty-seven languages. There have been some forty editions of it, or more, and over a hundred thousand copies have been printed. Even now an edtition of a million copies is being prepared in America. A wonderful work has been done by it. Above all, it bears that special imprimatur of the coming World-Teacher, and that is the thing that makes it most valuable—the fact that it shows us, to a certain extent, what His teaching is to be.[1]

[1] *Op. cit.*, pp. 76-78. Second Edition, 1927.

CHAPTER 4

THE PRELIMINARY PRAYER

C.W.L.—Dr. Besant concludes with a good wish for all of us:

> **May it help others as the spoken teaching helped him—such is the hope with which he gives it. But the teaching can only be fruitful if it is *lived*, as he has lived it since it fell from his Master's lips. If the example be followed as well as the precept, then for the reader, as for the writer, shall the great Portal swing open, and his feet be set on the Path.**

In reviewing this book, Dr. Besant said: "Very rarely are such words as these given to men; teaching so direct, so philosophical, and so beautifully put." Therefore assuredly every word of it is worth our most careful consideration.

At the beginning of the book, before we enter even upon the Foreword of Alcyone, is set the old prayer, translated from the Sanskrit:

> **From the unreal lead me to the Real.**
> **From darkness lead me to Light.**
> **From death lead me to Immortality.**

The use of the word 'real' in this case may sometimes prove a little misleading. When we say 'real' and 'unreal,' the idea conveyed to our minds is that one thing has a definite existence and the other has not. The unreal is to us purely imaginary. But that is not quite what the Hindu understands by this sentence. Perhaps we should come a little nearer to his meaning if we said, "From the impermanent lead me to the permanent."

The statement that the lower planes, physical, astral and mental, are unreal, often leads to serious misunderstanding. They are not unreal at their own level, and while they last. Physical objects seem perfectly real while we are on the physical plane, but when the body falls asleep and we use our astral consciousness instead of the physical, those objects are no longer visible to us because we have passed into a higher plane. Therefore people sometimes say they are unreal. But there is just as much reason to say that the astral plane is unreal because we do not see its objects when on the physical plane. Both physical and astral objects are there all the time; they remain visible to those whose consciousness is on the respective planes.

So far as we know all manifestation is impermanent; only the Unmanifested is absolutely and always the same. All manifestation, even that of the highest planes, will one day pass again into the changeless, so the difference between what we commonly call the impermanent and those higher planes is only a matter of time, which in comparison to eternity can be as nothing. The physical plane, then, is just as real as the nirvānic, and just as truly an expression of the Deity, and so we must not form the idea that one of these things is real and the other mere dream or phantasmagoria.

Another very commonly held theory is that matter is evil; but that is not so at all. Matter is an expression of the Divine just as much as spirit; both are one in Him—two sides of Him. Matter often operates to hinder us in our progress, but only when it is so used as to delay us on our way; as well might a man who happens to cut himself with a knife say that knives are evil things. Considering the flexibility of the Sanskrit words we might equally translate the first line as "From the false lead me to the true". 'True,' 'permanent' 'real'—these words seem all of them to be included in the meaning; so what we are asking is rather that from the outer, where the illusion is greater, we may be led to the inner, which is nearer to the absolute truth.

The second petition is, "From darkness lead me to Light,"—that is, of course, from the darkness of ignorance to the light of knowledge. The prayer is addressed to the Master; we ask Him to enlighten us by His wisdom. There is also a secondary meaning attached to that in India, for in these words one is also supposed to be asking Him to lead one to the knowledge of the higher planes, and there comes in a rather beautiful thought which will be found in some of those old books, that the light of the lower plane is the darkness of the plane above it That is wonderfully true. What is thought of here as light is dim and murky, compared to the light of the astral world, and that in turn is poor in comparison with that of the mental. It is very difficult to put these distinctions into words, because each time you rise one plane in your consciousness you get the impression of something quite stupendously greater than you have ever known before—greater power, greater light, greater bliss.

When a man makes a definite advance in consciousness, he thinks: "Now for the first time I know what life really means, what bliss is, and how splendid all these things are." So each plane is quite out of all proportion superior to the one below it, so that, for instance, to return even from the astral, the very next plane, into the physical is like coming out of the sunlight into a dark dungeon. When a man can function consciously on the mental he finds an expansion in many directions absolutely beyond that which he knows on the astral. When he can touch the buddhic consciousness, for the first time he feels a very little of how God sees things. One is then coming into touch with Divinity, and beginning to know how He who is in all, feels through all. It is said that "In Him we live and move and have our being," and that "Of Him and through Him and to Him are all things";[1] and all that is not merely a beautiful and poetic expression, but represents an actual fact. There is a glorious unity—not brotherhood alone, but actual unity—and when the lowest fringe of that can be touched one begins for the first time very dimly to understand how God feels when He looks on His

[1] Rom., XI, 36.

universe and says: "It is good." And so from the darkness of the lower planes we ask to be led to the light of the higher consciousness—and it *is* light as compared with darknesss. No phraseology could be more apt; no expression could give more exactly what one feels.

Then we say: "From death lead me to Immortality." That does not mean what at first sight the ordinary religious person would take it to mean, because the Theosophist's attitude towards death should be very different from that of the man who has not studied these things—quite the reverse, in fact. Death is not a horror, not a king of terrors, but rather an angel bearing a golden key to open the door into a higher and fuller life. Of course we always regret those who pass away; but the regret is for "the touch of the vanished hand and the sound of the voice that is still". And when we ask to be led from death to immortality we do not at all mean what a Christian would have in mind: that he should live for all eternity in his present personality in some form or other. We have, however, a very definite wish to escape from death, and its inseparable companion, birth. What lies before men is the round which the Buddhist calls the *sansāra*, the wheel of life. The prayer here is: from this cycle of birth and death, lead us to immortality—to the life which lies above birth and death, which no longer needs to dip into the lower planes, because its human evolution is finished and it has gained all that matter had to teach it.

Although people never seem to see it that idea is prominent in the Christian scriptures also. Modern

Christianity suffers from certain obsessions—I do not think we can call them by any other name—and one of them is the terrible idea of an eternal hell. That belief has cast a cloud of misunderstanding over a number of other doctrines, too. The whole theory of salvation has come to mean salvation from this non-existent, eternal hell, whereas it does not mean that at all, and all the passages which are supposed to refer to that, which seem so incomprehensible, become clear and luminous when it is understood that it really is the birth of the Christ in the heart that saves the man.

The Christ often spoke to the people of the broad road which led to death or destruction, and the many who followed it. His disciples came to Him once and asked: "Lord, are there few that be saved?" Then He said: "Strait is the gate and narrow is the way which leadeth unto life, and few there be that find it." Men have actually taken those very beautiful and perfectly true words, and interpreted them to mean that the majority of mankind will be cast into eternal hell, that very few indeed will succeed in attaining heaven; but it is absolutely ridiculous to attribute that idea to the Christ. What He meant was perfectly clear. The disciples were asking how many people enter the path of Initiation, and He said, "Few," which is as true in our day as it was then. When He said: "Broad is the road that leadeth to death, and many there be that follow it," He referred to the road that leads to the cycle of death and birth. Of course, it is true that that road is broad and easy; there is no trouble at all about following that line of development, and those who so do will attain the goal easily enough, somewhere about the end of the seventh round.

But strait is the gate and narrow is the way that leads to Initiation, to the kingdom of heaven. When Christ speaks of the kingdom of heaven He never means the heaven-world, the state after death, devachan, but always the body of the saved, the company of the elect, that is to say, the Great Brotherhood. When He refers to the conditions of life between death and rebirth, we find a very different set of words. Remember the passage written by S. John: " And lo, a great multitude, which no man could number, of all nations and kindreds and peoples and tongues, stood before the Throne and before the Lamb, clothed with white robes, and palms in their hands." When they spoke of that condition they told of a vast multitude which no man could number, not of a few who found their way with difficulty.

CHAPTER 5

THE SPIRIT OF THE PUPIL

C.W.L.—We come now to the Foreword of Alcyone himself:

> These are not my words; they are the words of the Master Who taught me. Without Him I could have done nothing; but through His help I have set my feet upon the Path.

He plainly attributes all his progress to the influence and the help of his Master. We have much of the help that he then received, because we have the words of this book, which are the Master's words; but the enormous help of His presence and personal guidance is also ready and waiting for every one of us, too. That must sink into our minds as a reality; we may be confident of it as an absolutely certain fact. As Alcyone was helped, so will all be aided who choose to make themselves ready for it.

> You also desire to enter the same Path, so the words which He spoke to me will help you also, if you will obey them. It is not enough to say that they are true and beautiful; a man who

wishes to succeed must do exactly what is said. To look at food and say that it is good will not satisfy a starving man ; he must put forth his hand and eat. So to hear the Master's words is not enough ; you must do what He says, attending to every word, taking every hint.

It is not enough to *say* : "I will do all that is written in the book"; its teaching must be made to permeate every part of one's life. One must be on the watch for opportunities. There is a little bit of poetry at the end of the book which expresses this very well :

Waiting the word of the Master,
Watching the Hidden Light ;
Listening to catch His orders
In the very midst of the fight ;
Seeing His slightest signal
Across the heads of the throng ;
Hearing His faintest whisper
Above earth's loudest song.

In the midst of all the noise, the whirl and excitement of the fight of life, one must listen all the while if one aspires to become a pupil of the Master. One must be eagerly looking out for opportunities to put into practice any of the teachings. This is not, after all, really difficult, because it is largely a matter of habit. *Ce n'est que le premier pas qui coute.*[1] When one has taken that, and has set up the habit, it is just as easy to be watching keenly all the time for this, as it is for the

[1] It is only the first step that costs.

business man who is looking for opportunities to make money. It is right that the man should keep up such constant watchfulness, for while he is doing business it is his duty to do it well. But if he can be eager about the temporary things, surely we might well be equally earnest about these things of the higher life.

It is very important that those who wish to reach the feet of the Master should understand His attitude. It is the same as that which is induced by Theosophical study. But the attitude is really what the study aims at, for Theosophy is a life to be lived, not merely a system to be learned. We must try, therefore, to bring our views into harmony with His, yet without forcing them at all. It would not be the wisest thing for any of us to adopt a point of view merely because it is the Master's, without understanding how He arrived at it. We should be quite safe in adopting it because He knows so much more than we do, but He would not wish it. Our intellect must be convinced, not merely our feelings influenced, by His thought.

The great requirement is to have it certain in one's mind that these things are the more real and permanent and important. The average Christian certainly says that the unseen things are more important, that that which is seen is temporary; but he does not act at all as though he believed it. Why? Because he is not certain of it. He is quite sure on the physical plane that money would be a good thing, and that the more he can get of it the better it will be for him; but he is not equally convinced that the spiritual things are real.

They belong to the group of subjects which he labels 'religion,' and there is not, somehow, the certainty and the practicality and the matter-of-factness about those things to him that there is in the affairs of ordinary life. We who are trying to make progress along these lines must introduce just precisely that matter-of-factness, that absolute and definite certainty, into these realms of the unseen. Mr. Sinnett said in his first Theosophical book: "These things must be as real to you as Charing Cross"; that is true; they must be as familiar as the things we see every day.

They may become so for us through reasoning about them, or through intuition, or best of all through direct experience. When we have completely convinced ourselves intellectually that a thing must be so, it grows into a fact for us. That is probably one of the advantages which the older students have over the newer ones. However enthusiastic the new ones may be, the older ones have had time to live into this thing and to make it, bit by bit, grain by grain, so to speak, part of themselves. Knowledge grows from more to more, as the poet puts it. There are some who as soon as they hear of the higher facts, spring at once into the state of absolute certainty about them, by a happy intuition, which is really their good karma from past lives. But for most of us, whose karma has not been quite so good as that, the steady growth tells very much. Of course, a person *may* be a member of the Society for thirty years and know no more at the end of the time than at the beginning. That is sad, because it is a waste of opportunity. But for those who have constantly thought about Theosophy and lived it, there is a feeling of certainty which has gradually grown. The experiences of life and thought on these things have accumulated for us proof after proof, until we see that they must be so.

In many cases the Theosophical ideas have appeared intricate and difficult at first, but later on simple and easy. They have become part of yourself. A child copies out a page of writing, and is very proud of it if there are no mistakes, but later on he will do the same thing without thinking of it—it has become a power. So long as we are making efforts to understand we have not yet realized the value of Theosophical truths; later on they will be a power in our lives.

Easier and more rapid is the path of the man who gets some personal experience. Few of us are entirely without that, and even one little bit of direct knowledge of that sort shows us—not, perhaps, that all the rest is true, but —that the rest is eminently probable. 'We have seen for ourselves that a part of what we have learnt is so; we recognize that the rest is probably so, since the entire philosophy is coherent; and this probability is so strong that it becomes for us practically a certainty.

If a hint is not taken, if a word is missed, it is lost for ever; for He does not speak twice.

A.B.—Many people fail to understand that those who hear these things again and again are worse off, not better off, than the people in the outer world who have not heard this message, if they do not try to carry them out. I do not say, it will be noticed, if they do not carry them out, but if they do not *try* to carry them out. It is the strenuous endeavour that is necessary, and it is this that is too often forgotten amongst us. It is true that the Master does not speak twice; He makes a suggestion; if it is not used, He lets it go; He does not repeat what He has said. Only His disciples, meeting the conditions of the world, repeat again and again the things that they have to say, until they produce an impression. If you were accepted disciples, your Master would not tell you to do a thing if it were not possible. If you did not take a piece of advice which He offered, He would not give it you any more. This is not because He is unkind, but because He cannot afford to waste any time; He has far too much to do. All this teaching was given to Alcyone, because he worked hard all the time. It is only those who are strenuously in earnest who can thus come into touch with the Master. I know that it is just this strenuous, unremitting effort which many of you find so difficult, but it is that which is needed, and without it you cannot enter upon the Path.

C.W.L.—We who follow the Master, and try to do some of His work in the outer world, have to speak twice constantly; we have to say over and over again the various things which are committed to us, because people are heedless and inattentive; but when one comes into touch with the Master Himself, he is not expected to be heedless any more; then a single hint should be sufficient, and certainly if it is not taken it will not be repeated, not because the Master is a proud Teacher, but because the pupil is not ready.

The method used by the Masters in training Their pupils should be understood. It is very rarely indeed that They issue any direct order. When I myself was taken on probation many years ago, almost my first question was, "What can I do?" The Master said in reply: "That is for you to discover." Then He explained: "I know quite well that if I tell you to do anything, of course you will do it at once. But in that case you will have only the karma of prompt and instant obedience; I shall have the karma of the deed. I want *you* to have it; I want you, for yourself, to do good things and to make good karma. It must be you who originate the idea, not I." The Great Ones very rarely give direct commands: but often from something that a Master says, or even from the glance of His eye, one forms the opinion as to whether He approves or disapproves of a certain thing; and those who stand round Him, more especially in the case of the Master Kūthūmi, learn very readily to note these things; they are always on the watch for any sort of hint.

The Master Morya was a King in the earlier part of his present incarnation, and He speaks with the command of a King. He more often gives direct orders, and if He disapproves of something, He generally says so clearly. The Master Kūthūmi has hardly ever expressed disapproval. His pupils have learnt to interpret His look, for He rarely says any word of blame. So it comes that they watch very carefully for anything whatever in the nature of a hint. When it is given they endeavour to take it, because they know that if it is missed that particular hint will not be given again. Nothing could possibly follow in the nature of blame or loss from not taking it, except to the pupil, who would be less likely to receive a hint on another occasion.

In *The Masters and the Path* it has been explained that the different Masters train their pupils in different ways, according to the rays to which they belong and the lines of work which they are destined to pursue. On the line of the Manu and Master Morya are people of the *kshattriya* kind—men of the governing type, judges, lawyers, soldiers, statesmen. On the line of the Bodhisattva and the Master Kūthūmi are those of the Brāhmana type—teachers, preachers, reformers. In addition to these there are five other great rays, with their special characteristics. A Chohan, who has passed at least the Sixth Initiation, stands at the head of each type, while under Him there are several Masters. Thus, on the second ray, for example, a pupil need not necessarily belong to the Master Kūthūmi; he might be attached to the Master Djwāl Kūl.

CHAPTER 6

THE FOUR INTRODUCTORY PATHS

C.W.L.—They tell us in the Eastern books that there are four main roads by which men may be brought to the beginning of the Probationary Path. They say that the most frequent method of such turning is through the companionship of those already on the Path. That makes them see its glory and beauty, and the necessity for following it. The influence of an advanced disciple is not limited to the words he speaks; it is the vibration of the life radiating from such a person that is so powerful. This fact is fully recognized in India, where there are many teachers of different sorts standing at different levels, of varying degrees of power, who are there called *gurus*. Each has his own set of followers, and teaches them his own ideas upon philosophy, and sometimes gives them *mantras* to recite, forms of meditation, and yoga practices to do. But it is not by any means mainly through these things that he helps them. The more important thing is that they shall be with him. If he is a peripatetic, wandering from place to place, they go about with him, just as the disciples of Jesus travelled with Him through Palestine. If he lives in one place, these disciples gather round him, sit at his feet and listen to any words of wisdom which he may drop, but the benefit they gain is not so much from what he teaches as from the influence of his presence.

This process is entirely scientific. The higher vehicles of the guru are keyed up to a higher rate of vibration than those of his pupils, who have come more recently than he out of the worldly life, where the vibrations are at a lower level. They are not entirely withdrawn from the selfish side of things, as he is. They must take themselves in hand, realize their faults and resolve to get rid of them and develop certain virtues, in brief, change their own characters, and that is usually a slow and tedious business. They can be quite immensely assisted in that process by being in constant contact with the *guru*, who has developed these virtues and extinguished those vices in himself. The pressure of the higher vibration is constant, whether they wake or sleep, and they are absorbing it and being attuned to it all the time. The principle of this is well known in physics: if you put close to each other two timepieces which are not moving regularly together in harmony, the stronger one will gradually bring the weaker into agreement with itself, or stop it altogether.

The second way of entering the Probationary Path is the hearing or reading of teaching upon the subject. A man who is interested in the matter gets hold of some teaching along these higher lines; it commends itself to his intuition, and immediately he seeks to satisfy his desire to find out more about it. This was my own experience. I came across *The Occult World*, and at once made up my mind: "If that be so—and it is so evidently—if there be these Greater People, and if They are willing to accept service from us, and to give us in return something of Their priceless knowledge—then I am going to be one of those who serve Them. I am going to pick up whatever crumbs I can, and the only thing worth doing from now on is to set to work to get into that position somehow." Of course there are many thousands who hear and read the teaching, and yet do not receive any impulse from it. That is a question of the man's experience in other lives. Only if he has already come into contact with the truth, and has convinced himself of its beauty and reality in a previous life, does he instantly feel it to be true when it comes before him in this life.

It seems to many of us amazing that everyone who gets hold of a Theosophical book is not converted. Theosophy is a wonderful teaching, and it solves a great many problems, and yet you know quite well when you try to lend Theosophical books to friends, half of them return them, and say "Yes, no doubt it is very interesting," but they have not really understood it at all. One's present understanding is the good karma of having studied it before; the more one has known of a thing before, the more he will see in it now. That is our experience with any good book that we may have read, say, twenty years ago. Read it again now, and see how very much more you will find in it than you did then. You are able to see in it that which you bring the power to see.

The third mode by which men are sometimes brought to the beginning of the Probationary Path is by what is called in the Indian books, 'enlightened reflection'. That means that by sheer hard thinking a man may come to see that there must be a plan of evolution, that there must be Those who know all about it—the evolved and perfected Men—and that there must be a Path by which They may be reached. The man who by such thinking comes to that decision then sets out to look for the Path; but those who traval by this road are probably few.

In some ways the most remarkable is the fourth way —the practice of virtue. That is an idea which would quite commend itself to the average Christian, because he often believes that all that is necessary is to be good. But the Theosophist recollects that in the early days of Christianity the purification, or saintship, which they now set before themselves as their goal, was considered to be only the first step. S. Clement says of it quite boldly that purity is merely a negative virtue, valuable chiefly as a condition of insight. Having achieved that, you are then fit to learn, to prepare for illumination, which was the second stage, and after that to pass into the third stage, called perfection. You will remember how S. Paul speaks of that. He says: "We speak wisdom among them that are perfect," but not to others.

This virtue leads to the beginning of the Path because, though the man who leads a good life through many incarnations may not thereby develop intellect, he will presently acquire sufficient intuition to carry him into the presence of the people who do know, to bring him in fact to the feet of some one who is a servant of the Master. It is admitted, however, that that method takes thousands of years and many lives. The man who practises virtue and does not develop his mind will reach the Path eventually, but it is a slow process. It would save him much time if he followed S. Peter's advice and aimed at knowledge as well.

CHAPTER 7

THE FOUR QUALIFICATIONS

Four Qualifications there are for this pathway :

> **Discrimination.**
> **Desirelessness.**
> **Good Conduct.**
> **Love.**

C.W.L.—These qualifications have been stated over and over again in the various religions, but this translation differs slightly from any that have been given previously. In the case of the first, discrimination, there has been little variation. I have already explained the words used for this by the Hindus and Buddhists, how they mean the same thing as conversion among the Christians, and how the pupil must unite the ego and the personality. On the Path proper the process has to be repeated between the Monad and the ego. The ego is a fragment of the Monad put down as far as the higher part of the mental plane; it also comes down for the collection of experience, to learn to receive and respond to vibrations such as cannot be sensed by the Monad at his own level. So the ego in turn has to learn that he is a part of the Monad, that he exists only for that Monad, and when that in turn is fully realized, the man is ready to take the Fifth Initiation and so become an Adept.

Those are the actual definitions of readiness for the two Initiations; for the First, that the higher and the lower self shall have been unified, that there shall be nothing but the ego working in this personality; and for the Fifth Initiation that there shall be nothing in the ego that is not approved or inspired by the Monad. Whenever the Monad touches our lives down here he comes in as a god from above. In all cases of Initiation he flashes down, and for a moment becomes one with the ego, just as they will be permanently one when adeptship is gained. At certain other times also the Monad comes down, as in the case mentioned in *The Lives of Alcyone*, when Alcyone took a pledge to the Lord Buddha.

By one or other of the foregoing means the man is led to discrimination—this knowledge of what is worth following and what is not worth following. Then he finds he has to develop the second qualification, to which the Master here gives the name of desirelessness. Dr. Besant previously translated it dispassion or indifference. This is the Hindu *vairāgya*, which means indifference to the result of one's actions. The Lord Buddha's statement of that is just a little different. For this second stage He uses the Pāli word *parikamma*. Karma or *kamma* always means doing or acting, and *parikamma* means preparation for action; so He calls that second stage preparation for action, the grade in which the emphasis is laid on learning to do right for right's sake, not for the sake of anything the man may gain from it in any way for himself. This must not be misunderstood. Many people say that indifference to the fruit of action means that one must perform duty without taking into account the effect on anyone else. As this book tells us later on, "that which is right you must do, that which is wrong you must not do," whatever the consequences may be; but it does not mean that people should go on doing just what they like without thinking how their action will affect others. In fact, it is that very effect which determines whether the action is right or wrong. The pupil of the Master does not think of the effect upon himself, but he does most emphatically think of that on others.

The third qualification, which is called Good Conduct, includes the six rules which the Hindus name *shatsampatti*. In the Pāli form, as given by the Lord Buddha, that qualification is called *upachāro*, which means 'attention' rather than 'conduct,'—one is to pay attention to conduct in the ways prescribed by those six jewels, as they are called. We shall come to the Master Kūthūmi's rendering of them presently, as we go through this book. By the Buddha they were given as *samo*, 'quietude,' that is, control of mind; then *dāmo*, 'subjugation,' that is, control of the body; then *uparati*, *titikkhā*, *samādhāna*, and *saddhā*, literally 'cessation, endurance, intentness, and faith'. I took the trouble to have all these words looked up in the principal dictionaries, and got these translations from the High Priest Hikkaduwe Sumangala Thero, who was then Head of the Southern Buddhist Church. The words also represent the current belief of that Church.

These are a little different from the translations which are given in this book. What is here called 'cessation' is translated 'tolerance,' because the cessation meant is from bigotry and superstition, the putting aside altogether of any idea that your way is better than anybody else's way, and the idea that any rite or ceremony is necessary. Endurance is simply cheerfulness in another form. Intentness is one-pointedness and balance, bringing all one's life to the focus of one's aim, and therefore also steadiness; and faith is confidence in one's Master and oneself. The qualifications are the same exactly in both cases, but the Lord Buddha spoke of them specially from the point of view of the necessity for wisdom, and the Lord Maitreya and the Master Kūthūmi are emphasizing more the necessity for love. In teaching Alcyone the Master also aimed more at giving the practical meaning than literally translating the old words.

The last qualification is called Love. It is in Sanskrit *mumukshatva*, which means "the intense desire for liberation from the round of births and deaths and for union with the Supreme". The Lord Buddha in His scheme called that *anuloma*, which means 'direct order' or succession. His meaning is that when the man has developed the other qualifications, he must desire to escape from the lower limitations and to become one with the Supreme in order that he may help.

Alcyone then goes on to say:

> What the Master has said to me on each of these I shall try to tell you.

And then begins the book proper.

PART II

DISCRIMINATION

CHAPTER 1

TRUE AND FALSE AIMS

C.W.L.—We now come to Section I of the book itself

> **The first of these Qualifications is Discrimination; and this is usually taken as the discrimination between the real and the unreal which leads men to enter the Path. It is this, but it is also much more; and it is to be practised, not only at the beginning of the Path, but at every step of it every day until the end.**

Those last few words show precisely the difficulties which stand in the way of most of those who see the glory and the beauty of the Path, and intend to enter upon it and come to the feet of the Master. They are all good, earnest, painstaking people, but the personality is wayward, and they have to face the great pressure of public opinion, as I have already explained. In addition there is also the fact that humanity is now but a little past the middle of the fourth round, and they are trying to do in it that which will be very easy to do at the end of the seventh round. Those who go on to that time will have, in their physical, astral and mental vehicles, matter far more fully developed than we have now, with all its spirillæ in activity instead of only about half, and all the forces surrounding them will be helpful and not hindering as they are now.

The Masters are on our side and Their forces help us. The force of evolution, slow as it is, also is on our side, and the future is with us: but the present is a very hard time to do anything of this sort. In the middle of the fifth round all the people whose influence is now bearing hard against us in an opposite direction will have been shunted out, and there will be none left but those who are going our way. In the seventh round things will therefore be wonderfully easy. One may then live in the outer world with all the advantages that can now be found only in a monastery under the direction of a spiritually developed man. Some might think: "Why then should we not wait for the seventh round?" Many among us have been drifting along comfortably and happily enough during the last twenty or thirty thousand years, and those who have not a keen desire from within to progress or to help the world may go on for another million years in just the same old line, and no doubt it will be very much easier in the end; but those who go through the dfficulties now will have the enormous privilege of helping forward evolution, and they will wear the crown of the helper. Remember the old Christian hymn which tells how a man went to heaven and, looking round, found himself somehow different from all the rest, and wondered what was the matter.

At last he met the Christ, and asked Him why this was so, and the Christ said in reply:

> I know thou hast believed in Me
>   And life through Me is thine,
> But where are all those glorious stars
>   Which in thy crown should shine?
> Thou seest yonder joyous throng
>   With gems on every brow,
> For every soul they led to Me
>   They wear a jewel now.

In the Christian Scripture it is said that they that are wise shall shine as the brightness of the firmament, as the light of the clear sky; but they that turn many to righteousness shall be as the stars for ever and ever—great glowing suns, sending out light and warmth and strength to thousands of other lives. That is the difference between doing the work now, and waiting to drift in with the current in the seventh round.

> You enter the Path because you have learnt that on it alone can be found those things which are worth gaining. Men, who do not know, work to gain wealth and power, but these are at most for one life only, and therefore unreal. There are greater things than these—things which are real and lasting; when you have once seen these, you desire those others no more.

A.B.—The question of the real and the unreal is a deeply metaphysical one, but we are not really concerned with that here, because the Master was teaching Alcyone as quite a young boy, and further the teaching was given on the astral plane. In such cases the Master is speaking to the lower mind as well as to the ego, and on this occasion he gave His teaching in a form suitable for the lower mind of a boy which had by no means reached its full development. However old the ego may be, the three bodies were young, so the teaching was expressed very simply, that on returning to his body the pupil might understand it in his waking mind.

The unreal is here taken to be everything which is not divine, everything that is passing in the phenomenal world, everything belonging to the personal self, including even the higher things for which men work for the sake of a material goal. Following the Master's thought, we may say that everything is unreal except that which is part of the will of God. Those who discriminate know the real things, so they work as agents of God, doing His will, He being the real doer. There is no suggestion that they should neglect material activity. Men should do their work better, not worse, because they are the agents of God, executing His actions in the outer world. "Yoga is skill in action," says the *Gītā*, and yoga is union with the Divine. Action must be skilful in the case of the man who has this union, for it is not he who does the work, but God in him. When Arjuna was asking Shrī Krishna about fighting, the Lord replied that He Himself had already killed the enemy, and He added: "Therefore fight, O Arjuna."

When the higher things have been seen, said the Master, the others are desired no more. That idea is familiar to students of the *Gītā*, in which it is said: "The objects of sense, but not the taste for them, turn away from the abstemious dweller in the body; and even taste turneth away from him after the Supreme is seen." When a man has seen the One, the very desire for the things of the senses dies out in him.

C.W.L.—It is a fact that when the greater things have once been seen one no longer has a taste for the lower things, but it must be absolutely that fact that induces one to refrain from following the latter. Very often people confound cause and effect, and think that to pretend not to care for the lower things—which, though quite good in their way, are yet so called in contradistinction to higher and spiritual things—at once puts a man on a high level. Of course it does not. It is another form of the very common delusion with regard to asceticism. A great many people follow what they call asceticism as an end in itself, and wrongly think that to avoid all the ordinary pleasures of life, to make oneself uncomfortable in various ways, is highly meritorious. That is a relic of the puritan idea which at one time dominated England and a good deal of Europe. It was distinctly of the essence of that puritanism that to be good you must be as uncomfortable as possible. Whenever a man was in any sort of way happy, he was surely infringing some of the divine laws, as he was not in the least meant to be happy down here; his body was a vile thing which had to be repressed in all sorts of ways, and if at any time it delighted in anything he was doing, he might be certain that that thing was wrong. That is all nonsense, but it does come from a perversion of the truth, and the truth is that those things which most people in the world enjoy and regard as great pleasures cease to be thought of as such by the man who, rising to a higher level, has altogether higher pleasures in view, which far more than take their place.

People in the world take great pleasure in all sorts of things which do not interest those who aspire higher—in horse-racing, for example, and drinking and gambling, and also in various forms of amusements such as dancing and card-playing, which are not necessarily harmful, but are rather like children's toys. As a little child grows up he abandons his toys. At the age of three or four he likes to play with bricks and dolls; when he gets a little older he takes to toy soldiers, kites, tops and marbles; when he gets again a little bit older he no longer cares for any of these things, but plays cricket or football, or some game of that sort which requires a great deal of out-door exertion. All these are stages through which the child passes, and each is quite proper in its turn. As he grows still older he abandons those things he had previously enjoyed, not because he thinks he ought to do so, but simply because they have ceased to interest him; he has found something which is more appropriate to his stage of development. But you can see at once that a little child of three would not become a big boy by choosing to ignore all the things of early childhood, and wanting to play cricket or football.

The highly advanced man does not care for a great many things which ordinary people think necessary, and the man of the world would probably find the life of the disciple intolerably wearisome, if he tried to live as many of us do, with no real interest outside Theosophy and the deeper problems of life. The average worldling would say that such people are always doing the one thing, and that they do not seem to know or care for anything else—which is quite true, because that includes all the rest. But he would not become an advanced man by pretending not to care for his own things, while all the time in his heart he really desired them.

> In all the world there are only two kinds of people—those who know, and those who do not know; and this knowledge is the thing which matters. What religion a man holds, to what race he belongs—these things are not important.

A.B.—The Master draws here a very luminous distinction. He divides men into two classes—those who know and those who do not know. That is the great division from the occult standpoint, and each should ask himself to which class he belongs. Both classes include many varieties of people, for outer distinctions and differences are things that do not matter. Those who do not know, work for what exists for one life only; but he who has once clearly seen the real things, is filled with the sole desire to work for the Logos, to fall in with His mighty plan and help in however small a way to carry it out. We can test our own knowledge to see whether it bears on that work or not. The mere brain knowledge which enables one to talk very intelligently, perhaps, and to teach others, is all unreal; the real knowledge is only that which is worked into one's life. There are very many people who make it their custom to sit quietly for a little time every night before going to bed, and review their day's work. That is a very useful thing, but if you do it, ask yourself not merely what you have done, what you have felt, and what you have thought, but what has been your attitude. If you have been submerged in the things you have done, the time has been largely lost: but if you had done the same things as part of the divine work—as acts of sacrifice—they would have helped and not hindered you.

The really important thing is this knowledge—the knowledge of God's plan for men. For God has a plan, and that plan is evolution. When once a man has seen that and really knows it, he cannot help working for it and making himself one with it, because it is so glorious, so beautiful.

C.W.L.—The spirit which makes men join political and temperance associations of various sorts which they think will help the world, is called forth in its very highest aspect the moment a man sees the real plan of the Logos for His system. He sees that it will be carried out one day, and that the time when that desirable consummation will be reached depends upon the number of people who are ready to work for it. If the whole world could be induced, in a few weeks or years, to see and to co-operate with it, everything that the Logos desires for His people would be very rapidly achieved. It is just because men are not yet sufficiently developed to see it, that we fall short so sadly, and so many sorrows and wrongs and wickednesses remain in the face of the sun.

Many students of Theosophy know something of the Plan. I do not say they have seen it yet, but they have been in contact with those who have, and know, therefore, what it is, and in what direction one must move if he would associate himself with it. But when the time of absolutely seeing it comes, it will be found that all that is said here of the enthusiasm is true. In the world, people often take up good causes and reforms with enthusiasm and vigour, but unless they know something of the larger plan of evolution, and see where their own work fits into it, mistakes may easily be made. They attach themselves to certain causes because they are impressed with their urgency and utility. Such is, for example, the cause of temperance, which they espouse because they have seen the tremendous evil caused by the drinking habit, and have realized in how very many ways the world would be quite infinitely better if that evil could be removed. They try to remove it, not by inducing men to give up the foolishness and wickedness of drink, but by prohibiting its sale, and so forcing the people into sobriety—a plan which by no means weeds out the desire, but only renders it impossible to gratify it. I am not for a moment speaking against the prohibition scheme; there is very much to be said in its favour. If we think it wise to place a restriction on the sale of arsenic or prussic acid, why should not the same be done in the case of a poison which is responsible for far more harm than both of them together? I am only pointing out that this remedy does not strike at the root of the evil; it tries to reform people by compulsion, not by persuasion.

Just in the same way people who have realized the awful suffering of the submerged tenth seek in all directions for a remedy for this great and crying shame; but unfortunately some think they have found it in extreme radicalism or even in anarchism. One cannot blame people for prosecuting unselfishly a line which they think will bring relief to their fellows. It is their heads which are at fault in such cases as this, not their hearts, which drive them to great personal loss and sacrifice in order, as they hope, to relieve the trouble of their fellow-men. They have to realize that there is a plan for human evolution, and to give themselves to its study, that their actions may become wise as well as unselfish. It is discrimination that is lacking; they see only one side of the difficulty, and so they plunge themselves into something which will lead to worse trouble than that which they are trying to assuage.

So, because he knows, he is on God's side, standing for good and resisting evil, working for evolution and not for selfishness.

C.W.L.—That is the touchstone by which we may recognize the people who know—it is not in the least by their religion or their race, but by the one and only fact that they stand for good and against evil. Wherever we find a man who is loyal to the highest that he knows, is standing for what seems to him to be good and resisting what seems to him to be evil, we must see in him a brother working on God's side, even though some of the work he does is hardly such as we could approve, or think of as being pleasing to God. There are numbers of people who are utterly good and loyal to their convictions and yet have most crushing limitations. These earnest, devoted persons actually sacrifice their energy, their whole time, and everything they have, to bring other souls to Christ, as they would put it; yet they have the most limited and bigoted conceptions. They show in some cases a feeling of bitter opposition, practically amounting to hatred, for those whose belief is a little different in certain ways from their own.

One of the most striking features of the work of the great Hierarchy is that in every such case its members extract the good and put aside the evil. They take up the force which that devotion and earnestness generates, and use every ounce of it, putting aside all the evil which, on this plane at any rate, so largely prevents the good from showing itself. There are many Christian communities where the bigotry so overshadows the loving-kindness that all the outward impression one gets is of its bitterness. The Brothers of the Hierarchy deplore the bigotry and see the evil done by it even more than others can, but nevertheless They draw out from it all the force of loving-kindness and devotion and good intention, utilize it, and give credit to those who pour it out; and every one of those people will get all the benefit that follows from his goodness, although at the same time for his anger and his bigotry there will also be exactly the due results according to kārmic law.

Wherefore it behoves us to be charitable in dealing with these other people and to try in all cases to fix our thoughts on the good things, to "pounce upon the pearls," as the Master said, instead of everlastingly flying at the flaws, as so many people do.

> If he is on God's side he is one of us, and it does not matter in the least whether he calls himself a Hindu, or a Buddhist, a Christian or a Muhammadan, whether he is an Indian or an Englishman, a Chinaman or a Russian.

A.B.—This is a thing that aspirants to the Path should never forget, for unless it is lived, you are still very far from the Portal. There no one will ask what your race is, or your creed, but only what you have added to your character in the way of qualities. All of us pass through different races in turn. We find ourselves now in a particular sub-race of a particular root race because we need to acquire the good qualities in which it specializes, and which it can therefore give to us, whatever they may be; yet at the same time many people are busy developing the weaknesses of that particular sub-race as well. It would probably be quite right to say: "No other race would be so suitable for me just now, to remove my defects and fill in my character," but it is not intended that we should take up, say, English methods and glorify them to the exclusion of all others, and feel that none can be as good as those. Each race has its part to play in the harmony; each contributes its share to the mighty whole. In whatever race you happen to be, the part of the harmony which is played by that race offers for the moment the easiest and most natural work for you. But you will pass through that and learn to play some other part later. If people understood this, they would be less prone to foolish pride of race, and criticism of other races.

When I hear some one complaining of some one else with the implication that the fault of the other exists because he is an Englishman or an Indian, it shows me at once that the speaker is still deluded by the unreal. The same thing occurs when a person excuses his own shortcomings by saying that they are those of his sub-race. You must try to acquire the best qualities of your race and sub-race, not its deficiencies. The Indian, for example, should try to acquire spirituality, harmlessness, tolerance, and capacity for action with non-attachment—for these are the qualities that the first family of the Aryan race was meant to show out.

Yet sometimes we find that non-attachment is accompanied by carelessness and slipshod work, rising from the wrong idea that because one should be indifferent to the fruits of action the action is unimportant. But what is really wanted is perfection of action with indifference to the fruits of action. With the Englishman, it is often quite the reverse. He is generally competent and careful in action; but is apt to get excited about the fruits of it, because he often lacks the quality of indifference.

It is the business of each to try to acquire what he lacks; the Indian should try to practise action, the Englishman indifference, without loss of the qualities which are already theirs. If this were done differences of race would work for the enrichment of all races, for each could learn from the other what he himself lacked.

C.W.L.—To be patriotic, to admire your own race, to feel that you owe something to it, and to be ready to serve it, are all good things. But take great care lest you show your admiration by depreciating the others. Our permanent relation is to humanity as a whole. We are citizens of the world, not of any one race. Yet patriotism is good, just as family love is good. In both cases, however, we must not let ourselves carry our virtue to such extremes as to put evil in the place of good. Truly family affection is a splendid thing, but that of the robber barons of the Middle Ages, which led them to murder other people for the sake of enriching their own families, was certainly a virtue carried to an excess, and become a vice. In exactly the same way patriotism is good, but if it leads to aggression against other races, it becomes bad. But if you can do something for your race, without injuring others; if you can show yourself to be a worthy member of it, so that it shall be the better for your passing through it, you may then have some cause for satisfaction. It is precisely the same with religion. We have all been through many of the great religions. Each one emphasizes certain virtues, but all are necessary for the progress of mankind.

Those who are on His side know why they are here and what they should do, and they are trying to do it; all the others do not yet know what they should do, and so they often act foolishly.

C.W.L.—Here is a touch of the teaching of the Lord Gautama Buddha that all evil comes from ignorance. The fact that those who do not know often act foolishly makes it true that the wicked man is always to be pitied, not to be disliked or hated. What impresses itself most upon people generally is that he is acting in selfishness—for his own interests, as he thinks—and they are a little apt to forget his ignorance of the facts. To take an instance—there have been certain great millionaries who won their way to temporary prosperity by throwing out of business a number of smaller people and beggaring them. They are regarded with execration by those people whose livelihood they have taken away, and everyone says how utterly selfish and brutal these people are.

Yes, but when they are so it is because they are ignorant. Such a man is doing exactly what he set out to do: to crush out those other people because he thinks he can do all that business better. Perhaps he can turn out better results, and make a fortune for himself at the same time, but he would never have set out to do it had he known that he was doing far more harm to himself than to any of the other people, that he was making for his own future a karma that would be quite infinitely worse than that of those men whom he crushed. Instead of execrating that man for his selfishness the wiser part would be to pity him for his ignorance.

> And try to invent ways for themselves which they think will be pleasant for themselves, not understanding that all are one, and that therefore only what the One wills can ever be really pleasant for any one.

C.W.L.—It is a great motto of utilitarianism to pursue the greatest good of the greatest number. It is a great improvement upon the previous idea that the good of only a few should be considered, and that the others were a negligible quantity. But the minority cannot be ignored; indeed every one must be taken into account, because all are one. This cannot be understood until the consciousness of the buddhic plane has been developed to some extent, and even then only by slow degrees can one learn how utterly all are one. We think of it as a sort of religious duty to believe it to be so, or as a sort of pious aspiration that some day all will become one. We say: "We have all come forth from the same great Father, and therefore we are all brothers, and we are all one." We do not, however, understand the reality and the depth of that until we experience it in buddhic consciousness.

Some suggestion of it may be given, nevertheless, if we say that all consciousnesses are one, that all the world is one, that all the love in it is the one Divine Love, that all the beauty in it is the one Divine Beauty, and all the holiness of the world is the one Holiness of God.

Christ expressed that when a man came to Him and called Him "good Master", He said: "Why callest thou Me good? There is none good but One and that is God." The goodness of each man is the goodness of God showing itself forth in him, and all the beauty and glory of the world, as we see it, in the earth and sea and sky, is nothing but part of the one Divine Beauty; and as we rise to different subplanes, from level to level, more and more we see that beauty opening itself out before us, until we learn to see all beauty through each beautiful thing. It is all one.

When that is learned, the glory of the Divine will be seen in and through everything, and all its other glories through each of those, so that when a beautiful landscape opens before us, it will not be merely the scene which we shall admire, but all that it suggests—the infinite whole of which it is only a tiny part. Then life will become wonderfully happy for us, and full of love. Through that happiness we shall experience something of the Eternal Bliss, and through that love we shall realize the Eternal Love. It is only in that way that great advancement can come, only when we realize that we ourselves are nothing but a point in the whole; then our consciousness is in a condition to merge into His, so that through us He may see all this beauty, and we, as in Him, may see it and realize it too.

They are following the unreal instead of the real. Until they learn to distinguish between these two,

they have not ranged themselves on God's side, and so this discrimination is the first step.

But even when the choice is made, you must still remember that of the real and the unreal there are many varieties; and discrimination must still be made between the right and the wrong, the important and the unimportant, the useful and the useless, the true and the false, the selfish and the unselfish.

C.W.L.—Those are all subdivisions of the great distinction between the real and the unreal, and their enumeration shows us how discrimination must ramify down into the smallest affairs of life, if we are to tread this Path. Little points are constantly arising which we have to decide this way or that way, so always we have to bear the idea of discrimination in mind, and keep constantly watchful. To stop and think all the time is wearisome. Many good people get tired when they try it; the perpetual strain of it is too great for them. That is very natural, but those who give in fail to achieve; therefore however wearisome it may be, we must continue the life of recollectedness.

Between right and wrong it should not be difficult to choose,. for those who wish to follow the Master have already decided to take the right at all costs.

A.B.—If anyone hesitates between right and wrong he does not really wish to follow the Master. Those who decide to do so must make up their minds to take the right at all costs on all occasions, small and great, no matter what the consequences may be. In the *Yoga Sutras* it is said of the five great qualities called *yama*, which include harmlessness, truth, honesty, and other virtues, which are prescribed at the very beginning of the Path, that "these are called the great vows, being universal," which means that they are to be kept under *all* circumstances, that no gain for himself or others could justify the disciple in breaking one of them. The man who has attained this position will never tell, or act, an untruth, however great may be the apparent advantage of so doing. This will be so not only in money matters but in everything; he will never take any more credit than belongs to him, for example. You must ask yourself whether you always choose the truth *instinctively*, for until this is so you are far from the first Portal. On this subject the Master does not think it worth while to say any more; it is so clear, so palpable.

C.W.L.—This idea refers not only to the question of conduct, but also to the fact that there are right and wrong ways to go about any piece of work that has to be done. He who is not strict in following this rule does not really desire success deep down inside. People sometimes say: "How I wish I were clairvoyant; how I wish I could see astrally, how must I begin? What is the first step?" The first step is to purify all the vehicles; you must be careful that the physical body takes no food but the most suitable. Many would like astral sight, but when it comes to the point they prefer what they call a good dinner. They feel that they must have that, because they are used to it, and for the time they forget all about their desire for astral sight. The feeling, however, is simply due to habit, and when we know about this peculiarity of the body we can proceed with confidence in the wearisome task of wearing down the old bad or unsuitable habits, and setting up new ones. It is encouraging that the principle of habit can be made a powerful ally in our work, although it is a hindrance in the beginning; for when once we have established good habits, they will go on automatically, and we can forget them, and give our attention to other things.

In conduct there is no question as to choosing between right and wrong. Anyone who is likely to be interested in this book, or who wants to reach the Master's feet, will not hesitate in choosing the right, when he sees it. Let us hope that none of us would try to cheat a fellow-creature—I hope we have got past that—or be guilty of the slightest untruthfulness, even to do apparent good. We should probably not be obtaining a living in any objectionable way, such as by the slaughter of animals, nor be of the number of those who wear articles of dress or adornment which can only be obtained by the killing of animals,—sometimes by the slaughter of, say, the mother-bird under peculiarly revolting circumstances. All people who continue to wear such things do not really desire to follow the Master; they prefer to follow the fashion.

CHAPTER 2

THE LIFE OF THE BODIES

But the body and the man are two, and the man's will is not always what the body wishes. When your body wishes something, stop and think whether *you* really wish it.

A.B.—Here the Master gives His pupil the decided order that when his body wishes something, he must stop and consider whether he himself really wishes it. Many people will find that stopping and thinking every day and all day long very difficult and irksome ; but the fact must be faced that it is an important part of the preparation. It is very difficult, I know, and therefore many aspirants get tired of making the effort.

Those who give up because they are tired do not achieve, that is all. The effort to do this must be great and prolonged—it all means such a regulated life, in which there shall be no hasty action, no hasty speech, not even hasty thinking, but all the pupil's activities, physical, emotional and mental, must be entirely under control.

C.W.L.—If one wants really to do his best in this matter of progress it is worth his while to make a careful study of his different vehicles and see exactly what they are. Here it is said quite clearly that the physical body wishes for things that the man does not wish for, and that is equally true of the astral and mental bodies. If the constitution of these vehicles is understood, one can see that what they are likely to want would be undesirable for the man. We are speaking of them almost as though they were separate persons, and in a way they are. Each of these bodies is built of living matter, and the life in them joins itself together, and acquires a kind of corporate consciousness.

In the astral body that forms what we sometimes call the desire-elemental, who is practically an entity composed of the joint life of all the astral cells that make up that body. Each cell by itself is a small, only partly-conscious life, struggling on its upward way—or, rather, its downward way, because evolution for it is to pass down into the mineral kingdom. When these lives find themselves all joined together in an astral body, they do to a certain extent practically club together and act as though they were a unit, and you get the effect of an astral body that has strong instincts of its own, so strong, in fact, that you could almost say that it has a will of its own. The way for it to evolve is to get stronger and coarser vibrations, connected with all those feelings and emotions which we do not want to develop, such as envy, jealousy and selfishness: that is why its interests are so often opposed to ours. The far more delicate, more rapid and really more powerful vibrations of love, sympathy and devotion, all belong to a higher part of the astral body, consequently they are of the type that the body itself does not want, though we do.

People of unregulated life, who want to be free, as they often call it, to say and do what they wish, are really slaves to their astral bodies. We must not blame the astral body for this, nor regard it, as the mediæval Christians did, as a tempting demon. It does not know anything about us or our existence; and it is not tempting us at all, but is simply trying to find expression for itself, to evolve, in its own way, just as all other creatures are doing.

People have sometimes asked the question, "Ought not we to give this elemental a chance for its evolution; ought we not to let it have its coarse vibrations?" No, that is mistaken philanthropy, and could not be done thoroughly, anyhow. The kindest thing one can do with the coarser matter—which is in our astral bodies because in some previous lives we have allowed the lower emotions to play strongly through us—is to shake it out, and let it fasten itself upon some savage, or a dog or a cow, where its vibrations can act with no harm to anybody.

The desire-elemental is in its way quite cunning. We cannot quite put ourselves in its place and realize consciousness at so very low a stage, but evidently it feels that it is surrounded by something finer than itself—the mental matter—and appears to find out by experiment that if it can get that to vibrate along with its matter, it obtains a much more intense vibration, and more of it, than it otherwise could. If it can make the man think that he wants what it wants, it is much more likely to get it, so it tries to stir up that finer matter. If it can thus induce an impure thought, for example, it will presently get the impure emotions that it likes, or if it can arouse a jealous thought there will presently be a feeling of jealousy rankling, which is what it wants; not, however, because it is evil, for to it it is nothing but a very strong coarse vibration such as it enjoys. In this way the elemental often proves more than a match for the human being, though it is very low in the scale of evolution. It is rather humiliating, when you think of it, to realize that you are being overcome and used as a tool by something that is not yet even a mineral. We have to face it and purify the astral body against its will by changing any bad habits that may be ours from the past, and putting in their places good emotions for the future.

There is a mental elemental and a physical elemental as well. The latter is engaged in the building up of tissue and looking after the body generally. If one gets a scratch, a cut or a wound, it is the physical elemental that at once hurries the white corpuscles to the spot, to try to build together new cells. There is a great deal that is very interesting about the work of this elemental in the physical body; some of its activities are eminently useful to us, but at the same time it is liable to have impulses which are not for our good.

For *you* are God, and you will only what God wills; but you must dig deep down into yourself to find the God within you, and listen to His voice, which is *your* voice.

C.W.L.—The idea of our unity with the One Self is difficult to realize. I will tell you how it was first brought definitely home to me, though it was not by a method that I can recommend to others. I was at the time trying to concentrate the whole of my power in the atomic part of the mental plane, in order to discover how far one could utilize what we call the short cuts which run between the atomic subplanes of the different planes. In rising through the planes one can travel up the physical plane from subplane to subplane to the atomic, from that to the lowest astral, and on by degrees to the astral atomic, and then to the lowest mental, and so on. Or one can take a short cut from the atomic physical to the atomic astral, and from that to the atomic mental.

I had heard, among higher pupils, of another kind of short cut, at right angles, as it were, to that. They said that if one's consciousness were focused in one of our atomic subplanes one could get a line of communication open to the corresponding cosmic plane. Therefore, by focusing oneself entirely in the atomic mental, there would be a possibility of coming into touch with the mental division of an entirely new set of planes, (that is to say, the cosmic mental plane) altogether above all the planes that we know.

I had not, of course, any hope of reaching such a plane as that, but there was a possibility of communication. I tried, and found that I was able to see—I cannot describe it, I am afraid—the corresponding subplane in the cosmic mental, two whole sets of planes above where we are. I could not actually reach it in any sort of way—I do not think even an Adept could do that—but I could see it. It was as though I were at the bottom of a well and were looking up at a star—but I could see that higher consciousness. The one thing that was then borne in upon me, with an intensity which I cannot describe, was the fact that if before I had supposed that I had a will, that I had an intellect, that I had emotions, they were not mine, they were His; it was His will, His feeling, not mine at all. I have never forgotten the experience, as it impressed that fact upon me with a certainty that I cannot describe.

That certainty that the Divine is within us can be gained also through the buddhic consciousness, as I have already explained. As soon as we achieve that, we find the sea of consciousness opening round us, and we know that we are part of it, and yet at the same time many others are in it and share it along with us; and presently, in addition to that feeling, we come to realize that this is all one consciousness, penetrating us and all others—that we are God. That realization gives one a sense of the utmost safety and confidence, the most tremendous impulse and stimulus of which one could possibly think. Yet I can quite imagine that at first it might alarm some people, because they might feel that they were losing themselves. They are not, of course; but remember what Christ said, "He that loseth his life for My sake shall find it." Christ represents the buddhic principle, and is saying: "He who for My sake—for the Christ development within him—will put aside the causal body in which he has been living for so long, will find himself, will find the far grander and higher life." It needs some courage to do it, and it is a startling experience the first time that one is wholly in the buddhic vehicle and finds that his causal body, upon which he has been depending for thousands of years, has vanished. When any one has one or other of the experiences I have described, he will know with absolute certainty that the Self is one. The idea cannot be conveyed, but it will be known when the thing is experienced, and nothing will ever again shake that certainty.

> Do not mistake your bodies for yourself—neither the physical body, nor the astral, nor the mental. Each one of them will pretend to be the Self, in order to gain what it wants. But you must know them all, and know yourself as their master.

C.W.L.—The Master speaks of these bodies quite definitely as though they were separate persons, referring, of course, to the elementals which we have already considered. Their empire is absolutely unchecked for most people in the world, who not only make no effort to throw off their dominion, but do not even know that there is any yoke to throw off. They do not separate themselves from their bodies. The disastrous teaching about man *having* a soul is responsible for much harm in this direction. If people could only realize that man *is* a soul and *has* bodies, at once they would begin to disentangle things a little. So long as a man has the idea that the soul is something vague floating above him, there is very little hope of doing good. When we find the elementals rising in us, we should say: "This emotion is a vibration in my astral body, and I will vibrate as *I* choose. I am the centre for the time being of this set of bodies, and I will use them as *I* want."

> **When there is work that must be done, the physical body wants to rest, to go out walking, to eat and drink; and the man who does not know says to himself: "*I* want to do these things, and I must do them." But the man who knows says: "This that wants is *not* I, and it must wait awhile."**

C.W.L.—You will notice that very strongly in the case of children. If a child wants to do a thing, it is heaven and earth to him; he must do it then and there in a moment, and if he cannot he thinks the universe is falling round him. Savages also are like that—creatures of impulse, which is so strong that just to do some trifling thing they will sometimes kill a man. The civilized man would say: "I will wait and consider what will happen." The child dashes off and plays, and far too often we who are older blame and scold him, not understanding the child nature. He says, "I did not remember." That is absolutely true, but we doubt it because we know that *we* should remember. We have forgotten our own childhood and that of the race. We ought to say, "I know you have an impulse, but really you must not do that just now. It will upset the arrangements of a great many other people. You shall do it some other time." That is the way education progresses. It is the same with the savage, who in course of time learns that certain impulses must not be followed. It takes him several births to do so, and he generally gets killed in the process, but gradually he becomes a little less savage and more civilized. But the advanced man is dealing with the body as a separate entity, as a thing he can manage.

> Often when there is an opportunity to help some one, the body feels: "How much trouble it will be for me; let some one else do it." But the man replies to his body: "You shall not hinder me in doing good work."

C.W.L.—Dr. Besant remarked with regard to this that there are very many cases where there is obviously a good piece of work to be done, but most people look at it and say: "Yes, that is a thing that must be done. Some one will do it some day; why should *I* bother about it?" but the person who is really in earnest says: "There is a piece of work that ought to be done; why should not *I* do it?" and he will plunge in and do it at once.

> The body is your animal—the horse upon which you ride. Therefore you must treat it well, and take good care of it; you must not overwork it, you must feed it properly on pure food and drink only, and keep it strictly clean always, even from the minutest speck of dirt.

C.W.L.—The idea that the body is an animal is really very useful; it sounds so obvious, and yet the more closely the simile is followed, the nearer we shall be to doing what is required. Suppose you keep a horse—I am taking it for granted that you are a reasonable and kindly person, and that while you want your work done, at the same time you want your horse to be as happy and comfortable as possible, and in good health. First of all, then, you want to make friends with him, to get to know the creature, and get him to know you and to feel that you are kindly disposed towards him. Then you find out what kind of food suits him best, and how much of it he needs, and give to him. You take care that he shall have enough, but you do not give him the things that will be bad for him. At the same time you work him, because that is the object of having a horse; yet you do not overwork him in any way. You find out what he can do, and set him to do it. You have taught him to trust you so that he will obey you, and when you suggest anything he will follow what you want, knowing that all will be well with him, and then he will trust you even when he is frightened. So you get the most work out of him with the least possible trouble. A bad trainer will sometimes terrorize a horse; but never after that will he get really good work out of him. You do not want that; you want to have a friendly arrangement with the creatures.

The body is exactly like that horse. We ought to find out the best way to deal with it. It is a great mistake to apply severe Hatha Yoga methods. We must be kind to it, and get out of it as much as we comfortably can, but never overwork it, for one may do harm in an hour that it will take years to repair. There is great strain and stress in modern life. Men constantly say in business: "I really must do a little more"; but very often that little overstrains the mechanism, and that which is overstrained does not return to its normal condition. It is very easy to do this harm, because the body is such a very delicate piece of machinery—a *living* piece of machinery. It is wonderfully recuperative, and in many cases what we know as "a good body" will stand a great deal of ill-usage. But the fact that it survives the ill-usage, and that the man lives through it, does not by any means prove that no harm has been done. On the contrary, very often a slight overstrain leaves a permanent mark. Therefore I would caution any who are attempting anything in the way of occult development to be very careful, and to realize fully that, as our President has said, what we have not time to do is not our work.

Then comes the question of nourishment. The theory that anybody can live on anything is not one that commends itself to the practical man. People differ enormously in their dispositions and capacities. It is an old proverb that what is one man's meat is another man's poison, and that is true in this matter of food values. I know there is a tendency to think that people who pay much attention to food are worrying themselves unnecessarily about purely physical things. Certainly I would say do not overdo it, but take the middle path and be wise. Each one owes it to his body to find out what it can take and what amount of that suits it best. Within reason we should give the body what it wants and likes, but never things which are bad for it, like alcohol or meat. Never try to force anything, but always aim at what is wanted with understanding of what you are dealing with, and thus gain the co-operation of such intelligence as the creature may have.

People very often have trouble in changing to vegetarianism from a meat diet. In England when people begin to be vegetarians they often misunderstand the whole matter; they have been living principally on meat, with cabbage and potato. Their idea of being vegetarians is to give up the meat and try to live on cabbage and potato. Now potato is practically all starch and cabbage is mostly water. A man cannot live on starch and water: other elements are needed—foods that will form flesh, bone and blood—and there are many different kinds of them, so assuredly one can with a little trouble find what kinds suit his body best, and then live principally on those. If any one has trouble with digestion he is probably taking the wrong things; he should try others, for there is always a way out, unless he is hopelessly diseased. When little children keep caterpillars in order to see them turn into butterflies they take a good deal of trouble to find what kind of a leaf the caterpillar will eat—they know that only one kind of leaf will suit it. Surely we might take as much trouble over the animal which is to serve us for so many years, and feed it properly on pure food and drink only.

Very great care must be taken about cleanliness. There are various reasons for it—not only for health, nor simply because it is the refined thing to do, but also because the Master particularly uses those who are in close relation with Him as channels for the outpouring of His force. That is generally confined to His pupils, who are in close touch with Him, but any person who is seriously trying to live by the principles laid down in such books as this, is under His eye, and therefore it is not impossible that such an one might be needed, and might be used as a channel for force. It might well happen that in any given place there was no pupil quite suitable for some kind of outpouring; but there might be some other person who, though not so far advanced, was suitable for that particular purpose. In such a case the Master would want to use him.

Many varieties of force are poured out by the Master for different purposes; sometimes one person is suitable as a channel and sometimes another. Watching the case of two pupils side by side, one sees that one is used always for one type of force and the other for another type. This outpouring is physical as well as astral, mental, and buddhic, and on the physical plane it issues mainly through the hands and feet. If, then, the physical body of the person selected failed him for a moment in this most important matter of cleanliness, the Master could not utilize it, because the man would not be a suitable channel. It would be like pouring pure water through a dirty pipe—it would be fouled on the way. Therefore those who are in close relation with the Master are exceedingly careful about perfect bodily cleanliness. Let us take care, then, that we shall be fit in this respect if we should be needed.

Another point about which we need to be careful if we wish to be of use is to avoid distortion, especially of the feet. Not long ago I stayed for a few weeks in a community where it is the custom to walk barefooted, and I was horrified to see the twisted and crippled appearance of the feet of many of the students, and to observe how seriously this deformity interfered with their usefulness as channels for the Master's force. The natural course for that force under ordinary conditions is to fill the whole body of the pupil and rush out through the extremities; but in cases where unhygienic foot-gear had produced permanent malformation the Adept could utilize only the upper half of the body; and as that imposed upon Him the additional trouble of constructing each time a sort of temporary dam or barrier in the neighbourhood of the diaphragm of the pupil, it inevitably followed that others who were free from this disfigurement were employed far more frequently.

> For without a perfectly clean and healthy body you cannot do the arduous work of preparation, you cannot bear its ceaseless strain.

C.W.L.—Under present circumstances preparation for the Path is truly arduous, and if it is hurried it is a ceaseless strain, which we cannot bear unless all our bodies, including the physical, are in good order. Therefore perfect health is a necessity for rapid progress, and wherever it fails there is a delay at once. Those who are in charge of the progress of any pupil always watch most carefully to see that there is no overstrain, and they will not put the least extra work upon one under their care until they see that he is perfectly able to bear it with a suitable margin.

> But it must always be you who control that body, not it that controls you. The astral body has *its* desires—dozens of them; it wants you to be angry, to say sharp words, to feel jealous, to be greedy for money, to envy other people their possessions, to yield yourself to depression. All these things it wants, and many more, not because it wishes to harm you, but because it likes violent vibrations, and likes to change them constantly. But *you* want none of these things, and therefore you must discriminate between *your* wants and your body's.

A.B.—I suppose that most thinking people clearly realize that they are not their physical bodies, but the examples that the Master gives here show how continually they identify themselves with their astral bodies. You may sometimes find yourself saying, "I am angry, or irritable." Even those who do not like to think of themselves as the lower emotions often still confuse them with the higher. Probably they will not say, "I am jealous," when they become conscious of the feeling of jealousy within them; for though men may identify themselves with their feelings they try to veil the lower ones, and in this case they deceive themselves into believing that their feeling is not jealousy, but love; "I am hurt because so-and-so, whom I love, loves some one else better than me."

Love is such a far-reaching, all-embracing virtue, that men like to shelter under it, and they manage to attribute to it all sorts of things with which it has nothing whatever to do. It is far better for us to examine our feelings honestly, and not to play with these serious matters and deceive ourselves with pretty words. In the case under consideration, you are not hurt because you love your friend, but because you desire to appropriate that friend to yourself. Whenever there is this feeling of being hurt it springs from selfishness, which is the opposite pole to love. You—the real Self—cannot feel jealous, but your astral body can; nor can you be angry or irritable; these are all moods of the astral body.

The Master also mentions further examples—greed, envy and depression. Aspirants for the Path are not so likely to yield to the first two of these as to the third. Often people are less careful about depression than about their other feelings because they are under the delusion that it affects only themselves. They think: "If I feel sad or low, after all it is only my business, and it concerns no one else." But that is not true; it does injure other people. The mechanism of this process is well known to all students of occultism. The vibrations of depression spread around, and affect the astral bodies and even the mental bodies of other people. This is a far more evil thing than is generally realized, because many of the people whom your thought may touch may be of a less-developed type, and may also be in circumstances in which they are exposed to conditions that tend to crime.

Those who are familiar with the history and statistics of crime know that a large number of crimes, especially such as murder and suicide, are committed after a period of deep depression. The prisoner in the dock often says: "An overwhelming feeling of despair came over me; I felt I could not help myself." There are many people in the lower stages of evolution who may be affected in this way; and some may suffer imprisonment and death, who yet were not really responsible, or only partly so for the crime committed by their hands. We are living in a world where few people understand these inner laws and very imperfect justice is rendered in our courts for want of simple knowledge of the rudiments of psychology.

Perhaps I feel this all the more keenly because I used to be subject myself to moods of great elation, and then of equally great depression when the pendulum swung back. Many people have the same temperament; one day the world seems full of happiness, the sunshine is bright, nature is beautiful, all things are joyful and fair. Then follows the inevitable reaction; a feeling of great sadness comes over you, and the whole world seems darkened. If you look at the matter quietly, you will realize that the outer causes to which you may attribute your changes of mood are not sufficient to account for such large results. Still, this temperament has some advantages. I certainly could not speak so effectively if

I had not brought it into the world with me; it is part of the orator's temperament to know these extremes of feeling. But, like every other temperament, it has its drawbacks as well as its uses. One must not yield to these violent alternations of feeling.

I doubt whether one can get rid of this defect by merely saying to oneself: "I ought not to feel depressed"; but even the worst cases can be overcome if one remembers that one ought not to yield to it because of its deplorably bad effect on other people. Do not therefore simply try to drive it away, but replace it with a strong thought of courage and cheerfulness, to which should be added the warmth of your unselfish feeling.

The astral body does not wish to do any harm, as the Master points out. It acts as it does simply because it is made up of elemental essence which is on the downward arc, and is evolving by violent and constantly changing vibrations. This constant desire of the astral body for violent changes is a thing that should help the student to realize that it is not himself, but something that brings about moods for no apparent cause, and not approved by the reason, because they are independent activities of the astral body. One must realize this, and not allow oneself to be the playground of all these changing moods. Study your own astral nature, and find out what are the undesirable things that it particularly desires. Then quietly determine that you will not allow it to have them. That done, do not think any more about them; do not brood over them. Pick out the opposite moods, and practise them all day long. If your astral body wants to be impatient, set your mind on patience; think patience in your morning meditation, and practise it throughout the whole of the day. If your astral body wants you to feel jealous, simply observe the fact, and then do not think any more about jealousy, but think of unselfishness and practise it hard, and then there will be no room for jealousy. Your mind cannot be filled with two opposing things at the same time.

Remember that all difficulties constitute opportunities for the would-be occultist. It is no credit for the disciple to show out love when all around are kind, or gentleness when all are considerate. The most ordinary person does that. Those who wish to be disciples must show out right emotion when the wrong is being shown to them; otherwise they are just like all the rest. This should be remembered in difficulty and temptation; the aspirant should spring forward to meet them as opportunities for the payment of debts. To a disciple, every trying person and circumstance he meets is not a temptation, but an opportunity. It is when he is returning good emotions for evil ones that the disciple resembles his Master; it is then that he is showing forth the Master's qualities.

Think, then, in your morning meditations, of the qualities that you want; if you are irritable, for example, think of patience. Then, when you meet an irritable or tiresome person during the day, you will at first respond to him with irritability through force of habit, but a moment after you have made the mistake you will think of patience. The next time you will think of patience while you are making the mistake; a little more practice, and you will think of it the moment before, and then you will feel the irritability, but will not show it; at last you will not even feel irritable. The first of those stages shows that your meditation is beginning to bear fruit.

I know many people who have set themselves to do this and have kept it up for a few days or weeks and then said: "I will not meditate along these lines any more: I am getting no results. My meditation is doing me no good. I am not making progress." It is exactly the same as if a person started on a three days' journey to some place, and after an hour or two sat down, saying: "It is no use my walking; I do not seem to be getting there." Everybody can see how silly such conduct would be down here in the physical world; the other is not a bit less foolish. Meditation *must* produce results, just as walking must carry you over the ground. It is as certain as that. Scientific rules act at all times, and every force you set going must produce results. If you do not at once gain what you are aiming at, it is because there is still more to be overcome, and the force is going into that, to neutralize it and then to conquer it completely. Do not think of the question of results. Just direct the thought to the quality of patience, or whatever it is that you are going to develop, and the results will take care of themselves.

C.W.L.—It is not, after all, very difficult with a little practice to realize that we are not this physical body, that it is only an overcoat, but the astral body—our emotions and desires—presents more difficulty, because it seems often to be a very intimate part of ourselves. One finds people in every-day life everywhere who feel themselves to be their emotions and desires; some are so full of them that if you could imagine these taken away there would seem to be nothing left—the whole person is desire and emotion. It would be very difficult for such an one to separate himself from his astral body, and yet that is what has to be done. The fact that the astral body is constantly changing its moods ought to help people to realize that it is not the Self, the 'I'. As soul one is not changing; one wishes always the same thing—advancement to be able to help others to walk alone the Path intended by our Masters. Surely, therefore, it is clear that this emotional body is not the Self.

The astral elemental gains a certain continuity because the permanent atoms attract round them just the kind of matter we possessed in our previous life. It is therefore difficult to turn round suddenly and check this creature. It can be done, however, and the best way is to discover by careful examination along what lines of undesirable activity one's astral body wants to run. Each person has his own difficulties. One perhaps is nervous and irritable or prone to jealousy, or is greedy for money. When he finds out, he must quietly set himself to check that particular thing. Suppose it is irritability, which is very common under the horrible conditions and the noise of modern life. The person should make up his mind that he will not be irritable. It is a good thing to take it as a subject for meditation; yet in that one should not set to work to combat the vice, but rather to meditate upon the opposite quality of patience. Never think of the evil thing and of fighting against it, because that stirs it up the more.

The same method must be applied also when you are trying to help others by your thought. If you are helping some one who has this fault, instead of dwelling upon his irritability and what a pity it is, and thereby intensifying it, you should think: "I should like him to be calm and patient." Then all the strength of your thought goes in the direction of making him so.

At first, when we meet an irritating person we shall probably be irritable, because we are in the habit of it; and afterwards we shall remember, "I did not mean to do that." It is something even to remember afterwards like that. Perhaps the next time, or the twentieth time, we shall remember at the moment, instead of just afterwards. In the third stage, we shall remember just before we say the irritable thing; the feeling of irritability is there, but we shall not show it. The next step is that we shall not feel the irritability at all, and then it is conquered and we shall have no more trouble with it in this life or other lives to come.

It is also necessary for the mastery of the astral nature that we should have no personal feelings at all that can be hurt or offended. The better feelings, such as sympathy and love, we may and must have to the uttermost. But it must be impossible for us to have our feelings hurt, to be offended. He whose feelings can be hurt is thinking about himself, and that we have no right to do if we have given ourselves to the Master. It may be that there are some people so thick-headed that they cannot see an insult—that is not desirable; but when you do see it, be wise enough to take no notice of it, which is always the better way. If people say nasty things about you, never mind; people have been saying nasty things about other people ever since the world began, and until we are all well on the way to Adeptship they will continue to do so. And after all it does not matter what another person says. It is a passing vibration of the air, and it is no more than that unless we allow it to be so. If a person says something about you which is unpleasant, if you do not hear it, it does not hurt you in the least. If you do happen to hear it and get into a fume of anger and horror and despair and all the rest of it, that is not the doing of the original sinner; you are hurting yourself. Take it quite philosophically. Say, "Poor creature, that is all she knows about it!" Be quite gentle and kindly about it. What other people say is of very little importance, because they never know. Remember "the heart knoweth its own bitterness". In each case a man has his own reasons for what he says and does and thinks; from the outside you never know the whole of his reasons because you are looking at them superficially, and usually quite wrongly. Until you reach the buddhic plane therefore, give him the benefit of the doubt, or more wisely still do not attempt to attribute motives to anyone. If you feel that a person's action is wrong the kindest thing is to say: "I should not do that; to me it seems to be wrong; but I assume that that person has his reasons, though I do not know what they may be."

When a person is rude, it is often because something has gone wrong, and the result is that he feels all out of tune—and you happen to be the next person who speaks to him. He is not really angry with *you*. Something else has upset him; perhaps he had not a good dinner. We have to learn to make allowances for other people and say: "Poor fellow, I suppose he cannot always feel as perfectly amiable and agreeable as I always am!" Probably that person will be rather sorry afterwards that he spoke a little rudely, or else he will not even realize that anything out of the common has been said. Any feeling of being offended or hurt must spring from a thought of self. If we were not thinking of ourselves we could not feel hurt or offended. This thought of self is precisely what we must weed out and cast away. Wherever there is a case of jealousy, there is also this thought of self. If the person were thinking only how much he loved the other, it could not matter to him how much that other loved some one else. The delusion of the separate self is at the back of nearly all our troubles.

The selfish man is now an anachronism—still carrying on what was useful and necessary for him twenty years ago, but it is not useful and necessary for him now, and he is simply behind the time. Our business is to be up-to-date. We are living for and thinking of the future that the great World-Teacher will make for us; and because of that we must brush away all these antiquated ideas.

When you examine yourself to find the faults that you intend to overcome, beware of being upset by delusions about remorse and repentance. Remember the story of Lot's wife, and do not look back—that is a very profitless occupation. You may say quite calmly when you have made some bad mistake: "That was a foolish thing to do; I will never do it again." Talleyrand is reported to have said: "Any man may make a mistake—we all make mistakes—but the man who makes the same mistake twice is a fool." A Master once remarked: "The only repentance which is worth anything is the resolve not to do it again." Remember; "The man who never made a mistake never made anything at all." You do not worry about what you did in past lives; why then worry about yesterday? Both are equally past. Remorse is a waste of time and energy—worse than that, for it is a form of selfishness.

It is easy to be loving and kindly to those who are so to us, but if we have made any real progress we shall pour out love even when we meet with the lack of it. The Christ said: "If ye love them which love you, what reward have ye? do not even the publicans the same?"[1] His command was to love your enemies and pray for them which despitefully use you.[2] That is the time when a disciple of the Master can show his true value; when he can do what the Master would do; when, although people speak ill of him, and ill-treat him, he still thinks of them kindly and lovingly, and makes excuses and allowances for their foolishness. That is what we have to do. It is not enough to return love and kindliness; we

[1] S. Matthew, v, 46.
[2] S. Luke, vi, 27-29.

must be able to pour it out upon people who as yet scarcely know what it means. It was said of the Christ that when He was reviled, He reviled not again; when He suffered, He threatened not; but committed Himself to Him that judgeth righteously.[1] We are all wronged and misjudged and misunderstood sometimes. No one need worry about it, for karma will see that all is put right. "Vengeance is mine; I will repay, saith the Lord."[2] Leave it to Him. Justice will always be done, and all that is wrong will some day come right, and those who now misunderstand will some day realize their error, and be sorry that they misunderstood. No injustice will be done: the total will come out as it should.

The Logos Himself is setting the example of Love all the time. Many people speak ill of Him; many misunderstand and flout Him. He makes no answer, but the steady outpouring of the divine love goes on for ever, and in so far as we wish to be an expression of the divine that must characterize us also.

Your mental body wishes to think itself proudly separate, to think much of itself and little of others.

C.W.L.—Here again we must differentiate between what the mental body desires and what we ourselves desire, and realize that we are not the mind. We are in the habit of saying, "I think so-and-so," but about nine times out of ten the fact is not "I think," but the mind thinks. Many of us have been trying to control and

[1] I Peter, II, 23.
[2] Romans, XII, 19.

train our thoughts, yet if we review them we shall see how few are worthy to be attributed to us—to the Self —and how many belong merely to the lower mind.

The lower mind flies from one thing to another, flits over the surface of a variety of subjects, but usually deals fully with none. It is not its desire as a rule to deal exhaustively with anything, but simply to pass from subject to subject in order to get constant change of vibrations. We shall probably find, if we look back, that we have, during even a short space of time, thought a great number of quite insignificant things. When you are walking along the street, for instance, you will find that though *you* are not specially thinking, there is something that is doing so all the time; that is the mental body. If you do not hold it in control, it will pass in review a vast number of things, useless to you, though not necessarily bad, unless they are self-centred or selfish. It has the habit of association of ideas, also, by which it will sometimes twist one's most beautiful thought and carry it away to something quite different and trivial. We must control and change all that. I know it is hard every moment to keep check upon what the mind is doing, but it ought to be done, because the mind is a mighty power, by far the strongest thing we have about us. If the will can be directed through the mental body there are few things one cannot do by its means. This enormous power can be ours, be we rich or poor, young or old—a valuable instrument in our service of the Master, if we will practise constant vigilance until new habits of mind are formed. Many things can be done with thought, which cannot otherwise be accomplished. Affectionate thought that is sent out to some one whom we know to be in need of assistance may be of far greater help than the gift of a sum of money—it may produce a life-long effect. The results of this may not even show on the physical plane, but it is none the less real work for the Master.

The background of the mind should be a thought of the Master, to which it will turn whenever the Self is not really thinking about something that requires attention. This thought should be as precise as possible. There are many people whose thought of the Master is a kind of vague beatitude, a sort of semi-ecstasy, a species of religious coma in which they are not really actively thinking of anything. Instead of vaguely bathing ourselves in a thought which has no precision about it, we should let our devotion to the Master take a definite form, such as "What can I do to serve Him, in what direction can I employ my thought-power?"

You will find again and again in this book the strongest insistence upon the fact that there is really only one thought, only one will, only one work for us. The one thought is the thought of service to the Master, the one will is to do that work, the one work is the devotion to Him, and for His sake to the world. Though there is the most complex variety in the work that will come in our way to do, it is all for Him and for the world. There is only one thought in the Master's mind—that of service; and if we wish to be one with Him that must be be our only thought, too. It implies that we shall make ourselves fit for service, and in that way it includes some progress for us, not because we want to be great, but because we desire to be good instruments.

Many people are developing their mental bodies. Great scientific men do it for the pure pursuit of knowledge. Sometimes there may be a side thought in the man's brain that if he makes a great discovery he will become famous, but I do not think that is true of most scientific men. There is usually a wish in the background to make the knowledge useful, but first of all there is in the scientific mind an intense desire to know. It is a noble line, and in it there are many noble souls, doing great service to mankind.

We too must endeavour to cultivate our mental bodies, to make them keen, active, useful. Why? Why does a carpenter sharpen his plane? Not in order that he may have a sharper plane than some other carpenter, but in order that it may cut the wood well, and that his work may be well done. It is precisely for that reason that our mental bodies must be trained. But we must all the time have in view the thought: "I am making an instrument for the Master's work." One who keeps this ideal will be free from spiritual pride, and so will avoid many of the pitfalls into which mere intellectual development does undoubtedly lead people.

Even when you have turned it away from worldly things, it still tries to calculate for self, to make you think of your own progress, instead of thinking of the Master's work and of helping others.

A.B.—The thing which has perhaps struck me most in this teaching of the Master is that it invariably centres round and returns to the idea of one thought, one will, one work. It seems to radiate that unity so strongly, that you feel that the Master can have only the one thought, that he has blended Himself so perfectly with the One that He could not think of anything else, that He could not forget it, whatever might be occupying His attention. That is the ideal for the disciple. He must think always of the Master's work and of helping others; that one idea must dominate all else. If it is otherwise, then it is your mind which is thinking, not you. But if you have that idea, you have everything else. Suppose you think of a virtue in meditation; why do you want it—to be admired, or to bring yourself nearer to initiation? Or do you want it in order to be a better instrument for the Master's work? That is the test by which you may know whether it is your mind or you which is thinking.

It is a good plan to put the test to yourself in a definite way. Suppose the case—and I do not think it an inconceivable one, though as a general rule the more developed a man is the more useful he is also—of a piece of the Master's work which called for qualities far inferior to others which you had developed. Would you be willing to take it and to work away at that, instead of going on using your higher talents and improving yourself on those lines? Would you be willing to be less, in order to be more useful? You would if you always kept in mind the one motive of being useful for the

Master's work. In that work there will be plenty of opportunity for the cultivation of our mental bodies, that they may be keen, active, useful. If we improve ourselves for this purpose we shall be in no danger of falling into the heresy of separateness. In the lower world we must continually keep our eyes open to turn to account the opportunities which other people have left aside because they thought them unimportant. A disciple always looks for the things left undone by others, that he may supply what is lacking. Such an attitude means that the mind is coming under control.

C.W.L.—The Master's work must dominate all else in our minds. If we find any other thought than that, any other reason coming forward for doing anything, then that which is putting forward a reason is the mind, not the ego—an important distinction to make. The mind is indeed proud and separate, and when it has quite given up all the earthly kinds of pride, its next stage will be to try to make us proud of our progress, of our position in relation to the great Masters, or something of that kind. When we have trodden that down, and are rid of any pride in these things, it will try to make us proud of not being proud. Do not blame the subtle mental elemental; it has no idea of you, but it is simply trying to get the varieties and kinds of vibrations which it needs for its own evolution.

When you meditate, it will try to make you think of the many different things which *it* wants instead of the one thing which *you* want. You are

not this mind, but it is yours to use; so here again discrimination is necessary. You must watch unceasingly, or you will fail.

C.W.L.—They say in India that the mind is the rāja or king of senses, and that of all parts of our nature it is the most difficult to control. In that respect we in the West are perhaps even worse off than the Indian, because we have been especially developing this lower mind, and have prided ourselves on the rapidity with which it can change from one subject to another.

However, by patient effort you may bring to bear upon this elemental the mighty power of the force of habit; you may get it into a groove, and induce it to understand that you, the ego, intend to preserve your dominant idea all the time, but that in connection with that idea there are infinite ramifications, for there is nothing that cannot be brought into the service of the Master. Then presently this curious unmanageable elemental will come to understand that, on the whole, it gets more by working with you, whom it does not understand, than by working against you; and afterwards it will work pleasantly and harmoniously along with you.

CHAPTER 3

RIGHT AND WRONG

Between right and wrong Occultism knows no compromise. At whatever apparent cost, that which is right you must do, that which is wrong you must not do, no matter what the ignorant may think or say. You must study deeply the hidden laws of Nature, and when you know them arrange your life according to them, using always reason and common sense.

A.B.—If you look honestly at it you will find that ordinary life is a series of compromises. Men are constantly doing a little less than what they know to be right in order to meet that deadliest of questions: "What will people say?" Knowing quite well in a given case what is best to do, they shift it a little, tamper with it, fall short of it, in order to make the way smoother for themselves. This fear of the opinions of others is partly due to a weakness which is amiable at its root—the desire to please. This desire is very common in India, but if you want to tread the occult path properly, you must never let yourselves be led by it into compromises, where principles or matters of importance are concerned, such as in the big religious and social questions. Take, for example, the case of child marriage. There are many cases in which these marriages are consummated too early. I have spoken again and again on the public platform about the cruelty of making a girl a mother before she is full-grown, and of the injury that such a practice does to the vitality of the race. Many a man knows that it is wrong, and openly says so; he asks why other people marry their children too young, and yet he still does it himself, because of what people would say if he did not. Out of such material as this you cannot make the occultists.

Putting aside for a moment the great questions on which the future of a nation largely depends, let us turn to the small matters of every-day life. Here also there must be no compromise. You must make up your mind as to what is right, and then keep firmly to it. I know that you cannot carry out your highest ideals immediately, any more than you can get from the bottom of a mountain to the top by taking one step. But if you mean to scale your mountain, every step must be taken with a view to reaching the summit, every step must bring you nearer to it. Never lower your ideal; that is fatal. As the Upanishad says: "One thing is the right, the pleasant another; right unto pleasant the wise man preferreth."

Try in little things to do what your conscience thinks right. You are not responsible for what another person's conscience thinks, nor for whether he follows his own conscience; but your are responsible for following your own, at whatever apparent cost. It is only *apparent* cost, mind you; you cannot lose by doing what you believe to be right. Of course, care must be taken not to identify your whims, prejudices and fancies with the right; as to that the Master gives a warning here, when he says: "Study deeply the hidden laws of nature." First find out what is right, and then live according to your knowledge.

The Master adds the important suggestion in the last few words of this passage: "Using always reason and common sense." Always consider the feelings of other people, but never let them interfere between you and what you know to be right. If you have to choose between hurting people's feelings and compromising with your own conscience, then choose the former. An occultist will always discriminate, in dealing with people, between the real person and the prejudices of his various bodies. He will never hurt a person, but he will hurt his prejudices rather than do wrong. Still, he will not hurt even his prejudices unnecessarily; but if he must do so, he will at the same time know that really the person is being helped, not hurt, and that he himself is being used as an instrument for breaking down a limitation which is cramping the man inside. Even in that case, his action will be gently and considerately carried out. Many people find this difficult. It is much harder to do a thing with quiet reason; a rush of emotion makes it easier. The emotion, be it good or bad, supplies an impulse which carries a man through without further effort on his part. If you would be an occultist you must not act through impulse, as ordinary men do; you must develop reason, power of discrimination, and in this effort you will begin unconsciously to unfold the buddhi.

C.W.L.—People usually have their prejudices—plenty of them; and they identify these with the right. Having been brought up along some particular line, it has never occurred to them to question it, so they are liable to think that the man who does not fall in with their particular method is wrong, especially when it is followed by the majority. Popular prejudices are usually very unreasonable, and therefore we cannot allow them to influence us in matters of right and wrong. I do not say that there are not often some grounds of reason to be found behind a popular prejudice, if we dig down deep to it—not probably the reason that people are alleging at all, but some other reason. But usually that fragment of truth is distorted and misapplied on account of the mass of error in which it is swathed.

The occultist never allows himself to be forced to do a wrong thing for fear of hurting other people's prejudices, but he will never offend those prejudices unnecessarily. Reason and common sense must rule in all things. There is something, let us say, that you want to do because you know it is a good thing, and important. Very well, but do not charge at it like a bull at a gate. He possibly gets through, but at the cost of considerable damage to himself and the gate. One should always show sweet reasonableness in all that is done. If we let ourselves become stirred up and angry about a thing there is a wave of emotion that carries us through; but to do the thing gently and quietly, without any feeling against those who oppose, is much more difficult; yet that is quite obviously the right way to do it.

One must not act on impulse, as most people do. They cannot bear this and that; they do not understand, and do not want to take the trouble to understand; they just drive ahead and take it for granted that they are in the right; but we have to consider others—to take into account their feelings, and to think, too, of the possibility that they may be in the right, and we in the wrong, in a particular case.

> You must discriminate between the important and the unimportant. Firm as a rock where right and wrong are concerned, yield always to others in things which do not matter. For you must be always gentle and kindly, reasonable and accommodating, leaving to others the same full liberty which you need for yourself.

A.B.—This is a very tender and beautiful passage, and it balances the previous one, which, taken by itself, might sound rather hard. Now, as the things for which people generally care most are those which do not matter the occultist can afford to let them have their own way, in many cases. What is important to him is a certain thing that has to be done; he points his will to the one thing in the middle that really matters, and with regard to the rest he lets people do exactly as they like. As he yields to them in those things, they realize what a delightful person he is to work with; and they gradually follow him quite happily on the important point, hardly conscious that they are following at all. In the world this quality is called tact. In occultism it is called discrimination.

It is this quality that the fanatic overlooks, and therefore he does not succeed, while the occultist always succeeds. This fanatic never knows the difference between the important and the unimportant, so he will not yield even in things which do not matter; therefore he rubs people's fur up all the wrong way, and then they will not follow him, however much he may be in the right, and however important his main object may be. If, instead of that, you smooth their fur down, they purr and come along after you. This is based upon a universal fact in nature. In both men and animals it is an instinct to pull in opposition to anyone who is trying to pull them. I saw a little instance of this fact the other day. A man was trying to pull a calf along, and, of course, the calf had planted its four feet firmly into the ground, stuck its tail out, and was pulling against the man for all it was worth. If that man had been sensible he would have stopped pulling, and then the animal would have stopped pulling against him, and with a little patting and coaxing he could have got it to follow him willingly.

There was a valuable lesson in that. If people will not do what you want, look for the fault in yourself; you will generally find that it is something in your way of acting that sets them against you. I follow this plan myself. When there is friction and trouble connected with my work in any place, I sit down and think it over, and try to find out what I am doing that produces these difficulties, and to discover some other way of doing the work. This is far better than trying to make people follow your way. You can force them to a certain extent, no doubt, but that is wrong in principle, and also in practice it only creates opposition and trouble. It shows a great lack of the qualities of leadership—a faculty which the Masters will want in us in the future. The Masters will want you to know how to lead, so that you may help people on, instead of hammering them along.

C.W.L.—Some seven hundred years from now many of us will have the opportunity of working in the development of the Sixth Root-Race, and in the meantime we shall have much to do with preparing the world for the coming of the World-Teacher. Some of us will be alive when He comes, and we shall work under Him; therefore we shall have to develop the qualities of leadership. The first necessity of a leader is tact.

Because the occultist never gives up in any work of importance, he always succeeds in the end, though he may meet with a check, and be thrown back for the time. The French Revolution was an instance of this sort. Those who stood at the back of the movement towards liberty in France were unable to control the mad passions of the people, so that terrible carnage and crime ensued, and the Star set in blood for the time. Never think for a moment that They approved of the madness, of the devilish lust for slaughter, of the unspeakable filth and cruelty, of the treachery and terrorism, of all the indescribable loathsomeness of that awful time. The power passed into the hands of a rabble, maddened by abominable tyranny and oppression, who showed themselves far lower than the beasts of the field. Never imagine that their incredible atrocities were countenanced by Those who were working towards civilization. But later on They managed to gain Their end in some other way, and at the present day that country and many others have all the freedom for which those people were struggling. That is so with all other great reforms that They introduce, and all the other work that They take up—They succeed in the long run, though not always just at first.

We shall have to do just precisely that—never accept defeat, always go on with the work—but to do it well we must acquire the art of helping skilfully. A great many good people want to drive everybody. But that is not the way—we must show others the delight and joy and glory of man's future and the Masters' work, and then they will come along with us of their own accord. If you cannot get on with certain people, look for the defect in yourself. Do not bother about their faults, although no doubt they have plenty, but see what it is in you that prevents you from getting on with them. You will probably find something if you look closely enough.

Try to see what is worth doing: and remember that you must not judge by the size of the thing. A small thing which is directly useful in the Master's

work is far better worth doing than a large thing which the world would call good. You must distinguish not only the useful from the useless, but the more useful from the less useful.

A.B.—As I have already said, the things which are worth doing from the standpoint of the real are those about which people usually care nothing at all. They are interested in unimportant things. The disciple is required therefore to practise this kind of discrimination, and must not waste his time in all the useless occupations which fill the days of worldly people.

Then comes a subtler point; you must not judge the value of a thing by its size. The acts of a statesman which are looming large in the eyes of the world may possibly be quite unimportant from the Master's standpoint—mere dust on the wheel. Some small thing done by an unnoticed person may be infinitely more important if it is exactly in line with the Master's work.

Then comes a still more subtle distinction—that between the more and the less useful. You cannot do everything, so you must do what in your own judgment will serve the Master best. Everything which helps the world is useful for the Master's work, but as your time and energy are limited you must take the more useful, whenever the choice is open to you. The Master gives a typical illustration of this in the next two sentences, when He speaks of feeding the souls of men in preference to their bodies. By helping the soul you are striking at the root of all the evils in the world, for without exception they grow out of ignorance and selfishness.

> To feed the poor is a good and noble and useful work; yet to feed their souls is nobler and more useful than to feed their bodies. Any rich man can feed the body, but only those who know can feed the soul.

C.W.L.—It has sometimes been brought as a reproach against the Theosophical Society that it does not engage itself in active philanthropic work such as the distribution of food and clothing to the poor. Some of our Lodges have done a good deal in that way, but it is not their principal work. Any man who is rich and kindly disposed could do that, but there is much work which only those who know can do. It may perhaps seem to some that we are rather conceited to arrogate to ourselves the title of "those who know". But we are not really praising ourselves in doing that. We can quite clearly see that there are plenty of good people who have nothing whatever to do with Theosophy who are intellectually far in advance of many of us; but it has been our karma to study these subjects, and because of that we know more about them than all those excellent people who have not studied them. There are many among those people of greater intellect, spirituality or devotion, who will go rapidly ahead when they acquire this knowledge that we have of the way in which our forces ought to be directed. They will pass us on the way, perhaps, but we on our part shall welcome them and rejoice to see it, for there is no jealousy on this path and every one on it hails the advance of a brother.

Meantime this Theosophical knowledge is the great talent which is put into our hands for use. If we did nothing for others with it, but simply hugged it to ourselves and enjoyed all that it brings us in the way of freedom from worry and trouble, comprehension of difficult problems, and so on, we should be exactly like the man in the Bible who buried his talent. But if we do our best to spread the light that comes to us and to help in every possible way, then at least we are putting our talent out to interest. 'One who knows' can feed the souls of the poor and the rich alike with his knowledge. This is in no way less practical than the other work, even from a material point of view. What is the cause of all the poverty and suffering in the world? Ignorance and selfishness. If we attack the ignorance and the selfishness by trying to put before men knowledge of the laws of life, and to show them why they must necessarily be unselfish, we are doing more even from the most material point of view to bring about the welfare and happiness of people on the physical plane than we should do by merely distributing food. Not for a moment would one say that that is not good and necessary, that it should not be done. The need of the moment must be met; but it is a greater service to remove the cause of all the trouble. We are doing what the purely physical plane helper could not do.

Wherever there has been any wisdom, any knowledge at all on these lines, those who know have been set free from the other work in order that they may teach. You may read, for example, in the Acts of the Apostles, how, in the early Christian Church, they had community of goods, and when there was some trouble about the distribution of the food supply, the Apostles were requested to settle the dispute—to deal with it themselves, in fact. They said: "It is not reasonable that we should leave the word of God to serve tables," and told the other people to elect from among themselves those who would do that work, and abide by their decision, but not to expect them, whose business it was to expound the word, to devote themselves to the purely physical side of things. It was not that those things were to be neglected, but that the proper people to attend to them were those who could do that but could not do the other work.

A.B.—We in the Society have knowledge which those outside have not, and therefore the spreading of Theosophy is the one thing we ought to do. Those in the Society who are not yet ready for that work—for lecturing or writing or teaching in some other way—should do other kinds of work while they are preparing themselves. I established the Order of Service for those who cannot teach, so that everyone who joins the Society may find something to do. The one thing that a person in the Society should *not* do is to be idle. All members should be active in the Master's work.

C.W.L.—It is hard to realize how many people are reasonably near the position where they might make rapid progress if only they could be awakened to it. I have myself, I suppose, seen it most among the young, because my work generally lies there. I see boys and girls by the score in almost any country who could make good progress along Theosophical lines, if the matter could only be put before them. But it is not, and they plunge off into the work-a-day world, and become very good people of the ordinary type. They will go on in that way for twenty or thirty incarnations, or more, though they are capable of taking up Theosophy and would be interested in it, if it were properly put before them. Surely that state of affairs throws a serious responsibility upon those who possess this knowledge. It is therefore our business to be capable and ready to put Theosophy forward whenever there is a suitable opportunity. There are plenty of people who might just as well enter upon Theosophical development now, as in twenty lives' time. It is, of course, a question of their karma, but it is our karma to give them the opportunity, to put the matter before them—whether they take it or not is their affair. Until we have done our best we do not know whether it is their karma to be helped or not.

> If you know, it is your duty to help others to know. However wise you may be already, on this Path you have much to learn; so much that here also there must be discrimination, and you must think carefully what is worth learning. All knowledge is useful, and one day you will have all knowledge; but while you have only part, take

care that it is the most useful part. God is Wisdom as well as Love; and the more wisdom you have, the more you can manifest of Him. Study then, but study first that which will most help you to help others.

C.W.L.—The Master here advises study, but He tells his pupil to choose so far as he can what will help him to help others. I take it that that means that one should try to understand Theosophy thoroughly and first of all, but should in addition acquire the knowledge and education of the time that make a cultured man. I know that there are many in the Theosophical Society who find themselves, for various reasons, uneducated, but yet are very earnest and devoted, who say: "Why should we bother ourselves about the details of education? We want to get at the reality of the thing, and to present the truths somehow." Yes, but the uneducated man is likely to present them in a form that will probably at once estrange and repel the educated and cultured. I have heard people say that an intuitional man who hears the thing badly put will rise above the form to the truth that lies behind; but unfortunately most men are not intuitional and we have no right, on account of our own laziness, to put an additional obstacle in the way of anyone who might otherwise be induced to take an interest in the subject. It is distinctly and emphatically our duty to make our presentation as nearly perfect as we can.

Work patiently at your studies, not that men may think you wise, not even that you may have

the happiness of being wise, but because only the wise man can be wisely helpful. However much you wish to help, if you are ignorant you may do more harm than good.

A.B.—Here is advice especially important for our younger members. I often come across young men at college who are touched by the new spirit; they are very eager to help, and often want to put aside their studies. "What is the use of these studies to us?" they ask. The advice I always give in such a case is: "Continue your studies and become an educated man. Although there may be many things among those you learn which have not much importance, the training of the intelligence is all-important. That is where the use of your studies lies; they render your mind logical and accurate. If you do not go through this mental discipline, afterwards you will be badly hampered in your work."

It is not enough to be able to recognize Theosophic truths; if you want to help others to know, you must have that intellectual training which enables you to present them properly. If a person is uneducated, one sees it at once in the way he presents a subject. There is no part of my own training which I am more glad to have gone through than the scientific part. First of all it has helped me to put things in a rational, logical way, which gains a hearing from intellectual and cultured people; and secondly, it supplies me with many illustrations, which appeal to the mind because they are drawn from subjects which can be definitely proved.

Those among us who are older can be of much use to the younger with whom they have opportunities of dealing if they will, without damping their enthusiasm, explain in a kind and sensible way the importance of their making themselves what the world calls educated. When one has the higher things, one is apt to be a little impatient with these lower studies. Therefore the Master says to His young disciple, who had still much of his intellectual training to go through: "Work patiently at your studies."

C.W.L.—History emphatically supports this counsel. Many good people, with the best intentions, have blundered in the most terrible manner, and have injured their cause, whatever it may have been, far more than any outside attack could have done. Theosophical work has frequently suffered from faulty or negligent presentation. We do not wish that Theosophy should be spoken ill of because of our personal defects or disabilities. If you are set to do work for the Society and do not do it satisfactorily, then go to work and learn to do it satisfactorily. If you are asked to read something and cannot do it, learn how to do it properly. If you cannot lecture—presently, when you know enough and take the trouble to prepare, you will learn to do that. But, at any rate, be doing something and try to do it well. It is our duty as Theosophists to master the correct grammar and the correct expression which will enable us to put these things acceptably before the people that we wish to reach. Any truth, however glorious, may be eclipsed, if clumsily and wrongly put. It is our duty to do our best in this matter. We must be educated if we are to present these truths properly.

CHAPTER 4

BE TRUE ALL THROUGH

You must distinguish between truth and falsehood; you must learn to be true all through, in thought and word and deed.

A.B.—One might wonder, if one were not following the Master's thought as well as His words, why this point comes where it does. Discrimination between truth and falsehood—surely this should have come first! The Master places it later because it is a very difficult thing. You must be true all through, He says, and it is not easy to make onself so in thought and word and deed. You will notice that thought comes first; this is the regular occult order, which puts thought first, then speech and action. The Lord Buddha also gave them in this order, as right thought, right speech and right action.

In thought first; and that is not easy, for there are in the world many untrue thoughts, many foolish superstitions, and no one who is enslaved by them can make progress.

C.W.L.—We think in Theosophy that we are absolutely free from superstition; I am not quite sure that

that is always true. There is a possibility, it seems to me, of a Theosophical superstition. The man who believes a thing because "it is written in the Bible" is no doubt superstitious to that extent, because he has no good basis for that belief. Still, it is only one step forward from that superstition to say, "Thus saith Madame Blavatsky" or "It is written in *The Secret Doctrine*". It *is* a step, because there is a great deal more evidence that Madame Blavatsky knew what she was talking about, than that, let us say S. Paul did, or any of the older writers; but the thing is no more our own because Madame Blavatsky said it, than because it is attributed to S. James or S. Peter. We must understand a thing and make it part of ourselves, grow into it and let it grow into us. So long as we are only reading things parrot-wise those things are superstitions. The very belief in the truth may be a superstition, if it has no better basis for us than that it is written here or there. When it becomes part of our mental system, we can say, "It is part of me and it is mine; I know why I believe it, and therefore my belief is an intelligent belief and not merely superstition." I am afraid there is a great deal of unintelligent belief even in the truth, in many cases.

A.B.—It is so difficult for a person to free himself from superstition, from taking the unessential for the essential (for this is the essence of superstition) that he is not expected wholly to do so until after the First Initiation. This shows that it is a deep and subtle thing, which works into the very nature of the man. No one who is enslaved by it, says the Master, can make progress. That is a sweeping statement, but we must observe the word enslaved. He does not say that no one who is in any degree superstitious can make progress, but that no one who is a slave to superstition can do so. Superstition is a great thing for holding people back. How many religious people one knows who are good, pious, philanthropic, who lead beautiful and earnest lives, but are superstitious! They think that their ceremonies, their formulæ, their ways of doing things, matter. But they do not matter a bit.

Let us take as an example the perfomance of a particular function, that intended to help the dead. The Roman Catholic celebrates the Mass for the dead; the Hindu performs the Shrāddha ceremonies for the same purpose. Both ceremonies are inspired by the same wish to help those who have passed over, and both effect their purpose, though they are widely different in form. Yet a Hindu or a Catholic in clinging to these *forms* would be superstitious. The goodwill and the earnestness that they put into it, the love that they pour out towards the departed—these are the real things, and they produce the result. The good wish matters very much, but the specific character of the outer form does not, for the garment of their wish is local and unimportant. That outward form depends on where you happen to be born, for you are born into a religion as into a race and country. Of all the superstitious belief in rites and ceremonies, in the efficacy of mere outward forms, you must rid yourselves. For a long time this belief was very important, a good thing, because it is the only thing which can get people out of sloth, carelessness and indifference. These outward things are crutches; they are necessary for those who cannot yet walk alone, but when once you can walk without them you must cast them aside.

> Therefore you must not hold a thought just because many other people hold it, nor because it has been believed for centuries, nor because it is written in some book which men think sacred; you must think of the matter for yourself, and judge for yourself whether it is reasonable.

C.W.L.—Those are the words of the Master Kūthūmi. They were also, twenty-five hundred years ago, the words of the Lord Gautama Buddha, when men came to Him asking: "There are so many teachers and so many doctrines put before us, and they all seem good; how are we to know which is the best: how can we decide among them?" His reply to that question is given as follows in the Kālāma Sutta of the *Anguttara Nikāya*:

> Our Lord Buddha has said that we must not believe in a thing said merely because it is said; nor in traditions because they have been handed down from antiquity; nor rumours, as such; nor writings by sages, because sages wrote them; nor fancies that we may suspect to have been inspired in us by a deva [that is, in presumed spiritual inspiration]; nor from inferences drawn from some haphazard assumption we may have made; nor because of what seems an analogical necessity; nor on the mere authority of our teachers or masters, But we are to believe when the writing, doctrine, or saying is corroborated by our own reason and consciousness. "For this," says He in concluding, "I taught you—not to believe merely because you have heard, but when you believed of your own consciousness, then to act accordingly and abundantly."[1]

[1] See *A Buddhist Catechism*, by H. S. Olcott, question 131.

One of the exercises set by the Masters for Their pupils is to find out how much they really know and how much they only believe. It is a good practice to observe how much of our mental furniture we can definitely claim as belonging to ourselves, how much is ours because we have thoroughly understood and assented to it, and how much we have accepted from others almost without having thought about it. In every case people are born into religions as they are into countries. It is the same with a great number of customs. For example, when you go out to dinner you must wear a certain dress. It is the custom, and one does not want to go against custom in a matter which is of no importance, in which there is no question of right or wrong.

A.B.—It is a very useful exercise to examine the contents of the mind from time to time, and observe, first, how many things you believe simply because many other people believe them; second, how many things you believe only because they are old beliefs; third, how many things you believe because they are written in some sacred book. And when you have swept out these three classes of belief, notice how much remains, and these will show you what real basis you have for your beliefs. That is one advantage of going through the Freethought experience, as I did. No one who has not been through it can quite understand, I think, what it means to have to give up one's religious beliefs if they have been really sincerely held; what the final crash is like, when the foundations that you have been standing upon give way. It very nearly killed me; I was physically prostrate for weeks. But when once you have done it thoroughly like that, you need not do it over again. So, when I came into touch with Theosophy, although I felt sure of it with a perfect inward conviction, I tested it all with my mind as I received it.

> **Remember that though a thousand men agree upon a subject, if they know nothing about that subject their opinion is of no value.**

C.W.L.—That is a matter which is very hard for the modern world to realize. People seem to think nowadays that, if you only pile up enough ignorance you will somehow get knowledge out of it. But you do not. The ignorant must have those who know to direct them.

A.B.—In one way, the multitude of books that we have at the present day is a disadvantage. It induces reading without thinking, which produces superficiality and fickleness of thought. That is why I always advise people to read a little and then reproduce what they have read, not by memory, but out of the clear grasp of the subject that they have obtained. Only what you have thought out is really yours, and only by thinking over and understanding what you read and hear, can you make it your own. Otherwise, the more you read the more superstitious you become. You go on adding more beliefs to those that you already have, none of which has any sure foundation.

I once employed a man who kept accounts very badly. Whenever he got his accounts into a muddle, he began a new account book, and hoped in that way to get them straight again. In the same way, people nowadays always want something new because they have not gained any real satisfaction out of their superficial acquaintance with what they already have. Those among our members who quote Bishop Leadbeater's books and mine all over the place are also superstitious. However true the statements they quote may be, they are not true *to them*; for if they had grasped them they would not need to fall back upon us as authorities. If they quote what we say at all, they should only quote our words as opinions, and not try to force them on anyone. There is only one authority in the world, and that is wisdom.

He who would walk upon the Path must learn to think for himself, for superstition is one of the greatest evils in the world, one of the fetters from which you must utterly free yourself.

C.W.L.—That superstition is a very big and subtle thing is evident from the fact that it is the third of the fetters which men must cast off on the Path after the First Initiation. The Pāli name for it is *sīlabbataparāmāsa*, "belief in the efficacy of rites or ceremonies of any kind".

Your thought about others must be true; you must not think of them what you do not know.

C.W.L.—If we think of other people what we only suppose about them, the thought is probably the merest speculation. We really know remarkably little even about those who are very near to us, still less about casual acquaintances; and yet there is constantly much profitless babble about the doings and sayings and supposed thoughts of other people, and most of it, fortunately, is hopelessly untrue.

A.B.—Opinions about other people are mostly untrue. We can only think truly of another when we really know him, when we can see his thought and understand it. That knowledge is impracticable to most people, yet they have very definite opinions about others; they constantly judge them and think unkindly of them.

A little further on the Master says: "Never attribute motives to another." That is an enormously important piece of advice which, if carried out in the world, would do away with at least half the trouble that exists. If a person does a thing which you do not understand, leave it at that; do not invent possible motives. A person does something, for what reason you cannot know; but you hunt round for a possible motive, generally an unworthy one, and fasten it on to the act; then you blame him for what you have thought and done yourself. By thus attributing motives men add to any evil force that may possibly exist in the mind of the person criticized, or they supply it if it is not already there. Christ said: "Resist not evil"; this is a case where that applies; it is not our business to search in people's minds for evil to battle against; leave the thing alone and it will die.

Do not suppose that they are always thinking of you.

C.W.L.—This happens perpetually: whatever some other person says or does is taken as referring to ourselves. Because we are always thinking of ourselves we imagine that other people must be thinking of us also; but if we are always thinking of ourselves, it seems more sensible to assume that other people are probably thinking about *themselves*, not that they are thinking about us. They make themselves the centre of their own circle, round which all their thoughts and emotions revolve, and they think of everything as it affects them. They are running round themselves in a circle all the time, and because they are running round themselves they think everyone else must be running round them, too. But they are not. Each man is in his own circle—an equally vicious one, no doubt. Probably nine-tenths of the cases in which people take offence at what others do and say, are rooted in this idea.

If a man does something which you think will harm you, or says something which you think applies to you, do not think at once: "He meant to injure me." Most probably he never thought of you at all, for each soul has its own troubles and its thoughts turn chiefly around itself. If a man speak angrily to you, do not think: "He hates me, he wishes to wound me." Probably some one or something else has made him angry, and because he happens to meet you he turns his anger upon you. He is acting foolishly, for all

anger is foolish, but you must not therefore think untruly of him.

C.W.L.—That is plain commonsense, but how very few people ever practise it! When I was a priest in the Church of England I once preached a sermon about some ordinary trial or temptation which I thought might come in the way of the farmers and labourers who were my congregation. I explained how a man might get into trouble along a certain line. After the service a farmer came into the vestry in a towering rage, and asked me what I meant by preaching a sermon directed at him. Of course, poor man, he gave himself hopelessly away. I had never before supposed that he was guilty of this particular thing, but evidently it was a sore point, and my remarks had gone home to him. I have no doubt that to this day that man really thinks I singled him out, and preached about him.

In this crowded life which we are all living, it is inevitable that there should be a certain amount of friction, which need not be taken seriously, or regarded as of great importance. As we walk along the streets of any great city thousands of people, each full of his own business, are pushing ahead and not thinking in the least of others. Inevitably it happens that people jostle each other, but it never occurs to anyone to take it seriously as an insult; that would be ridiculous. The same thing is bound to happen mentally and emotionally. Where there are great crowds there is inevitably a certain amount of mental and emotional jostling. We ought to take that in exactly the same spirit, realizing that the man who happens to tread on our mental corns did not mean to do so in the very least but that he was following his own line of business and not thinking of us. We must not take all such little frictions as serious things, any more than we do the daily jostling in the street.

At the same time, while we hold that attitude with regard to the absorption of other people in their business, it is our duty to see that we in turn are not so absorbed in ours as to forget the little courtesies that make life go so much more smoothly.

The Theosophist ought to be distinguished from the rest of the world by his courtesy, and by his calm and unchanging cheerfulness. Be gentle, be patient; there is always time to be friendly and gentle, however much one may be hurried. One should decline to be swept off one's feet by the waves of irritability which come from overstrained nerves, which are so common in these crowded times.

A.B.—The suggestion that the Master makes here is very wise. Do not suppose that everybody is thinking about you, because you are thinking about yourself. The other people are also thinking about themselves and not of you; they are concerned with their own affairs just as you are with yours. It would add greatly to the happiness of nations if people would only take up this idea and put it into practice. When some one jolts up against you in the bustle and hurry of life do not think that he means to injure you, or that he has any personal intention at all. Unless you are sure that a person meant to harm you, it is much better to think the reverse.

Suppose a man speaks angrily to you. If you would remember then not to attribute wrong motives to him, and not to get angry also, you would make very rapid progress in self-control. Generally people remember this afterwards. If a man is self-controlled he will not *show* irritation, but if he is *perfectly* self-controlled he will not even feel it. Even if the other man is at fault, it is, after all but a weakness of his, and he who would be an occultist must remember to be charitable to the weaknesses of others. One must also remember that the angry speech, or the hasty and irritable answer, very often means that the person who makes it is under a great tension arising from some trouble or anxiety, and is not quite strong enough to bear the strain and show no signs of it; his nerves are highly strung; that is why he acts as he does.

It is true, of course, that he acts foolishly, as the Master says. But we must make allowances. Most of the little difficulties that people have arise in this way. A heavy strain on a person will cause him to take offence at almost anything. Think how many troubles there are in the world—troubles of all kinds constantly pressing on people and worrying at them. We do not know the troubles of all those around us, of course, because no sensible person goes about proclaiming his difficulties. Ordinary dignity forbids that. But if we would remember that they exist, and make allowance for them, we should obtain that perfect peace which the Master is aiming at in this teaching.

> When you become a pupil of the Master, you may always try the truth of your thought by laying it beside His. For the pupil is one with his Master, and he needs only to put back his thought into the Master's thought to see at once whether it agrees. If it does not, it is wrong, and he changes it instantly, for the Master's thought is perfect, because He knows all.

A.B.—An accepted pupil can always test his thought by laying it beside that of the Master. If he feels a jar he knows that the thought is wrong. To use a physical analogy, it is like a false note in music. The pupil does not need to call the Master's attention; he simply puts his thought beside the Master's, and if it does not ring true, he casts it out at once, and sets to work immediately to bring his thought into harmony with that of the Master. He does not argue about it, nor try to make out that his thought may be right after all, because if it is faulty, its error at once becomes apparent. Those who are not accepted pupils cannot quite do this, and that presents a difficulty to many aspirants. As the consciousness of the pupil is one with that of the Master, the latter will not accept anyone against whose thought He would afterwards find it necessary to build a wall.

C.W.L.—It is said that the pupil is one with his Master. That is true in a sense which only the Master knows perfectly. The pupil knows it too, but less perfectly. Those who have not yet entered into that relation cannot understand the intensity of that unity. The pupil becomes an outlying section of his Master's thought, belonging to Him in a way not at all unlike that in which the personality belongs to the ego. The ego puts down a small piece of itself—that is not quite correct, but it is more accurate than the idea of reflection would be—into the conditions of the lower planes, where even the best of physical, astral and mental bodies can give only a very imperfect expression of him. That ought to be a comfort to us when we feel depressed at our own various weaknesses down here. One may say to oneself; "At any rate the ego knows better than that; therefore I need not despair. It is only needful for me to bring more of myself down into this lower manifestation to make it a purer expression of what I really am up above, and then my defects will become less."

In the same sort of way the pupil not merely represents the Master; he is the Master in a very real sense, but the Master under tremendous limitations—the limitations not only of the lower planes, but also of the personality of the pupil, which is by no means perfectly transcended. If the disciple's ego had gained perfect control of its lower vehicles, so that they were nothing but reflections or expressions of the higher, he would be able to express the Master far more perfectly than he does now, but even then there would be a limitation of what must be called the *size* of him, because the pupil is a smaller ego than the Master whom he follows, and therefore can be only an incomplete representative of

Him. Still, whatever thoughts the pupil has, those are in the Master's mental and astral bodies also. Partly for that reason all pupils have to pass through a period of probation, during which the living image of the probationary pupil is constantly before the eye of the Master. The Master wants to know exactly what are the thoughts and feelings of His prospective pupil, because otherwise He might find constantly obtruded into His own astral and mental bodies thoughts and emotions which were out of harmony with the work He is doing all the time. It is only after He has seen for some considerable time that such thoughts and emotions as would not harmonize are very rare in the pupil, that He accepts him, and makes him a part of Himself.

Even then the Master still retains the power to interpose a veil between His consciousness and that of His pupil. It is the latter's earnest desire not to be shut off, but still we are fallible people down here on the physical plane, and it may often happen that some thought or feeling comes to us which should not. The Master does not want that, so He shuts it quietly away from Him. There is, it is true, a later period at which the Master renounces even the power to do that—when He accepts the pupil as His 'son,' but that comes only when He is quite sure that there will be nothing that needs to be excluded.

On account of this intimate association with his Teacher's consciousness the pupil is able to lay His thought by the side of the Master's thought. It is not necessary to call the Master's attention at all; he is not seeking His opinion on the question in hand. He is simply going back along the line of that oneness to discover what is the idea in the Master's mind with regard to this particular question. "How," you may ask, "would the pupil do it?" There are various ways, according to the extent to which he has realized the unity. He would make a vivid image of His Master; he would raise himself into it with all his force, and then would think his thought and see whether there was the slightest jar or disharmony, and if there were he would, of course, alter his own thought at once.

There is here a great difference between the occult and the worldly point of view. In the world if there is a difference of opinion between yourself and another man, you at once proceed to argue in favour of your opinion, or try to justify it. In occultism we never argue; we know that the man who stands on the higher level knows better, and we simply accept his view. It would never occur to us for one moment to set up our own opinion against that of the Master, because we know (it is not a matter of opinion; but of actual knowledge) that He has access to all kinds and sources of information that we have not; therefore He knows what He is talking about. His opinion is based on far greater knowledge than our own. Afterwards we may try to find the reasons which gave rise to it—that is quite another matter—but in the meantime we do not oppose it, and we should never think of doing so. When the pupil lays his thought beside the Master's he does not argue. When you have an instrument out of tune you do not argue that perhaps that is a better pitch; you tune it up.

In the occult world we never criticize, we take it for granted that every man who is working for the Hierarchy is doing his utmost; and if he is doing his best, then to his own Master he stands or falls—not to us. Of course it may sometimes be possible, if we see failure in some direction, to make a little suggestion in the most delicate way we can: "If so-and-so were done, do you not think that things might perhaps be a little better?" The way in which people recklessly criticize others of whose troubles and difficulties they know nothing whatever is entirely foreign to occultists or those who aspire to become such. We simply do not go that way at all; we should consider it wrong.

Those who are really in earnest about getting on the Path would do well to follow the custom of the Masters' pupils in this matter. We should not plunge into criticism of people who are doing their work; most people are doing the best they can from their point of view. We may possibly have a much higher point of view, but at any rate they can work only according to their own light, not according to ours. When an official is appointed, for example, to do something in our Society, we should give him his chance; if he does not do the work satisfactorily, then we may in due course give the work to some one else, but in the meantime we should not hamper the man. He should be given a chance to show what he is made of, to try the ideas which are in his mind. It is a bad thing to be always interfering.

It would be a very much worse thing to be always in a critical frame of mind—constantly looking for holes, always trying to find weak spots. That is not the way in occultism. We often hear people say, "I cannot help criticizing; that is my nature." If that is your nature it is a very bad nature, and you had better try to transcend it. When you say a thing is natural, human, you mean it is what the average man would do; but if a man has really taken himself in hand he is trying to be a little more than the average. We are here to change our natures. There need be no pride in this; the aspirant is seeking to raise himself above the average in order that he may be able to advance that average—which he could not do if he were on the same level or below. Anyone who wills to do so can give up the bad habit of criticism.

Sometimes one would like to say to people, "Do get out of the way of your higher self and give him a chance to do what he can. You are letting the lower personality stand in the way of what the higher would and could do quite easily." No one should ever say, "I cannot." If you take that line, you have already prejudged the case, and foredoomed yourself to failure. Set up rather the thought-form, "I can do this thing, and I will do it"—then it is already half done. People often fail in their efforts; that is very natural. While they continually try, however, force is being accumulated, and this will presently bring success. We must not think when a failure comes that everything is lost; for the force which has been gained, though it may not be enough to bring immediate success, is all the same a substantial gain, and if we go on putting more and more to it the time will come when success will crown our efforts.

There is a vast gulf between these two attitudes: to sit down and despair, and to get up and do something. It has been said that the world is divided into two parts: the people who go and do something, and the people who sit still and say: "Why was it not done some other way?" We ought to be among the former, and not mind in the least what is said by the other kind of people who never move a hand to do it themselves.

> **Those who are not yet accepted by Him cannot do quite this; but they may greatly help themselves by stopping often to think: "What would the Master think about this? What would the Master say or do under these circumstances?" For you must never do or say or think what you cannot imagine the Master as doing or saying or thinking. You must be true in speech too—accurate and without exaggeration.**

C.W.L.—If we could keep that always in mind, never to think or say or do anything that the Master would not think or say or do, there would not be much need of correction in our lives. We might make some errors, perhaps, as to what we thought He might think or say or do, but on the whole ours would be a life wonderfully pure and near to Him. No doubt many people may feel: "If I had to stop and think that, I should never say anything." The world would probably not be greatly the poorer if they did not, for most of what is said is not particularly useful. If a man each time before he speaks really seriously sets himself to think: "Would the Master say what I am going to say?" he will speak a great deal less. The process of referring to the thought of the Master may be slow at first; but presently it becomes a habit, and then it takes place like a flash.

Thought moves with the rapidity of light, probably even faster, and if, as the physicists tell us, light travels about 1,86,000 miles per second, your thought of England, for example, which is 12,500 miles away, would be there like a flash of light. The speed of thought is one of the questions of occult physics amidst which we are only stumbling as yet. We are trying all the time to learn new facts about occult science, and are making experiments blunderingly, much as did the old alchemists, out of whose effort emerged the beginnings of chemistry, which has slowly evolved into a great science comprising many thousands of facts. I believe that out of the stumbling experiments which are now being made by only a few people, there will arise, as the years roll on, a development of occult science generally which will be of great importance to the world.

Usually our thoughts do not move as fast as they might, because we have not practised using them apart from speech and action to any great extent. It is one of the fruits of meditation that it trains us to use thought apart from these other things. From success in that one obtains really wonderful results. Dr. Besant has made a study of this. I have heard her say that when she is giving a lecture in public, while she is speaking one sentence, the next comes before her thought in three or four different forms, and she deliberately selects that one which she thinks will be most effective, while she is speaking the previous sentence. Very few people could do that. It is a matter of using thought altogether apart from action, and with a rapidity which would be hard to calculate—but it shows what may be done. It is quite worth while to try to practise using thought as thought. The pupil, following out the excellent practice of thinking before he speaks or acts, will find it not only fruitful in bringing his life into harmony with that of his Master, but also a useful training in swift thought.

Never attribute motives to another; only his Master knows his thoughts, and he may be acting from reasons which have never entered your mind.

C.W.L.—Every man is an enigma even to those who are nearest and dearest to him, and if sometimes, long afterwards, you do get at his reasons for having done something, they are usually surprising—something which would never have occurred to you has been the controlling influence in his mind. I have seen that many times more, perhaps, in India than anywhere else, because the Indian mind differs greatly from ours in many ways, and most of our Hindu brothers are moved to action by ideas that never would have occurred to an Englishman. Their mind is infinitely more subtle, and its activities are based upon a set of traditions foreign to our ways of thought. If, therefore, even in our own race it is never advisable to supply a motive to anyone for what he or she says or does, it is far less safe in a foreign country, where you are dealing with another civilization altogether. Hopeless misunderstandings occur because we supply motives, and we must not do it. It is not our business to know why a certain thing was done. We need not trouble about it.

If you hear a story against any one, do not repeat it; it may not be true, and even if it is, it is kinder to say nothing.

A.B.—If, having heard this, you go and tell a story against some one, you are disobeying the Master's direct command, because it has been passed on to you, and so is directed to you personally. It is easy enough to hold your tongue; it may be difficult to control your thought, but surely you can control your body! The story that you tell may not matter much, but if it is untrue and you repeat it, you are telling a lie, and that matters very much for those who are striving to prepare themselves for Initiation. It sounds hard to call it lying, perhaps, but it is a fact, and we have to face facts.

It is obvious that we cannot spend our lives in enquiring into the truth of such stories, so the only safe course is never to repeat them at all. Quite apart from the question of injuring ourselves and our own prospects, and even supposing you know such a story to be true, it is kinder to say nothing. Why should you wish to harm any person? Why should you wish to repeat anything which shows another in an unfavourable light?

Of course, if we happen to find out that a man is a rogue or a swindler and is bent upon doing injury to unsuspecting persons, it is our duty to expose him, or at least to warn those who are in danger from him; but that is a matter altogether different from those which form the pabulum of common gossip. This is, however, a duty which should be exercised only with the greatest care and forethought, and certainly without the slightest ill-feeling or indignation.

Think well before speaking, lest you should fall into inaccuracy.

C.W.L.—This has been preached for many years and yet even our own people go on making inaccurate statements. People sometimes talk in a most exaggerated way. If a thing is a hundred yards away they say it is "miles off". If a day comes that is hotter than usual, they say it is "boiling". Our command of English is poor if we are not able to find words to express different gradations of thought without plunging into these wild, meaningless superfluities. It is a lack of education as well as of accuracy, and I do not think we ought to be careless about this matter. Not without significance the Christ is reputed to have said that for every idle word that men shall speak they shall give account in the day of judgment.

Be true in action; never pretend to be other than you are, for all pretence is a hindrance to the pure light of truth, which should shine through you as sunlight shines through clear glass.

A.B.—Truth in action is a very difficult thing to carry out. It means never to do a thing before people in order to impress them with a high opinion of you, and never to do when you are alone anything of which you would be ashamed in the company of others; but to be perfectly honest always. Let people see you just as you are, and do not pretend to be anything else. Most of us have a kind of ideal of what we should like other people to think us to be; consequently there are all sorts of small things which we do when we are alone, but would not do if others were present, because they are not quite the things that we feel they would expect of us.

Whenever you are inclined not to do a thing because somebody is there, check the feeling: if it is right, never mind other people's opinion about it; if it is not, never do it at all. I know the feeling well, for I used to have it. I used to feel that I must behave before people as they would expect an author and lecturer and all the rest of it to behave. In the past, I sometimes found that this feeling came up about some quite harmless thing. To give an example; on board ship, where I never feel well, I was at one time in the habit of playing patience—a most harmless recreation, I consider. It came into my mind one day to wonder what the passengers would think when seeing me play it on a

Sunday, knowing I was a teacher of occultism—whether it would shock them. Then I thought: "It does not matter whether people see me or not. If wrong it ought to be dropped; if right, their opinions do not alter the fact." Madame Blavatsky was remarkable in this way. She always did what she wanted, and cared not in the least what people thought about it. If people thought her behaviour was not what they considered that of an occultist should be, what on earth did it matter? They knew nothing whatever about it, anyway.

An occultist does not go about with a grave and solemn face, taking care to do things in a very dignified manner, though that is the notion which many people have of him. The popular views are entirely false on the subject. An occultist is supremely natural. I think one reason why it is important, at the present time, to lead a perfectly true and frank life, is that it may serve in a small degree to prepare the way for the great Teacher who is coming; it may make His path a little bit smoother. For the Great Ones are not always what the people expect them to be. They do not run in moulds prepared for them, but They come to reform the world, generally to alter radically the popular outlook; and while They are very considerate of people's feelings, They are not always so of their prejudices. We, by living frankly and openly, may help to prepare the people's minds, so that when the Lord Maitreya comes they will already have loosened some of their prejudices, and there will be a chance of their being less offended than might otherwise have been the case. Let us, then, lead a perfectly open life, always provided that we do not fall below our ideal. We must not make the mistake of thinking that it does not matter how we act before people; but we must be equally careful and honest in private and in public.

C.W.L.—It is quite true that we should never pretend, that there is a falsity about any kind of pretension, but take care that in the effort to avoid it you do not run into the opposite extreme. Sometimes people say, "I want to show myself just as I am naturally," and then they proceed to show the worst and coarsest and most vulgar part of themselves. They are not showing themselves naturally, but a very low and poor and degraded copy of what they should be. That in man which is highest and best and noblest is nearest to the real self; therefore, to be natural we should be at our best.

Sanctimoniousness is a form of untruth. If you find a person giving himself out as an occultist, and at the same time talking very largely about his own loftiness and tolerance, hinting at his great powers, and trying to win the admiration of credulous people, like the hypocrites of old who "love to pray standing in the synagogues and in the corners of the streets, that they may be seen of men" and the scribes and Pharisees who "for a pretence make long prayer,"[1] you may know that he is not a real occultist. The genuine occultist is never sanctimonious, though he is determined to live far above the standard of what is usually called the "natural" man.

[1] S. Matthew, vi, 5, and xxiii, 14.

People often fail to recognize a Master because they have a rigid idea of what a Master must be, and the real, living Master may not be like that at all. He does not adapt Himself to our prejudices and ideas; He is that which He is on His own plane, and if we are hidebound by our own prejudices we may not know Him when He appears. Some have already made up their minds as to what the World-Teacher will do and say, and how He will carry Himself. Do not risk shutting yourself off from Him by preconceptions. We know that He will teach the doctrine of love, but the manner and detail of it will be settled entirely by Him. Let us recognize Him to the full, and be ready to follow wheresoever He will lead.

CHAPTER 5

UNSELFISHNESS AND THE DIVINE LIFE

You must discriminate between the selfish and the unselfish. For selfishness has many forms, and when you think you have finally killed it in one of them, it arises in another as strongly as ever. But by degrees you will become so full of thought for the helping of others that there will be no room, no time, for any thought about yourself.

A.B.—The Master here describes what is I believe the only way to become perfectly unselfish. It is possible to get rid of one particular form of selfishness, certainly, if we turn our efforts to its eradication, but, as the Master says, it comes up in another form. Working in this way, you may spend a long time in killing one form of selfishness, and then find yourself like Hercules when he was killing the hydra—as soon as he had cut off one head, another grew. But the way that is recommended here goes straight to the root of the matter.

One of the valuable results of devotion lies here—I am inclined to think, the greatest of all: the thought of another person, who is the object of devotion, occupies the whole mind, and the man becomes unselfish without any special effort. That is the proper way of growth, to "grow as the flower grows, unconsciously, opening its heart to the sun". Efforts are all signs of weakness; if you can find clever ways of getting round yourself, as it were, it is a great advantage. You circumvent your thoughts and turn your force into a good channel, and the undesirable quality gets starved out. This is the best way of getting over one's faults; for thinking of them, even regretfully, strengthens them.

Be full of thought for others, and then, as the Master says, there will be no room, no time, for thinking about yourself. Then, too, you will be happy. I have found that this is true in my own case. If ever I found myself inclined to grieve, to feel the least regret about anything which affected me personally (I do not think that I am ever inclined to do so now, but at one time I was) I filled my mind at once with the thought of helping and of working for others. Grieving over things which affect oneself is selfish, and it only serves to make one unhappy. Yet it is what many people do. They sit down and say: "Oh, how sad it is. How hard it is. This thing is very hard on me. That person does not care for me, does not look after me, does not love me"—and so on indefinitely.

All that is selfishness. The remedy, both for your own grief and the selfishness, is to go at once and do something for someone else. Go and work. Your mind cannot be filled with two things at once, and the moment you cease to think of yourself you begin to be happy.

When you can say: "I do not want anything from anybody around; I love them and need nothing in return"—then you will be happy. What people generally call love is a little love underneath with a great coating of selfishness over it. The moment that there is pain through love, it means that selfishness is also there.

That is a hard lesson for the warm-hearted and the affectionate to learn, I know, but it has to be learned; and when learned it brings happiness and peace. I speak to you from my own experience. Learn to love all, without asking anything in return, and when you do that you will find plenty of people to love you; but so long as you keep on grabbing, their natural instinct is to draw back. A hard lesson it is, but once learned it brings a peace that nothing can shake, not even when a person you love dearly is for the time being disagreeable. What does it matter? You know he will come round again some day, and in the meantime you go on pouring out your love on him just the same. If you suffer, just make up your mind not to trouble about it. Say to yourself: "I do not mind how much my lower nature suffers." What are we—our lower selves at any rate—that we should care if we suffer, or that we should claim to be loved? By taking up this attitude towards your suffering you will overcome it.

C.W.L.—To think about a fault is to strengthen it. That is the mistake often made in the Christian system, where men are urged to repent of their faults and to feel remorse for them. The more sorry one feels and the more he turns his fault over in his mind the stronger it grows. But if one goes ahead and does some work for someone else, the thought-form is not intensified; it dies a natural death, drops away, and is forgotten. Morbid introspection often magnifies small failings into great sins. It reminds one of little children who constantly pull up their plants by the roots, to see how they are growing. Thus, a person eagerly takes up some good and noble work, then begins to doubt himself, and says: "I am not sure that my motive was pure; I must have done it because I was inwardly proud," or, if he relieves suffering, he thinks: "It was not really unselfish; I could not bear to see the suffering, and so I relieved it." In the Church of England they say: "Lord, have mercy upon us miserable sinners." We may be sinners, but we need not aggravate the offence by being miserable about it, and so making others miserable too. Never brood over the past, but set to work to do better in the future. It is useless to wish that you had not done so-and-so; much better to say: "I did that; it is a pity; never mind, this is the present condition of affairs, and I must see what I can do to make the best of it." I do not say that it may not be possible at some exalted level to alter the past, but it certainly is not practical for us to take that into consideration.

In the Lord Buddha's Noble Eightfold Path, the last step but one was Right Remembrance. He said to His people: "You must be very careful what you allow yourselves to remember. If you say you cannot help remembering everything, then you have no control over your memory, over the mind which is a part of yourself. It is as though you went along the street gathering up all the rubbish which came in your way; you are sweeping into your memory all kinds of useless and undesirable things. You should remember the right things and be particularly careful to forget the others." Then He enumerates elaborately and definitely the things that people should forget, and among these He mentions all unkind words spoken to them, all fancied slights and injuries. Those are among the things which one should permanently and absolutely forget, whereas, among the things one should remember are all the kind words that ever have been spoken to one, all the kindly deeds, and all the good qualities one has ever seen in one's neighbours.

We must learn to love all whom we contact. I do not say all alike; that is not expected. The Lord Buddha Himself had His favourite disciple, Ananda, whom He loved more than the others, and the Christ had His beloved disciple S. John, who leaned upon His breast at the Last Supper. We are not expected to love people all alike, to feel towards everyone the same love that is felt for father or mother, wife or child, but to hold the attitude of active goodwill or love towards all, and of hate to none. We are to hold this attitude also without asking any return for it; the moment one begins to make demands he sets up a claim; he is introducing the factor of desire again, and once more thinking of himself, not of those he loves. To pour out love and not expect any return is the only thing that deserves to be called love. Without that unselfishness people get entangled with jealousies, envyings and many other desires, and their love, instead of showing the pure glorious rose-colour, is seen as a sort of brownish-crimson, a poor-looking thing, and unpleasant also in form, because instead of outraying like sunlight, it is hooked and grasping, and makes a closed curve, often affecting no one but the sender.

The worlds are moved by the divine unselfish love that pours out in great open curves, and never returns and does not mean to return. It is poured out in other dimensions and other planes, to do the work of God in God's own way. This is the lesson to be learned—it is hard because it means the destruction of the lower nature, but it is the path to peace.

> You must discriminate in yet another way. Learn to distinguish the God in everyone and everything, no matter how evil he or it may appear on the surface. You can help your brother through that which you have in common with him, and that is the Divine Life; learn how to arouse that in him, learn how to appeal to that in him; so shall you save your brother from wrong.

A.B.—This is the final lesson in discriminating between the real and the unreal. However evil a thing is from the outside, God is there, for it could not exist at all if God were not at its heart. This truth is told again and again in the Hindu scriptures. "I am the gambling of the cheat," says the Lord in the *Bhagavad-Gītā*. That statement sometimes shocks people dreadfully; but it is true, because the cheat has something to learn in that way which he is refusing to learn in a better way. If a person cannot learn quietly by precept, he must learn from experience of natural laws. What we call the laws of nature are the most material expression of the Divine Mind.

The laws of nature stand there like rocks; if a man goes and bruises himself against them the pain that results teaches him to avoid a similar mistake in the future. When a person will not learn by precept or example (and there are plenty of both of these in the world) he must do so through the pain that comes from breaking the law. He must be carried on at all hazards towards unity, for the divine will is for evolution, and his own innermost will is one with the divine. I think that is the meaning which underlies also the words of the Hebrew singer: "If I ascend up into heaven, Thou art there." So far it is plain; we all know God is in heaven, but then: "If I make my bed in hell, behold, Thou art there also." [1]

See therefore the divine in everything around you; the rest does not concern you. In that way, and in that way only, you can help your brother, for the one thing you have in common is the divine life; all the rest is different, but in that you are at one, and you can use that as a lever for helping him in all ways. When you want to help a man to overcome a fault, remember that

[1] Psalm, cxxxix, 8.

he is just as anxious as you can be to get rid of the wrong thing in him; it injures him, and if you can only reach the real man inside, you will find that he wants to be rid of it. This is the right way to help; the inside way never hurts or offends anybody.

C.W.L.—All that exists on this plane, as much as on any other, is a manifestation of the divine Life: and therefore all of it—the good and the evil alike—must be an expression of God. Nothing can exist of which God Himself is not the heart and root. That fact is emphasized in all the scriptures. We have it in the Christian Scriptures: "I form the light, and create darkness; I make peace, and create evil; I the Lord do all these things."[1] People cannot understand how all that men commonly call evil can somehow be also divine, yet we must face the fact. There are black magicians and evil people of all sorts and kinds, but the life in those people is the Divine Life, because there is no other life.

If a man introduces evil into his life by his own stupidity, by his wrong-headedness, out of it good will nevertheless come; it is the only way to evolve that particular man. The cheat will cheat; he has it in his mind to do that. He is under the Divine Law still, and although he is doing wrong, out of it good for him will come, because he will learn by doing that, and by failure, to step into the right path. It is, as it were, the last resort, but it is a resort, and therefore we must acknowledge it to be within the Divine Plan.

[1] Isaiah, 45, 7.

There is a sense in which everything absolutely *is* God. Still it is not exactly in that sense that these words are written; it is the divine spirit in every one which makes him man. If you can see through the personality which is so warped, which has gone so far wrong, and get at the divine life in the man, you can appeal to that. We must remember that the "evil" man, as a soul, wishes to make progress just as much as we do. He wishes to get rid of the evil which is haunting and obsessing and troubling his personality, and therefore if we can get back to that soul through all this outer crust of hardness and evil, he will rush forward to help us in our endeavour to assist the personality.

I have been a priest and lay-helper most of my life, and have worked in some of the very worst parts of England. I have seen many men whom one would think hopeless criminals; but I have never seen one who had not some spark of good in him somewhere. It might be his love for a child, or his love for a dog, that seemed to be the only human touch in what was otherwise a brute, and a dangerous brute; but there is the One Life stirring in him somewhere, and if one can get into touch with him at that point there is just a chance that he may be helped upward through an appeal to that one thing.

A.B.—The Master's last words on the subject are: "So shall you save your brother from wrong." Here He makes the strongest appeal; it is to that which is the very object and end of life to the disciple, for his one aim is to become a saviour of the world. Far stronger is it than any appeal to the disciple for his own personal advantage could possibly be. The Master lives only to help the world; and the more we can bring service into our lives the more we shall reflect in them the beauty of His.

PART III

DESIRELESSNESS

CHAPTER 1

THE REMOVAL OF DESIRE

A.B.—We come now to the second qualification, which in the Sanskrit is *vairāgya*, for which, speaking in English, the Master uses the word desirelessness. That is a very accurate translation. In the past I have used the word dispassion, but henceforth I shall translate the term as the Master does.

There are many for whom the Qualification of Desirelessness is a difficult one, for they feel that they *are* their desires—that if their distinctive desires, their likings and dislikings, are taken away from them, there will be no self left.

A.B.—Practically all those who sincerely desire to tread the Path feel the truth of the first sentence, in which the Master says that the qualification of desirelessness is a difficult one. The difficulty arises because people identify themselves with their desires. So long as a desire which is not gratified makes you unhappy, so long are you identifying yourself with your desires. It is well to recognize this, admit it to yourself; for it is quite easy to think that you have separated yourself from your desires, when in reality you have not done so. Very many people like to think that they have conquered the desire-nature, when their whole life, their every act, shows that it is not so. It is far better to recognize the fact, if you have not yet done so, and then you are prepared to adopt the remedy.

The first step that should be taken is to dwell on the idea; "I am not my desires." Here you can call to your aid what I have already explained with regard to moods; your desires, like your moods, are changing, and anything that changes is not the Self, who is not subject to fluctuations. For instance, I have known people who think one day: "How delightful it is to be at Adyar; how beautiful to think of all the great things that are going to happen"; and the next day they feel depressed, discouraged. Now, neither of these changing moods, neither the enthusiasm nor the depression, is yourself; both are merely passing vibrations of the astral body, roused by some contact from the outside.

It is for this reason that people are advised to meditate every day; for you cannot meditate properly until your desires are quiescent. If you meditate regularly and faithfully, you will little by little realize a Self behind your desires, and as you go on meditating, and also during the day practise the attitude required, you begin to realize that Self all the time. Then you will no longer identify yourself with your desires, and constantly feel: "*I* want: *I* wish; *I* desire"; but will think: "It is not I; it is the lower self."

This is the first great lesson which the Master gives about the second qualification. You are not required to have desirelessness perfectly before Initiation, but what the Master does expect is that you should have it to a great extent, and what He expects is law. All the swinging between the two poles of depression and elation must go before you can reach Initiation.

C.W.L.—Large numbers of people make no effort to distinguish between their desires and themselves, but say: "I am as God has made me. If I have a bad temper, or a weak will; He gave it to me. If I am not strong enough to resist temptation, that is how I was made." They do not understand that they have made themselves by their past lives, but they are in the habit of taking their character as a sort of inalienable something which is given to them, as one may be born blind or with a lame leg. They do not realize that it is their business to change a nature which is undesirable in its character. They do not know that they can, and furthermore, often they do not particularly see why they should.

There is usually no adequate reason held up to the average man why he should take all the very great trouble necessary to change his character. Some may say that unless he does so he will not go to heaven, but many reply that the conventional heaven would bore them inexpressibly, and they are hoping for something different. It is obvious, in fact, that though teaching concerning the heaven-life has been widely spread, it has had little practical influence on most people's character probably because it is so lacking in verisimilitude. The only theory that I have ever heard that seems to me adequate as an inducement to effort is that of Theosophy. It shows what is worth doing, and shows us that there is every opportunity and sufficient time for complete success. If a man understands God's plan, and seeks to co-operate with Him, he has the strongest possible motive to throw himself into the work of evolution, and to fit himself for it. He sees then that it is possible to make the most fundamental changes in his character and disposition, and that success is absolutely assured.

The never-changing desire of the ego is for progress, for the unfoldment of the higher self, and the bringing of the lower vehicles into tune as its instruments. Whenever we find other desires which are not part of that, and do not agree with it, we know that those are not from the soul, and so we do not say, "I desire this" but, "My desire-elemental is moving again; he wants so-and-so; but I, the ego, wish to progress; I wish to co-operate in the divine plan. These changing moods and desires are not mine." As long as an ungratified desire can cause unhappiness a man may know that he is still identifying himself with the desires of the elemental.

But these are only they who have not seen the Master; in the light of His holy Presence all desire dies, but the desire to be like Him. Yet before you have the happiness of meeting Him face to face, you may attain desirelessness if you will.

A.B.—This recalls once more the verse in the *Bhagavad-Gītā*: "The objects of sense, but not the relish for them, turn away from an abstemious dweller in the body; and even relish turneth away from him after the Supreme is seen." All desire dies when a glimpse of the one desirable object has been obtained. Hence to realize the presence of the Master will rid you not of desires only, but of desire itself. Desire is a root that sends forth many shoots; you may lop off the shoots, but while the root remains it will send forth new ones. But union with the Master will finally rid you of the root of all desires.

Even before that, however, the Master says you may attain desirelessness if you will. Those three words "if you will" are specially important. They show us where the difficulty lies. It is not the ability, it is nearly always the will to do a thing, which is lacking. If you could put into your work on the path the same amount of will that you put into your worldly work, your progress would be rapid indeed.

C.W.L.—We have here one of the specially beautiful sentences in this very beautiful book. It is true that when you see the Master and realize what He is, all lower desires are simply not there any more; your whole being is filled with something higher.

Many people speak of their wish to attain desirelessness, and are yet all the time hugging the objects of desire and would be unhappy without them. They do not in reality wish for this desirelessness; they only think they do; on the surface they do, but deeper down, in the personality they do not. It is well to question ourselves on this matter, to search deeply and see whether we have really got rid of all these lower desires. A Theosophist often thinks that he has, and thinks that it is merely an elementary matter ; but a great many of these elementary things go very deep. Superficially one gets rid of them, but they crop up again in different forms, and it is hard to be sure that one has really disposed of them. Fortunately, it is not expected of us that we shall be utterly free from them at this stage. Initiation may be attained with the roots of some of these things still within us, but after that one must weed them out entirely. Still, it is better to root them out utterly even now, so that our progress may be smoother and more rapid. It is practicable, for the Master never suggests to us anything that we cannot do, though He does set before us many things which will tax our endurance or moral strength, because that has to be done if we want to get on rapidly.

Discrimination has already shown you that the things which most men desire, such as wealth and power, are not worth having ; when this is really felt, not merely said, all desire for them ceases.

A.B.—Desires for wealth and power clothe themselves in a variety of ways, not only in connection with money and social or political influence. Wealth is the thing which most people want above all others; but it is not in itself a good thing to have, for it only fosters desires, and does not give happiness, as may be seen by looking at rich people, who are by no means a happy class of beings. It is the same with power, social or political; it is all dross and tinsel, not gold. The *Gītā* says that the wise man is content with whatsoever cometh—which means that he will cheerfully make use of what is available, and not waste his time and energy in craving for something different.

Few people attain high social or political positions, but the temptation of power is often present without that. Power includes all wish to control other people, to interfere with them and tell them what to do, instead of minding one's own business. Though there may not be much desire for social or political power, there still is frequently an unhealthy desire to make others do what we think they ought to do. That must go if we mean to make progress. Those who mean business will soon find out, as many of us have done, that we have quite enough to do to manage our own lower selves, without trying to interfere with anybody else. The Self in others is the same as the Self in us, and the way in which it chooses to manifest in them is their business, not ours. Therefore all tendencies to interference must be weeded out.

You have no right to interfere except when it is your duty, and that is only when you have a certain limited control over a person who is placed under you by nature, as in the case of your own children, or by karma, as in the case of servants or workmen. Your control of a child should be protective control, exercised when and as long as there is weakness which needs protection;

and it must gradually disappear as the ego inside becomes able to take possession of his own vehicles. With your equals—I use the word in a wide sense—you clearly have no right of interference.

C.W.L.—People often want to interfere with others only because they think they can manage affairs better than those others can; but after all they do not *know* that. The divine power is working through each man; we had better let it do so in its own way. Remember how the Christ reminded the Jews that their Scriptures told them, "Ye are Gods", and that they were all children of the Most High. It may be that the other man is not doing his work in the very best way, or possibly that he is making some mistakes, but so long as he is honestly and earnestly doing his best it is well. Let him have his innings, even if he is not so good a batsman as you are. Sometimes one may very tactfully, very respectfully and delicately, offer advice, but there are many cases where even that would be an impertinence; one should never under any circumstances attempt to force an opinion on any one. Our first care should be that our own affairs are well managed, for each man is responsible to himself.[1]

[1] S. John, 10, 34, and Psalm, 82, 6.

CHAPTER 2

THE ONE GOOD DESIRE

Thus far all is simple; it needs only that you should understand. But there are some who forsake the pursuit of earthly aims only in order to gain heaven, or to attain personal liberation from rebirth; into this error you must not fall.

C.W.L.—The desire for personal liberation from rebirth is found chiefly in India, because most of the people there believe in reincarnation. To the average Christian, heaven is also a release from earth. These instructions were given to an Indian boy; therefore first of all and most of all they refer to Indian conditions, though the ideas can be applied to our Western world as well. We Theosophists are not particularly likely to make violent efforts in order to gain the happiness of the heaven-world, in which men spend hundreds and even thousands of years between incarnations. Many of us would prefer to avoid it altogether and return quickly to work upon earth, and that is possible to those who really desire it. That does need a certain amount of strength, however, as we must then carry the same mental and astral bodies over into the new physical body.

It is not that the astral body and the mental body are capable of fatigue, like the physical brain. There is, however, another consideration: the astral and mental bodies that we have in this life are the expression of ourselves as we were at the end of the last incarnation. As we go on through life we modify them considerably, but that cannot be done beyond a certain point. There is a limit to which, for example, a motor-car is susceptible to repair or improvement, and very often it is better to buy a new car than to try to bring the old one up to date. It is somewhat the same with the astral and mental bodies. A radical change in them would take a great deal of time, and might perhaps be only partially accomplished after all. If a man's capacities in this life have greatly increased, it might be better for his progress that he should get a new astral and mental body in which to express himself, instead of trying to patch up and alter the old one. Therefore quick reincarnation is not always quite a practicable thing. Yet we may take it, as things are now—with the special need of workers on account of the coming of the World Teacher—that any person who has worked well in this life and is earnestly desirous of taking an immediate incarnation in order to continue in service, may be able to achieve his desires.

There is an ordinary course of life after death for all men, and for those who pass through it there is no need to make any special arrangement; but if a man wishes to depart from that he has to make what amounts to an application, or it has to be made for him. It has to be submitted to a higher authority, who can give permission if He thinks it desirable ; but He would quite certainly refuse it if He did not think it to be in the best interests of the person. I think those who have anxiety on this subject may set their minds at rest, however, for those who have worked well now will certainly have further opportunities of continuing that work. A man who wishes rapid reincarnation must make himself indispensable, so that he will be known as one who would be useful if he did come back at once. That also, incidentally, is the best way to bring the mental and astral bodies into the required condition.

> If you have forgotten self altogether, you cannot be thinking when that self should be set free, or what kind of heaven it shall have. Remember that *all* selfish desire binds, however high may be its object, and until you have got rid of it you are not wholly free to devote yourself to the work of the Master.

A.B.—We must remember that the astral and mental planes are material, though they are made up of subtler matter than the physical. They also are objective, and full of objects of desire. The desire for heaven, which is in the lower mental plane, is therefore just as much a desire of the lower self as is the desire for earth—only it is further off and more impalpable. The advantage of the former desire over the latter is that it gives a check to the desire-nature, because it cannot be gratified at once ; so it helps the man to get rid of desire in general, and at the same time it causes him to select more refined pleasures, and to dwell upon those in his thought rather than the coarser ones. There are many men to whom it would obviously be useless to say, "Kill out desire". If you want to help a man who is addicted to the pleasures of eating and drinking and sex, you may put before him the desire for heaven, in order to help him to starve out the lower desires. Therefore it is that all religions make so much of the teaching of heaven and hell. Even the Lord Buddha spoke of these when he was addressing the ordinary people.

Those who wish to tread the Path must give up not only desire for heaven, but also that for personal liberation from the round of births and deaths, that is, for *moksha*. The reason is quite simple, and the Master gives it here. If you have forgotten yourself altogether, you cannot be thinking of those things which affect yourself. You must be free from desire for those things, if you mean to devote yourself to the work of the Master.

There are many people who wish to serve, in one way or in another, but the disciple must wish to serve the Master in the way He wills, and where He requires the service. Such unconditional service is not possible while the heart is bound up in anything. As one of the Upanishads says: "Until the bonds of the heart are broken, man cannot attain immortality." That sounds a hard thing to say, if we think of the bonds of the heart as including the qualities of love, to which we attach the greatest value. It does not say, however, that the heart must be broken, but that the bonds must be broken, so that the heart's love may be boundless. Do not misunderstand me, and think that I have said that to love is not desirable. It is not the love which binds, but the elements of selfishness which are too often mixed with it. The love of the Self in one man for the Self in another is in its very nature everlasting; we could not change that even if we would, but when love for the Self is mixed with love for the form, it begins to bind, and thus even love itself may become a bondage.

There is no way to reach the condition that makes you free for the Master's work but by constant effort to break every bond that restricts you. If you find in your love anything which can cause you pain, there is selfishness in it, which must be eliminated. Get rid of it, and your love will remain, stronger, nobler, purer; and such love can never interfere with the Master's work. Suppose you have a wish to go to a certain place because there is a particular person there with whom you like to be; well, give up the idea of going. That is just one instance of the way in which you may deliberately break the bonds that tie you by selfishness to special persons and things. Break off such ties.

I say this only for those who are in dead earnest—not for those who wish to go gently and quietly along the road of progress. There is no blame attached to this latter course, mind; each is free to go forward slowly or swiftly as he chooses. But I am speaking now for those who mean business, for those who are wholly in earnest. The Master is always looking out for this earnestness, and does not find too much of it. Once more I am speaking from my own experience, for I have had difficulty in this way. Then I began to train myself, and when I found that I had a great wish to be with some one, I would try to keep away from that person. If you have tact and strength, you can often untie yourself inside, so to say, without showing others that you are doing it. You remain just as loving as before, and your outward manner shows no alteration, but you are loosening the personal bond inside your own heart. It is by thus clearly seeing what ought to be done and then deliberately doing it that some of us have made more progress than most people. You will find such an effort easier if you keep in mind the fact that you cannot devote yourself entirely to the work of the Master until nothing remains that can bind you.

C.W.L.—This passage shows us that desire for heaven belongs to the personality. It is not, however, by any means a bad thing at an earlier stage of development than that of the disciple. It has its place in the evolutionary scheme. The primitive man is full of thoughts about eating and drinking, and similar pleasures. It would be quite useless to talk to him about desirelessness, as he must first pass through a stage of higher and more refined desire. The utmost we can say to him is: "Try to refine your desires; there are other and grander things than these of which you are thinking, and you cannot rise to those in the future unless you are prepared to check the outrush of your feeling." Men can rise only step by step, and only the strongest can climb the great heights of the Path rapidly. Yet those who read the words of this book, and wish to do as Alcyone has done, must resolve at once to get rid of all selfish desire, because it binds. As I have said, even love itself is a bond of the heart if there is in it a grain of selfishness, but when it is utterly free from any thought of selfishness it is a power of the heart. Until the bonds are broken, until the selfishness is weeded out, even love itself may be a hindrance as well as a help.

There has been much misunderstanding in India and elsewhere on this subject, on account of the confusion of love (which is unselfish) with desire (which is selfish). Some philosophers try to harden themselves so as to be indifferent to what happens, to escape suffering by avoiding love. But that is the wrong way; it produces men half-developed, intellectual but unemotional. We must have the power to express even great surges of feeling, but they must be reflections of the higher emotions of the Self, strictly under control, not astral waves sweeping us along at the will of the desire-elemental. To control emotion by killing it is something like that other idea of trying to avoid bad karma by doing nothing at all. The Master's way for us is that we should become increasingly useful to humanity through our actions, emotions and thoughts, and the more we can do in all three ways the better it will be for all concerned.

When all desires for self are gone, there may still be a desire to see the result of your work. If you help anybody you want to *see* how much you have

helped him; perhaps even you want him to see it too, and to be grateful. But this is still desire, and also want of trust.

A.B.—This is what the *Bhagavad-Gītā* calls not working for fruit. The result is the fruit. If you are really working you have no time to notice results, no time to stop and look at a piece of work which is finished. As soon as one thing is done there is something else at hand to be done. You are wasting time if you are looking at the results; if you are thinking of what you have already done, how are you to carry on the next piece of work? And when it comes to personal help, which is the pleasantest of all to give, because there is personal love at the back of it, do not look to see if the person whom you have helped appreciates what you have done. That is like running after one to whom you have made a present, in order to see if he is grateful, and to claim thanks. One who acts like that has not given; he has sold. It is barter; so much help for so much gratitude. You must not barter here! Remember how the Christ drove from the temple those who were selling, although they were selling things for sacrifice, saying to them: "Make not my Father's house an house of merchandise."[1]

C.W.L.—No one is busier than the occultist. The moment he finishes one thing he goes on with another, and he does not stand gazing to see what has resulted from what he did before. Suppose you were acting as a

[1] S. John, 2, 16.

nurse or a helper on the battle-field; you would have to do the best you could for one case, and instantly turn to another; you could not stop to watch for half-an-hour to see exactly what was going to be the final effect; you could not even stop to see whether the man was likely to recover or not. It is just the same with the Master's work; we have not time to stop and think about the ultimate results, and above all we have no time to think about ourselves in connection with those results. It is but human to desire that our efforts should meet with success, and to be elated when it comes, but we must rise above such human frailties, because the goal at which we aim is superhuman. If a thing is well done, we may rejoice in the fact, but we must feel just as glad if the success is another's as if it were our own.

It speaks here of sometimes wanting the man you have helped to see it too, and be grateful. If one has any feeling of that sort he is not giving at all, but selling. The only giving which is recognized in occultism is giving as God gives, pouring out love as the sun pours out life.

When you pour out your strength to help, there must be a result, whether you can see it or not; if you know the Law you know this must be so.

A.B.—In the book *Of the Imitation of Christ* it is asked: "Who will serve God for naught?" The disciple must work for the sake of the work, not for seeing the result, and even without the happiness and satisfaction of thinking, "*I* am serving". He must give himself to the world because he loves it. There *must* be a result, of course, because we live in a world of law; that is why we need not make it our concern. Very often the nature of our work is such as not to bring about immediate results on the physical plane, but to bring something nearer to accomplishment; some one else will put the finishing touches to the work, but without those who have toiled and seen no results the thing could not possibly have been done.

You cannot do important work without trusting the law, because all great work is slow work. Consider, for example, the work of a Manu: thousands upon thousands of years go by before anything you would call a result is seen. Even in building a big house the same rule holds good, for deep foundations are necessary. Our work is largely the laying of foundations, which are not seen; later some one will come along and put a row of bricks above the surface; those will at once be seen. Are the foundations useless, then?

Results are inevitable. Therefore work in a quiet, scientific way, and you will never be disappointed. All disappointment is due to a desire for fruit. You may go on working strenuously for a long time without seeing any consequences, and one day the result will flash into sight. A chemist making a saturated solution goes on dropping a salt into the water, and for some time the liquid remains to all appearance unaffected; then the last grain is added, and the whole suddenly turns solid. So it is with our work; suddenly it will be manifest complete. We are preparing for the coming of the

Great Teacher. We must put all our force into this work, quietly, confidently, patiently; sacrificing ourselves wholly to the work. When the Lord Maitreya comes, He will take up all that we have done, and the result of it will then be manifest to the world.

C.W.L.—It often takes the work of a number of people, following one another, to achieve some great result. When there is a great reform to be introduced in the world, it usually happens that one man, or one group of men, will see the need and begin to talk and write about it. He or they will be ridiculed, and it will seem that their work is without result, but they will convert a few people to their cause, and these will carry it on, until at last society accepts the reform. What was done by the later men would have been impossible without the apparently resultless work of the pioneers.

Very often it may be the nature of our work to bring something near to its accomplishment. Somebody else will step in and put the final touch to the work; his efforts will then be recognized, and he will be considered as having done the whole thing. Never mind; we must care nothing whatever about getting the credit, but be happy to be allowed to do the work. One must not think: "That is rather hard on me." Our karma will take care of what we have done, and it does not matter what the world does or says about it at the present time. One who works scientifically, understandingly, without a thought of the result, except that somehow, somewhere, all good work must do good, will never know disappointment.

When the Lord comes He will take up all our work, carry it on and complete it; and so it will appear that it is all His work. In a sense it all is His, as we have been inspired by Him; yet a great deal of it will have been made possible by the unseen, or apparently profitless work done by a number of humble people beforehand. That we should have a chance of being among those people is assuredly the very greatest privilege we could desire.

In all cases, when one knows the laws of nature one can use them. This is as true of all the work that we are constantly doing on the inner planes, as of that in which we are engaged on the physical plane. Every thought of ours makes a form on the astral or mental plane, and this goes to the person or thing of which we are thinking, and hovers around or discharges itself, for good or ill according to its nature and quality. It is no more trouble to make a helpful thought-form than a harmful one. It all depends upon the attitude of the mind. One may think: "My attitude of mind matters only to me, and only just now." But it matters to others as well, and also it will matter to you the next day, the next month, or even the next year, because it generates thoughts which react upon you. Every thought intensifies itself, by calling up repetitions of itself. It rests with us to make forms which will be beneficial in every way; for though they be invisible to ordinary sight, they infallibly do their work.

So you must do right for the sake of the right, not in the hope of reward; you must work for the

sake of the work, not in the hope of seeing the result; you must give yourself to the service of the world because you love it, and cannot help giving yourself to it.

C.W.L.—Love is indeed the greatest of all motives. All through the teaching of this book, and of some later ones which have been moulded to a large extent upon it, it will be observed how strong and constantly repeated is this need of love as the motive in life, as the explanation of everything, and as the remedy for all ills. It is because that will be the key-note of the teaching of the World Teacher Himself when He comes, that it is already so strongly foreshadowed in that of those who are trying in their small way to prepare for Him.

Another thing the student will note is that all through this book the Master takes it for granted that we are all utterly in earnest, and that the work is the one thing for us. That is certainly the very best way of bringing us into that frame of mind, if there are still some lingering fragments of other ideas hanging about us. The fact that in His mind there is clearly no thought of anything but service, is the greatest incentive for us to make ourselves what He desires.

We often get in our own way; we have to stand aside and give the Self in us a chance to work, for as long as we have some reservations, as long as there is something which we are not prepared to give up for the sake of the Master's service, we are standing in our own way. It is a rare thing to find one who has no reservations whatever, who will give himself utterly to the service of the Master, who will stop at nothing, but give all. It is rare, but the man who has that quality will go far and very fast.

CHAPTER 3

PSYCHIC POWERS

Have no desire for psychic powers; they will come when the Master knows that it is best for you to have them.

A.B.—The term "psychic powers" properly includes all the manifestations of the powers of consciousness through organized matter, in the physical body, or the astral, or the mental. All powers of the intellect are therefore psychic powers. The distinction which has grown up between the ordinary powers of the mind shown through the brain, and the various kinds of clairvoyance and similar powers, is an unfortunate one. One hears many people speaking against the acquisition of psychic powers, while they themselves are using them all the time through the physical body. They denounce astral vision while they are using physical sight. It is illogical to denounce astral sight, unless you are prepared to take up the logical position of some of the Indian yogis, who regard the use of both physical and superphysical senses equally as a hindrance. These men are quite rational; they do not value any of the senses, because they consider that these only bring them into closer touch with the worlds of illusion from which they wish to escape. I do not agree with those people. I think that it is better to be healthy and to have the use of one's faculties on all planes; but unless their thorough-going attitude is adopted a good deal of the talk against psychic powers is foolish.

What is true is that in the early exercise of one's astral senses there is always a possibility of being misled. But one's physical senses also may deceive one. Certain sight-illusions, for example, are due to bad digestion and liver disorders, though I would not include in this category many things which the average doctor does, which are in reality instances of etheric or astral sight. The commonest illustration of the way in which our senses deceive us is that of the rising of the sun; you know that the sun does not rise, but you see it doing so.

The senses have always to be corrected by the reason, which is higher than all sense perceptions. Your astral vision constantly deceives you, when you begin to exercise it. That is why anyone who is being trained by a Master is put through a definite and thorough course of practice. He is asked what he sees, and his replies at first are mostly wrong; then his mistakes are pointed out to him, and explanations are given.

Suppose that a person who is not being trained by a Master awakens that sight. This frequently happens, for in the normal course of evolution the astral senses are unfolding, so that many people are beginning to possess them. Such a person is in the same position on the astral plane that a baby is in here. You know how a baby will stretch out its hand to grasp a lighted candle which is at the other end of a room. The baby's mistakes get corrected naturally by his elders ; he will find out that certain objects that attract him are at a distance, by being carried to them. So our astral baby—as we may call the person newly functioning with his astral senses—makes many mistakes, which would not matter in the least if he were in the midst of his elders. Neither would they matter so much if only people would have common sense. But unfortunately the person who receives an astral communication, or sees an astral vision, too often thinks himself distinguished from all the rest of the world by being vouchsafed a special revelation. They are thus not in a position to learn from their elders in this sort of knowledge, as a baby is willing to be taught by grown-up people, and so a good deal of trouble arises.

C.W.L.—Those who become pupils of the Masters are put through a long course of training with regard to this matter of higher sight and higher impressions generally. I suppose that to many that training would be very wearisome. An elder pupil will take the younger and pass before him a number of different objects and ask him what he sees. The young pupil is generally quite wrong at first, because he has got the thing out of focus. He does not know the difference between the astral body of a dead man and of a living man, nor that between the man himself and a thought-form made by some friend. In these and many other ways the untrained observer is liable to deception. Patiently the teacher will show him these things again and again, and show him how to recognize them, pointing out the minute differences.

No one should think that because this training is necessary the astral senses are especially unreliable. All senses are unreliable until they are trained, and even then when they are not used along with the rational intelligence. Every morning in fine weather, if we are up in time, we may see the sun rise; we know perfectly well that it does not rise and yet we see it doing so. Sometimes illogical people say with regard to things a little outside the range of most people's experience that they will not believe in what they cannot see, but if they see they will believe. Some go further and say that they will be convinced if they can touch the thing. A simple test will show the fallacy of this. Take three bowls and put into them water at different temperatures; very hot, icy cold, and of temperate degree. Put one hand into the hot and the other into the cold water; let them remain there for a few minutes, then move them both into the temperate water. The hand that has been in the hot water will tell you that this bowl of water is very cold, and the other hand will tell you that it is very hot. This demonstrates that the senses are not always to be implicitly relied upon. Their testimony must be checked by the use of reason, and this has to be done just as much with the astral and mental senses as with the physical.

If a man wishes for psychic powers he must work at their development and it is often a matter of years before the man is perfectly certain of his accuracy in all cases. It is difficult to realize the extent of the area over which this clairvoyant vision extends. Take one example only: in the astral plane there are two thousand four hundred and one different varieties of what is called elemental essence, and if one wishes to be reliable and to do his work well and quickly, he must learn to distinguish one from another, and know when they are to be used. The work can be done without any of this knowledge, but wastefully—on the principle of emptying a bucket of water over a man to wash his little finger.

We are told, however, that waste of energy is precisely one of the things we must avoid. Energy is capital, and we are bound to make the most of it. We are responsible for any waste of it, just as we should be if we let it lie idle and did nothing with it.

It would be of no use for a pupil of the Master to say: "I know already." That is not the spirit in which we approach these things. We are always eager and anxious to acquire further information, but always that we may serve the better, in order that we may be more useful. That is the idea, and most assuredly there is no knowledge which comes amiss in the work we have to do. Everything he knows enables the occultist to illustrate points, and often to understand points which otherwise might not be clear to him. They say at the end of this evolution we shall attain all knowledge; we shall get rid of ignorance. All our work is tending in that direction, and we shall certainly need to be most wonderfully well informed to do the higher work well when our turn comes. Meantime, it is wisdom to use to the full the powers one has, and to have no desire for psychic powers until the Master sees fit that we should develop them.

> To force them too soon often brings in its train much trouble ; often their possessor is misled by deceitful nature-spirits, or becomes conceited and thinks he cannot make a mistake ; and in any case the time and strength that it takes to gain them might be spent in work for others.

C.W.L.—The deceitful nature-spirits, of which there are many different kinds, are a very real feature in the case. Most of them are rather small creatures, and they think it is very amusing if they can make a great big man do what they say, when they order him about. They do that very often merely by pretending to be Julius Cæsar, Napoleon Bonaparte or any great and well-known personage whose name happens to occur to them, and it is great fun for them to see big people who belong to a higher stage of evolution than their own doing what they suggest. It is perhaps a little hard on the people, but they should have brought their reason and common sense to bear on their visions.

If you hear an astral voice sometimes, do not immediately jump to the conclusion that it is that of the Master or of a great Archangel. Dead people often manage to communicate and offer advice, and nature-spirits play their little tricks frequently, so it is more likely in most cases to be one of these. So, take the voice quite calmly; it is an interesting phenomenon, not necessarily because of what you may get out of it, but because anything a little out of the ordinary is in itself interesting, and there is generally something to be learned in connection with it. But do not start by denying that there is a communication—that again is an unwise thing to do. One may think of a thing as improbable, but it is not safe to say it is impossible. Listen respectfully to the revelation, but, unless you have good reason to do so, do not let it affect your conduct in any way. Action should be the consequence of one's decision, following upon one's own reasoned thought, not of something said by somebody else, one does not know who.

A great number of people have revelations which they think are going to remodel the world. Though they are usually quite good, there is generally nothing very striking about them, and they are apt to be somewhat indefinite in outline, and vague in their teaching. As far as they go they are generally an improvement upon the very limited and cramped orthodox theories. They are nearly always along Theosophical or New Thought lines —Theosophy and water, the water predominating. They are usually given out with perfectly good intentions, by some dead man, who has now realized certain broad facts of life which he wishes to impress upon those whom he has left behind. He thinks that if these higher ideas were accepted the world would be a much better place, and he tries to impress them upon the people on the general theory of Dives in the parable, that if some one came to the people from the dead they would repent, forgetting, of course, the sage answer of Abraham: "If they hear not Moses and the Prophets, neither will they be persuaded though one rose from the dead."[1]

Such a man forgets that he himself paid no attention whatever to spirit messages when alive. If such come our way—they are sure to, more or less, if we are what is called psychic—we should receive them quite respectfully, but at the same time without undue excitement. Many of those who receive the message think that they are going to revolutionize the planet, but that is not easily done. When they are brought to our notice, we apply to them, if necessary, certain means of testing the truth and validity of such communications. Most people have not those means immediately at their disposal, but if they will just apply plain common sense to their superphysical experiences they will get along very well in regard to most of them. There are two attitudes which are adopted by most people; either they receive them blindly or else they scoff and say it is ridiculous. Both these extremes are silly. Everyone who has studied these things knows that they do come, but for the most part only from people who can tell us nothing new and accurate. A dead man, if he is wise enough to do it, may learn certain things which as a living man he could not get to know, but nearly all the dead neglect this opportunity, and go on contentedly with the limitations and prejudices they had on earth.

[1] S. Luke, 16, 31.

Experiences of the super-physical are now on the increase, because the time of the coming of the World-Teacher is drawing near, and that fact is widely known on all the planes. In the physical world there is a strong expectation of His coming, quite outside the Theosophical ranks. There are many people who feel the nearness of His approach, and consequently are more likely than before to be the recipients of such communications. They invite them by their attitude of expectancy. Therefore it is quite certain that there will be a great deal of information and misinformation spread abroad with regard to the coming of the Lord. He Himself said a long time ago that there would be many false Christs who would come. The average Christian probably thinks of the false Christs as anti-Christs, deliberately deceiving the people. But most of them will be entirely well-meaning people, who have really persuaded themselves that they are overshadowed by the Christ, and the very fact that they are well-meaning will render them more dangerous, because people will feel their earnestness, and be carried away by that.

The Theosophical attitude about false Christs may be expressed somewhat thus: it is a pity that people should be misled into thinking that some one who is very ordinary is the World-Teacher. Nevertheless, if the teachings are good and the people follow them heartily and nobly, their lives will be improved. The fact that they have wrong impressions on certain points will not prevent them from receiving the karma of their good lives. It would be better that they should see the truth clearly, but we must not make the mistake of thinking that people who are in error with regard to a certain important truth are necessarily wrong in every other respect—because they are not.

I hope, however, that we who are students of Theosophy shall be free from this particular error, because we are expecting the coming with a clearness and a definiteness which most of the sects have not. As the time draws nearer more than ever shall we have to use our own common sense, never denying the possibility of anything, but exercising judgment and reason always. We may adopt the attitude of Gamaliel: "If this counsel or this work be of men, it will come to nought; but if it be of God, ye cannot overthrow it; lest haply ye be found even to fight against God."[1] Let us take whatever comes of good, from any source whatever.

The Masters influence many people, and care nothing about whether the instruments that They use know Them or not; therefore we must be prepared to find that quite outside Theosophical organizations other forces are working towards the same great goal. And while we follow our line and serve our own Society firmly, strongly, faithfully, loyally, keeping to that because it is obviously the way for us, yet we should be careful not to condemn or to speak against any other forms of manifestation outside it, which may be tending in the same general direction, and we must not expect such manifestations to be all pure or perfect. In all sorts of ways

[1] Acts, 5, 38-39.

spiritual power will be outpoured from now on to the time of the coming. The Hierarchy itself is pouring upon the world floods of influence which may perhaps touch but little the man who is entirely wrapt up in worldly matters, but which mean a great deal to those who are sensitive; to those who are ready to profit by it, it will mean the making of a new heaven and a new earth.

That there will be unusual happenings is certain. *The Light of Asia*, which is a very faithful transcript of the Buddhist books, referring to the life of the Lord Buddha, relates again and again how various non-human entities knew of His coming and rejoiced in it, and how devas and nature-spirits everywhere felt His wonderful magnetic influence and gathered round when anything specially great was going to happen—at the time of His birth, when He was about to attain Buddhahood, and at the time of His first sermon. There is much truth in that idea. Whenever any great manifestation of the higher power is taking place, the other and more sensitive evolutions feel it much more than humanity does. Because men have given themselves largely to the development of the lower mind, and for a long time have neglected the hidden side of things and been so entirely wrapped up in themselves, they are generally at present less sensitive than some of the lower creatures. I have known cats and dogs that were more sensitive to higher influences than human beings—not that they could get so much from them, but they were aware of them when human beings were not.

When the Lord comes He will no doubt take up the experiments made by those who have prepared for Him and carry them through to a successful conclusion, so probably He will leave the world in all sorts of ways different from the condition in which He will have found it. He will not only preach His religion, but it may well be that all sorts of other reforms as well may be introduced as a consequence of His teaching. One cannot say definitely, of course, because there will probably be opposition this time, as there was before.

I do not think we can assume that He will carry the world before Him. Probably many teachers will have to come before His pure doctrine wins the allegiance of the world in general. When He came two thousand years ago men barely heard of Him. We must expect the life of the Teacher and those around Him to be anything but easy. The world at large is always ready to take up and circulate evil reports, so we may as well be prepared for a vast amount of petty annoyance and discomfort, if nothing worse. All sorts of vested interests will obviously find the changes which He may propose unpalatable to them. The vested interests murdered Him last time after only three years of teaching. How it will be this time we cannot know, but we hope that at least a nucleus of people will exist in every country, who may be able to make it profitable for Him to stay and work with us longer than three years. The Order of the Star in the East has definitely set itself the work of preparing for Him, with a full knowledge of what it means and what lines His teaching is likely to follow.

There may well be also other individuals and organizations inspired to work in the same way, often without any means of obtaining such knowledge as we are privileged to have. We hope that our service will make possible what was not possible before. We hope, but we cannot say. We can only do our best.

Those who are destined by karma to work with the great Lord of Love are now of necessity coming into incarnation. We often hear, therefore, of the birth of extraordinary children. They must come now, in order to be in the prime of life when the Lord arrives. It is likely that they will differ in certain ways from other children, so do not be surprised when you hear of young people who remember previous births, or have other superphysical experiences of their own ; all these things are quite natural and to be expected, because of the special time in which we live. Dr. Besant once gave directions as to how people should treat such cases as came within their ken. She said : " Do not be excited with regard to any such things, and do not recount alleged identifications of such children too readily, for very few people know who they were in previous births. Remember that all such children are unusually sensitive, therefore you must be very kind and very gentle in your dealings with them. There must never be a harsh word or gesture of any sort ; you must never startle or alarm them, for they feel much more acutely than other children. You must guard them from crowds or from the neighbourhood of undesirable people. You should let them know but few people, and should surround them with harmonious magnetism, which should not be changed too often. You should not send them to school, but you should surround them with a specially loving home atmosphere."

A.B.—Here the Master adds a further reason why one should not desire to obtain psychic powers: the time and strength that it takes to gain them might be spent in work for others. Notice how constantly the advice that the Master gives has for its aim service and the getting rid of selfishness in every form. Instead of using time and strength to acquire psychic power for yourself, give them to the service of those around you. If the Master sees that you are thus using every power you already have in the service of others, so that more can be entrusted to you because it is certain that you will also use those unselfishly, then He will step in. If you can honestly say that you are using every faculty *you have, be sure you are on the threshold of having fresh powers entrusted to you. But there are very few* who can say *it*, and *if you* are not one of *those* you had better set to work to attain this condition.

This is the meaning of the parable of the talents—the name is equally applicable whether you take the word talent in its modern meaning or in its original one of a certain measure or weight of money. A man went away on a journey, entrusting some money to his servants; one had five talents given to him, another two, another one. On the employer's return, he asked how the talents had been used. Those who had five and two talents respectively had traded with them, and were able to return them with interest. But the servant with one talent only had hidden it away, and now he brought it and handed it back. Then the lord took it away from him; while the other servants who had been faithful in small things he made rulers over many things. And he said: "Unto everyone that hath shall be given, and he shall have abundance: but from him that hath not shall be taken away even that which he hath."[1] It seems paradoxical, but the occult meaning of the words is clear. He who uses his powers to the full shall be entrusted with more; he who does not use his powers, and who therefore from the occult standpoint does not possess them, shall lose even the possibility of using them; they will atrophy.

No one should complain that he is not receiving from the Masters all the help to which he thinks himself entitled. There is only one way in which to satisfy your wish to come into touch with the great Teachers, and that is to be useful to your fellow-men. That is the only claim which the Masters recognize; they look not at the capacity of a person, but at his usefulness. I came into touch with the Master in this life when I did not know of His existence, and so was obviously not thinking of reaching Him. It is true that I had been His disciple for many lives, but it was not that which caused Him to reveal Himself to me; He did so because I was straining every nerve to help the people about me—the poor, the miserable, the down-trodden—because it was worth while for Him to pour His strength into me, when it was passed on to thousands.

[1] S. Matthew, 25, 29.

So, instead of crying out to the Master in your meditation, asking Him to reveal Himself to you, see what good work there is that ought to be done in your town or village, and go and do it. It does not matter to the Master whether or not His instrument knows that He is using it. There are many great helpers scattered throughout the world who are assisted and inspired by the Master. Many outside the Theosophical Society are so inspired.

> **They will come in the course of development—they *must* come; and if the Master sees that it would be useful for you to have them sooner, He will tell you how to unfold them safely. Until then, you are better without them.**

C.W.L.—People often say: "I hear of these wonderful powers which make their possessors so much more useful. I want to be useful. I should like to have them too." There is nothing wrong in that, only one had better follow the advice which is given here, and wait until they come naturally, or until the Master Himself tells one how to open them. Is He likely to do that? Yes; when you are ready. My own experience tells me that. I had none of these powers, and was not thinking about them, because we thought in the early days of our movement that they could be developed only by those who were born with a certain amount of psychic faculty to begin with, and I had none. One day, however, the Master Himself, when visiting Adyar, gave me a hint in that direction. He advised me to try a certain sort of meditation, and said: "I think you will get good results from it." I tried it and got the results. The same thing will be said to everyone who works for the Master, when the right time comes. We may take that as quite certain. In what form He will signify His wish cannot be foretold, but He will do it in some way.

The best way to make oneself fit for such an effort is unquestionably to use for service to the fullest possible extent all the powers one has. Any person who is doing that without thought of self is likely to receive some new powers.

It is the old parable of the talents again. You remember those who made good use of their talents were able to go on, and were given charge of far greater work. It was said to them, "Thou hast been faithful over a few things, I will make thee ruler over many things: enter thou into the joy of thy lord."[1] Very few people stop to think what that means—the joy of the Logos, the joy of the Masters. It is not vague pleasure or bliss, or entry into heaven. The making of the worlds is joy to Him; it is the play of Bacchus in the Greek Mysteries, and of Shrī Krishna among the Hindus. The Logos has chosen to throw Himself into this mighty work of evolution; that is the joy of our Lord, the joy of carrying out this splendid plan of pouring out His love through the universe; and if we are to enter into the joy of the Lord we must take part in that work and the bliss which it brings. If we are not using *all* the powers that we have, the Master will not help us to obtain others.

[1] S. Matthew, 25, 21, 23.

He will wait until He sees that we are making full use of what we already have. People do not always understand that. They want to become invisible helpers ; we tell them always, "You must be visible helpers first. If your whole life is full of helpfulness on the physical plane where you are fully conscious, then quite certainly you will be useful also in the other planes."

CHAPTER 4

SMALL DESIRES

You must guard, too, against certain small desires which are common in daily life. Never wish to shine, or to appear clever.

C.W.L.—Most people rather like to appear clever, to appear to the best advantage. But no man who has met the Master face to face could ever think about shining himself. When he has seen that glory he realizes in a moment that any light he can show is as a farthing rushlight compared to the sun. Therefore the idea does not occur to him, or if it was there before it is now dissolved. The man who thinks that his tiny light is going to make a vast impression in the world is the one who has not yet seen the higher lights, and therefore has not the means to compare.

Yet in every possible way we must make the best of every quality that we have, in the Master's service. What light we have is not to be hidden under a bushel. It is not only the mighty beacon of the World-Teacher that is needed; let the lower lights be borne along the shore. The great light shines out so brightly that it dazzles some; others never lift their eyes, and hardly know of its existence. The lesser lights, which are nearer to their own comprehension, may appeal to these. There may be many whom we can help who as yet are not at all ready to be helped by greater people. So each has his own place; but never desire to shine for the sake of shining, that would be foolish.

> **Have no desire to speak. It is well to speak little; better still to say nothing, unless you are quite sure that what you wish to say is true, kind and helpful. Before speaking think carefully whether what you are going to say has those three qualities; if it has not, do not say it.**

A.B.—People who want constantly to talk have not enough to say to be able always to talk sensibly, and so they say things which are not worth hearing, and thus add to the tremendous stream of gossip which there is in the world. Thus they do incalculable harm, if they allow the tongue to be their master, instead of themselves mastering the tongue. Then comes a teaching which I have often heard from the Master: think before you speak whether what you are going to say is true, kind and helpful, and if it has not those three qualities do not say it. This will make you slow in conversation, so that gradually you will find that you talk less, and that will be a good thing.

Talkative people fritter away their energies, which ought to be employed in useful action. The person who talks a great deal is generally a poor worker. You may think, perhaps, that these remarks about speaking might very well be applied to myself, as I am constantly lecturing. But I do not speak much outside my work. I have lost the capacity for small talk, so that people often find fault with me for my silence. In the West I have often to force myself to talk, because silence is frequently mistaken for moroseness or pride, or a disinclination to make oneself agreeable. Naturally, then, my facility of speech is not great unless I have something definite and useful to say. Speak, by all means, when you have good cause to speak, when you have something to say that is worth saying, when it is done out of kindness to others. It is not such speech, but useless talking, that must be stopped. Every useless word is another brick built into the wall which separates you from the Master, and that is a serious consideration for those who want to reach Him.

He who speaks much cannot be truthful. I do not mean that he is consciously and wilfully untruthful, but he cannot always be accurate, and inaccuracy is untruth. There is scarcely anything worse than to have around you an atmosphere of untruthfulness, such as is always created by inaccurate speech. I often receive letters, for example, which are a mass of verbiage, with perhaps a little kernel of fact in the middle of it all. In all the ordinary affairs of life we learn to discount exaggeration; so also, when I receive a letter containing a complaint against somebody else—and there are many such—I judge how much ground there is for it largely by my knowledge of the writer's character and also by sensing the mood in which he was when he wrote it.

The Manu said that he who had mastered the tongue had mastered all; and a Christian teacher said: " The tongue is a little member, and boasteth great things. Behold how great a matter a little fire kindleth! And the tongue is a fire, a world of iniquity: so is the tongue among our members, that it defileth the whole body."[1] To master the tongue is to master the lower nature. The small troubles which people have are mostly the result of their idle words; the reaction from them. Little headaches, indispositions, depressions and so forth arise in this way. If people who have these would learn silence, they would soon improve their physical health, partly because they would no longer lose all the nerve-energy which now trickles away in talk, and partly because they would not have constantly to pay the little kārmic debts which result from their idle words. It will be remembered that Pythagoras imposed two years' silence on his pupils; that fact should weigh with us, because he was the Master whom we now know as Kūthūmi, the teacher of Alcyone and also of Bishop Leadbeater.

In India there are many yogis who are called *munis*; they have taken a vow of silence, as their name implies. The value of that has always been recognized in this country. I know one man who has carried out this vow for ten years, and it has given him great peace and dignity; because of it he is leading a far more spiritual life than he could have done without it. Of course, most of us cannot take such a vow when we are living

[1] James, 3, 5-6.

in the world and have all kinds of work to do in it; but we can and should follow the spirit of it, keeping silent whenever it is possible to do so without giving offence.

The need of constantly watching and judging is also valuable as a training in greater self-recollectedness. You must say something, but you have to determine not to say more than will fulfil the occult rule as to kindness and usefulness. It is a good practice to make a resolution on this point for one day at a time; determine in the morning that you will speak no idle word during the day—that will be one day to the good, at least. Our Jain brethren make use of similar exercises in order to learn watchfulness and self-recollectedness; they determine in the morning that during that day they will not do a certain thing—which may be quite unimportant in itself—and they do not do it, and the habit of watchfulness thus engendered does away with carelessness. The Lord Buddha also spoke very strongly on the subject of carelessness, the lack of thoughtfulness which leads men into so many blunders.

C.W.L.—People who are all the time chattering cannot always be speaking sensibly or profitably; furthermore, they cannot be truthful. If people are always talking loosely, quite certainly some of the things they say will not be true, though not intentionally false. They make all sorts of inaccurate statements, and afterwards say: "I did not mean to be inaccurate, so it does not matter." It is not what you mean, but what you do that produces results. If you do a foolish thing, the fact that your intention was good does not alter its character, nor relieve you from the karma of it. The good intention, if definite, will be beneficial to you, but the foolish thing will bring you bad physical karma. A man will say something, and later correct himself: "I see I was wrong; it is not quite like that." He has told a falsehood: he did not mean it, but he has made an assertion which is not true. To say that he did not mean it is like the plea of a man who happens to shoot some one by accident: "I did not know the gun was loaded." He ought to have presumed that it was loaded until he knew it was not.

It would be a good thing if we set ourselves just for one day to make quite sure that we spoke nothing that was not true, kind, and helpful. It would be rather a silent day, but perhaps the world would not lose much, and it would be very good for us. Of course, it would be impossible to carry on a rapid and animated conversation because we should have to stop and think. These rules are based upon the laws of the higher life. If a man wants to make more rapid progress, he must try to keep these higher rules. He must change himself to suit them, even when they seem to bring him into conflict with ordinary life and its methods. That may appear hard, perhaps; but if, after carefully thinking it over, he feels that the demands of the higher life are too hard for him, let him wait a life or two before trying to make real progress. We cannot do the two things: have an easy life without any effect and exertion, and have the rapid progress; but we can do either one, and there is no blame attached to the man who feels that as yet he is not equal to the strain.

It is well to get used even now to thinking carefully before speaking; for when you reach Initiation you must watch every word, lest you should tell what must not be told.

C.W.L.—That might possibly be misleading if one did not understand the facts with regard to Initiation. If anyone thought of divulging the real secrets of Initiation, before he uttered the words he would have forgotten that there was anything to betray. Therefore the real secrets are perfectly safe; they have never leaked out, and they can never do so. Still, there is great danger for the Initiate who may become careless. He may put himself in a very awkward position indeed. I myself am possessed of certain information of various kinds, as to which I cannot see that any particular harm would be done if it were published in the daily newspapers; but I was told not to repeat it so I do not; I do not know why. A promise is a promise, and must be kept as a sacred thing. If there are any who do not feel that way about it, they had better give up at once all thought of occult progress.

Much common talk is unnecessary and foolish; when it is gossip, it is wicked.

C.W.L.—Often what we must call unnecessary talk is nevertheless spoken with intent to help to pass the time pleasantly for some one. It is, perhaps, the unfortunate custom of our period to spend a great deal of time in talking which really might be employed much more profitably in thinking. There must be times when we say things which are not absolutely necessary, just in order to please other people who would misunderstand us if we were persistently silent. Yet outside that there is a great deal of unnecessary talking which does not fall under that head at all, done apparently just for the sake of saying something. That is a mistake. Real friends can be silent and yet enjoy one another's company, and realize a close community of thought; but if people are in a condition where they are afraid of gaps in the conversation and must keep on talking, then unfortunately there will be a great deal said which would be much better not said. Garrulous people are not the wisest, and are not, as a rule, notable for thought.

So be accustomed to listen rather than to talk; do not offer opinions unless directly asked for them.

C.W.L.—Some people cannot hear a statement made which they think to be wrong or incomplete without instantly contradicting it and creating disharmony and argument. We must realize that it is not our business to correct opinions, or to try to put right everybody who is wrong. It is our business to go about helping people as much as we can in a quiet sort of way, and if our opinion is asked on the subject to state it very calmly and temperately, and not in a spirit of opposition. We need not assume that our opinion is of great interest to anybody else; sometimes it is not, and then it is wrong to thrust it upon people. A man may be quite sure that the fact is so-and-so, and we may know very well that it is not so, but it is better to let him talk; it probably pleases him and does not do us any harm. He may choose to believe that the earth is flat or that the sun goes round it—it is his own affair. If one were in the position of a schoolmaster and were appointed to teach certain boys, then one would gently and quietly correct them, because that would be one's duty; but no one is appointed as a schoolmaster to the general public.

Of course, if we heard some one's character being taken away it would be our duty to say, "Excuse me, you are not quite right; that is not true" and as far as possible put the thing right before people. That would be a case of a helpless person being attacked—then it is one's duty to defend him.

One statement of the Qualifcations gives them thus: To know, to dare, to will, and to be silent; and the last of the four is the hardest of them all.

C.W.L.—The Rosicrucians held that he who would make occult progress must resolve to know, dare, will and be silent. We must know the truths of nature, and dare to use them. To use the great powers that become ours on this Path we must have a strong will that can control them, and control ourselves too. Then, when these things are done, we must know enough to be silent about them.

CHAPTER 5

MIND YOUR OWN BUSINESS

Another common desire which you must sternly repress is the wish to meddle in other men's business. What another man does or says or believes is no affair of yours, and you must learn to let him absolutely alone. He has full right to free thought and speech and action, so long as he does not interfere with any one else. You yourself claim the freedom to do what you think proper ; you must allow the same freedom to him, and when he exercises it you have no right to talk about him.

C.W.L.—One should not interfere with other people's beliefs and actions, as long as their actions are not obviously to the common harm in any way. If a man comports himself so as to be a nuisance to his neighbours, it may sometimes be our duty to suggest something ; but even in such cases it is often best to go away and let things quietly right themselves.

We of the Anglo-Saxon race boast much of freedom, but we are not in the least free really, for we are hidebound by custom to an almost inconceivable extent. We cannot dress as we like, or go about as we choose.

A man might prefer the ancient Greek—it is probably one of the most beautiful costumes in the world—but if he put it on and walked down the street he would probably have a crowd of people round him, and might be arrested for blocking the traffic. In any land of liberty he would be quite free to dress and act as he liked, so long as he did not make himself a nuisance to others. But there is no real freedom at all; we cannot depart from the line which other people take, or at least only very slightly, otherwise a great deal of trouble and disturbance is caused. It is a pity, because real freedom would be so very much better for all concerned, especially for those who want to interfere with others.

A.B.—I suppose that most of us who are earnest and enthusiastic are so sure of the value of what we have learned, so convinced, and rightly so, of its supreme importance, that we want other people to feel the same; and sometimes we should almost like to force them to see as we do. That is a fault of almost every enthusiastic nature. But a man can only receive gladly what he already knows inside, though he does not yet know it in the brain and therefore cannot yet articulate it to himself. Until that preliminary stage has been reached he is not in a position to accept a truth presented to him from the outside, and to try and force it upon him does far more harm than good.

In the same way conscience cannot be created from the outside; it is only the fruit of past experiences. Therefore the acceptance of all teaching and advice implies that the outer presentation has stirred knowledge already possessed by the man inside, and it has then flashed down into the brain. All that the teacher can do along these lines, therefore, is to bring to a man's physical-plane knowledge that which he already knows on other planes. One of the great Teachers has pointed out that many people are taught much Theosophical knowledge while out of their bodies during sleep. The real man then learns, and the knowledge that is thus acquired can then be regiven to him by a physical-plane teacher, whose words help the man to bring it down into his brain. That is all that the physical-plane teacher can do.

We have all to learn by repeated disappointments that we cannot help a man along the way which he is not yet ready to tread. Thus we become much quieter—ready to help when help can be useful, also ready to stand aside and wait when our help would be no help at all, that is, when the person could not profit by what we could tell him. This attitude often gives the ignorant the idea that we are indifferent, whereas the truth is that the person who is more advanced knows exactly where he can help and where he cannot.

For those who cannot see exactly where help can be given the policy ought to be tentative. Suggest a thought; if it is met with indifference or is repelled, you see that you cannot help the person whom you are addressing along that particular line. Then you must wait or try some other way, as the case may be. That is much better than forcing upon him all that you know; do not drown or choke the person mentally by pouring all your knowledge out upon him or trying to ram it into him. People are often very willing to claim freedom for themselves but extraordinarily reluctant to give it to others. That is a serious fault, for other people have fully as much right to their views and to the expression of them as we have.

Sometimes the fault is the other way. Do not run into the other extreme of thinking that you must accept other people's opinions. You have the fullest right to disagree. You may say quite frankly, "No, I do not agree with that," or you may keep silent; but what you must not do is to attack another for holding his own opinion. When you hear a person making some statement, use your own common sense first of all; always exercise your reason on every statement you hear. Leave other people free, but do not enslave yourself.

If you think he is doing wrong, and you can contrive an opportunity of privately and very politely telling him why you think so, it is possible that you may convince him; but there are many cases in which even that would be an improper interference. On no account must you go and gossip to some third person about the matter, for that is an extremely wicked action.

A.B.—You may sometimes be able to help a person whom you know to be morally doing wrong, but here great circumspection is required, since it is so easy to do more harm than good in such cases. Help so given must certainly be offered only in the private and utterly friendly way which the Master indicates. If the person is self-opinionated we can but leave him to learn by experience, which fortunately is a great teacher.

If a person has got hold of some mistaken idea, and he comes and expresses it to you, it is not necessary to say that it is wrong, unless you are sure that he has more confidence in your judgment than in his own, or at least is willing to consider seriously what you say; in many cases, he is bound to find out the error for himself, and then it is better to let him do so. People often come to me and make some great announcement of what is going to happen, according to their belief; generally I listen quietly and politely and do not express an opinion. When the prophecy fails of its fulfilment, the person who made it sees that he made a mistake, but one leaves him to draw the conclusion for himself. It is inevitable that such things should happen when many people are coming into touch with occultism. Sometimes they become confused, because many of their former standards of judgment are swept away, and they wonder how many of their criteria are going to fall to pieces among all the earthquakes that are taking place. The only thing to do under these circumstances is not to hurry, but to keep calm and cool and steady; gradually things will become clear, that which is false and mistaken will pass, and the real things will remain.

If you see a case of cruelty to a child or an animal, it is your duty to interfere.

A.B.—In the case of cruelty to a child or an animal interference is a duty, because strength is taking advantage of weakness, which it ought always to protect, because weakness cannot protect itself. Whenever, therefore, a child or an animal is being ill-treated, the duty of one who is stronger is to step in between and not allow an infringement of its rights, nor permit the liberty of another to be taken away. So whenever you see a case of cruelty to a child you should interfere, and try to make your interference effective.

> If you see any one breaking the law of the country, you should inform the authorities.

C.W.L.—A great deal has been said about that passage, and various people have taken exception to it. This is curious because, as a matter of fact, if you conceal a crime you become an accessory to that crime, before the fact or after the fact as the case may be, and you are so regarded by the law. People say, "But are we to spy upon others to see whether they are breaking the law?" Certainly not; you are not constituted a detective to go and find people breaking the law.

Law gives cohesion to a country; it establishes order for the good of all; therefore it is the duty of every citizen to uphold it. Still, one must use common sense. No one is expected to obey obsolete laws, though they remain on the statute book. Nor need anyone go out of his way to report minor delinquencies. Let us take, for example, the question of trespassing on another man's property; if you see a man taking a short cut across another man's park, I do not think you are thereby bound to go and report the matter. If you are asked about it, then, of course, you must say so. Or take the law against smuggling things through the customs. I should say a good citizen would obey that law, and not think of endeavouring to smuggle in goods of any sort. At the same time it seems to me that if some fellow-traveller is trying to smuggle some cigars or something like that through, it is not exactly my business to inform the authorities, because that is not a matter of the breaking of a law which injures anyone else.

I would not myself break it, because I think that when a law is made it should be obeyed, and if it is a bad law we should endeavour to use constitutional means to change it. We have in some cases laws which it would be difficult to obey. In some places there is a law of compulsory vaccination. Personally I should object to being vaccinated, and should refuse to submit to it except by major force. I should be prepared if necessary to go to prison rather than have that done, because it is an evil thing. These are all matters on which each person must pass his own judgment.

In India it is especially laid down what crimes must be reported if seen—they are, of course, all the serious crimes. If one were to see a murder or a robbery it would be one's duty to report it, but with regard to a host of minor things, one does not legally, in India, make oneself an accessory by not reporting them.

A.B.—It is the duty of every citizen, whenever he sees the law being broken to put a stop to the wrong,

This is one of the elementary duties of citizenship. Yet the other day an objection was raised to this teaching. A student came to me and said that here was a thing in the book which he could not accept; it seemed to him to suggest a general prying about, a spying into other people's affairs. Of course, it intends nothing of the kind; but when you see the law broken you must interfere, because the law is what gives cohesion to a country, establishing and preserving order, and binding its people together. It is the duty of every citizen therefore to uphold it; no one has the right to conceal a crime which he knows is going to be committed, and if he does so he becomes a partaker in it. This is so generally recognized that a person who knows of the crime and fails to report it is held legally to be an accessory to it and is punishable by law. I could only suppose that my objector had not considered what he was saying, for a country whose citizens do not recognize this simple duty and act accordingly goes down, because of the lack of public spirit.

If you are placed in charge of another person in order to teach him, it may become your duty gently to tell him of his faults.

C.W.L.—That is obvious. A child, a pupil, or a servant is placed in our charge because we are older and wiser. If we do not tell him of any faults which he commits he is losing the advantage of our wisdom and experience; therefore we should be so far failing in our duty towards him, neglecting to do that which we are placed there to do.

Except in such cases, mind your own business, and learn the virtue of silence.

A.B.—Think how different society would be if this were practised! Instead of being constantly on guard against his neighbours, a man could live his own life freely and openly, for people would leave one another alone to act as each might think best, and mutual tolerance and goodwill would replace interference and criticism. Our fifth race, which dominates the world to-day, is aggressive, combative and critical, but we have to try to live the life of the future, that of the sixth root-race, which is to be reached by tolerance and active goodwill. This will lead on to the general idea of brotherhood, on which the sixth race will be established.

C.W.L.—It does not seem difficult to mind one's own business, but very few people do it. What is meant here is that a general attitude of tolerance and goodwill should replace what is so painfully common at present—the spirit of interference and criticism. If a person does something quite unusual I am afraid many people fly to the conclusion that he has some nefarious reason for so doing. It does not at all follow; he may have his own private reason, and anyhow, unless he is doing something clearly wrong or interfering with others, we should let him go his way and do what he will.

Like some of the other common present-day faults, this springs largely from an excess of our fifth race and fifth sub-race qualities. Our race is developing the critical faculties of the lower mind, and that carried to excess makes us liable to be aggressive, combative and argumentative. Those who aim at occult progress are supposed, however, to develop the next quality—buddhi, the unifying quality, that which gives synthesis rather than analysis, and tries to see the points of contact rather than those of difference. The development of that will be the business of the sixth root-race, and also, in a subsidiary way, of the sixth sub-race, which is now dawning in America, Australia and some other places.

In the Theosophical Society we uphold the idea of brotherhood, and this is a way of practising it—find something not to blame but to praise. Something to praise as well as something to blame can be found in everybody and in everything, if you look for it; and there is every reason why we should concentrate our attention on the good qualities, not on the blameworthy things. We might try thus to bring down the side of the balance a little. We can afford to leave the fault-finding to the rest of the world, who are certain to continue to attend to the business of blaming, and will do it with more gusto than we possibly could. It is a valuable exercise to pick out the good things, because until we begin to look for them we do not really understand how many good things there are in everybody. When we do this, we shall begin to find all kinds of beautiful qualities in people whom we have been regarding very unfairly. It is easy to form an opinion of people whom we do not know well, based on only one or two things: we saw them looking angry, and therefore think of them as irritable people; or we saw them one day looking discontended, and so put them down as usually that sort of people. Probably we have simply stumbled upon them just at an awkward moment, and their life in general may not be at all coloured as we conceive it to be.

If we must err now and then, let it be on the good side; give a person credit for a little bit more than his due—that will not hurt him or us. A Master once said, "In everyone there is good, and in everyone there is evil." Beware of thinking of a person as bad; for you may expect him to act badly, and then, when he does not do so, you may be disappointed, because it shows that you were wrong in your judgment. It is much better to think too well of hundreds of people than to think too badly of even one. Let us live the buddhic life at least to the extent that we look for the things which are good and not for the things which are evil, not only in the interests of truth and justice, but because we know that our thoughts are powerful, that to think of another as bad tends to make him so, but to see the good in him diminishes the evil and helps that good to grow.

One of the chief things we have to learn is not to let the lower mind run away with us and make us attribute unworthy motives to other people. Our experience of human nature has shown us that it is a fallible thing, that people are not always swayed by unselfish considerations; therefore the natural tendency is to look for something selfish in the way of a motive, rather than for something high. But we must not allow ourselves to be dragged down to that level of suspicion and unkindness; not only for our own sakes, but for the welfare of others it is necessary that we should look first for the highest motive, and, even when we do not see it, should give the person credit for meaning well. When we think of a bad motive we are intensifying it by our thought, for the mind is very receptive. If a man has slipped back a little, and we give him the credit of meaning well, he will soon become ashamed of the lower motive and will replace it by the higher. Besides, in attributing the best possible motives to all our friends we are sure to be right in nine cases out of ten. Of course, the outer world in its cynical way will say to the man who does this. "You are a simple fellow." It is better to be the simple fellow who does good in this way than the clever one who cannot think well of anybody.

Practically no one is intentionally wicked. One should therefore avoid the common mistake of thinking that those who do what we should call wrong, do so through wicked motives. We must guard against doing injustice by supposing, for instance, that those who eat meat think anything about it, and are doing what they know to be wrong. They are not usually acting against their better feelings; they are following the custom without thinking about it. Such people are quite good; indeed, good people burnt one another in the middle ages, with no more thought. But one of the Masters said: "Our object is not to make good people, but to make mighty spiritual powers for good."

PART IV

GOOD CONDUCT

CHAPTER 1

CONTROL OF MIND

The six points of Conduct which are specially required are given by the Master as :

1. Self-control as to the Mind.
2. Self-control in Action.
3. Tolerance.
4. Cheerfulness.
5. One-pointedness.
6. Confidence.

[I know some of these are often translated differently, as are the names of the Qualifications ; but in all cases I am using the names which the Master Himself employed when explaining them to me.]

A.B.—As Alcyone says, the Master's translation of some of these qualifications is a little different from that to which we have been accustomed. The first three are not unlike the translations that I have been using for a great many years, but the last three are somewhat dissimilar, though of course the essential meanings are unaltered. The third of these points of good conduct

I have always translated "tolerance", as the Master does here, but that rendering is not acceptable, I know, to a good many people. The Sanskrit word is *uparati*, which means literally "cessation". We take the cessation as referring to qualities like criticism and discontent, and the positive side of this virtue is therefore tolerance.

The fourth, *titikshā*, I have always called endurance; of course, the idea of cheerfulness is the same, for a person who has endurance will necessarily be cheerful. Here the Master, who is—if I may venture to use the word—particularly sunny, gives the translation that emphasizes this aspect of the quality, and it is well that all should meditate upon it. Then comes one-pointedness; that is the Sanskrit *samādhāna* which I have given as balance—and again the idea is the same, for the one-pointed person is balanced, and vice versa. Lastly comes *shraddhā*, which I have always called faith. Here it is confidence; but once more the meaning is unchanged because I have always defined faith as utter belief in the God within and in the Master. It is well to note the differences as well as the likenesses, because these help us to grasp the meaning better.

1. *Self-control as to the Mind.*—The Qualification of Desirelessness shows that the astral body must be controlled; this shows the same thing as to the mental body. It means control of temper, so that you may feel no anger or impatience; of the mind itself, so that the thought may always be

calm and unruffled; and (through the mind) of the nerves, so that they may be as little irritable as possible.

C.W.L.—Control of temper is precisely one of the things which are difficult for us, because we are trying the new experiment of raising ourselves in evolution (which means much refining all our vehicles and making them more and more sensitive) while remaining in the midst of the life of the world. Our victory is so much the greater because of these difficulties, the overcoming of which shows that we have progressed further in strength of will than has the monk or the hermit.

Sometimes people succeed in weeding out the angry feeling, and yet find it difficult to control the outer vehicles entirely; there may still be a movement of impatience when really the feeling which used to be behind it has absolutely gone. It is not so bad as having the feeling and not showing it, but we must get rid even of that, because it misleads other people. If you look clairvoyantly at the astral body of the average man in the street, you will see that the whole thing is a swirling mass, and instead of having definite striations, and colours clearly marked and circulating as they should be, it has on the surface fifty or sixty little vortices or whirl-pools in violent agitation, each of which, because of the rapidity of its motion, makes a hard knot resembling a wart. If you examine these vortices you will find that they all arose in the little outbursts of temper, or small worries, or feelings of offence, jealousy, envy and perhaps even hatred, which the man has had some time within the last forty-eight hours. Larger vortices, lasting much longer, are made when the man renews a number of times the same kind of thought about the same person.

While a man is in that state it is quite impossible for him to think with the clearness and definiteness that might otherwise be his; if he wants to think or write on any subject, his views are bound to be coloured and distorted by these vortices, even though he has forgotten the feelings which caused them. Men forget their feelings of annoyance, and do not realize that the effect is still there; most of them keep up their stock of vortices at much the same level.

Prejudice shows itself in this way very clearly to astral and mental clairvoyance. The matter of the mental body ought to be in rapid circulation; not all over it, but in certain zones or areas. Broadly speaking, it tends to arrange itself according to its density, so that the coarser matter, while circulating to some extent all over the body, tends to gravitate towards the lower part of the ovoid, so that people who have a preponderance of selfish thought and feeling look like eggs standing on their larger ends, while those who are notably unselfish or occultly developed resemble eggs standing on their smaller ends. There are four zones or slices in the mental body, just as there are departments in the brain which deal with particular types of thought.

Imagine a man who is very illiberal in his religious thought. The mental matter, instead of flowing freely in that particular department, piles up until it actually projects and becomes a heap, and begins to fester and decay. As his thought on religious subjects must pass through this division of the mental body, it can never be true, because its vibrations are overcome by what is literally the mental disease that has fastened upon it. His view is bound to be prejudiced, until he sets to work and cures himself by deliberate control and purification of the mind. Only then may he learn to think truly—that is, to see things as does the Deity, who knows absolutely the whole of His system exactly as it is.

Prejudices are not necessarily against persons or things; quite often they are in favour. Even so, they are a form of untruth, and they show the same corruption in the aura. One of the commonest cases is that of the mother who cannot believe that there ever before was such a baby as hers since the world began. Another example is that of the artist who is incapable of seeing good in any other school of art than his own.

All those things, from the point of view of psychic force, are like open sores, through which the will-power of the man is leaking away all the time. That being the condition of the average man, when you get a person who is by nature a worrier, you have naturally a still worse case—a person who is all one sore, and has no force left, for all is spent. If we want to conserve our energies and do good work with them, as must be the case if we are to be occultists, the first thing to do is to check all these sources of waste. Suppose we want to put out a fire; we must have a jet of water. It must be pumped at high pressure, and there must be absolutely no leak in the water cylinders and pipes. That means for us calmness and control of mind.

The average man seems to have little or no will-power; when trouble comes he simply lies down under it and groans and complains, instead of directing his will to deal definitely with it. There are two reasons for this weakness. The degree of power that comes down into any man varies according to his realization of the true Self—the extent to which the One Self, the Deity, is unfolded within him. In essential nature we are all of equal strength, but men differ in the extent to which they have unfolded the divine strength in themselves. The ordinary man has not developed much of that, and even what he has he is wasting.

Many among us would like to realize more fully the presence of the Master, and to bring various other good influences from the higher planes down into the physical brain. Such influences must come down through these different vehicles—must be reflected from one to another. Look at the reflection of a group of trees on the surface of a lake or river. If it is quite calm we get a perfect picture, in which every leaf is clearly seen; but the least ripple distorts the picture altogether. If there is a storm, it is completely destroyed. That is exactly true with regard to the astral and mental bodies. They must be kept calm and held still if through them any true or valuable influences are to come from above. People constantly ask, "Why don't we remember all that we do in our sleep?" That is one of the reasons—because their vehicles are not quiet enough. Now and again they may become calm enough to bring something through, but even then the impression is usually somewhat distorted, because the medium is not perfectly clear. It is like looking at something through cheap bottle-glass instead of good plate-glass; it altogether alters the proportions of things.

When we have become calm we can work in the midst of disturbance and trouble, but of course it is always a strain to hold the bodies calm under these conditions. It is so great a strain that some people cannot do it at all; but they must gradually acquire strength.

The occultist learns through self-control to work on two planes at once, that is, to be partly out of his body at the same time that he is working on the physical plane; so that while he is writing or speaking he may be doing other things with his astral body. I have heard it said, for example, that when I have been lecturing various people in the audience have seen astral entities standing on the platform and coming up and speaking to me. That is correctly seen so far; it is often the case that they come up in that way, desiring answers to questions or wanting something done, while the lecture still goes on. That is only a small and passing example, but often there are much more serious pieces of work to be done, in which the occultist uses his consciousness in that complicated way.

This double concentration is performed to some extent quite frequently in ordinary life also. Many ladies can knit and go on talking, because the knitting is a mechanical action to them. I had much to do once with one of the great banks in London, and I have seen there men, who were used to it, rapidly and steadily adding up long columns of figures, and at the same time singing a song for the entertainment of their fellows. I must admit that would be impossible to me, but I have seen it done over and over again.

A.B.—In the section on desirelessness the Master has dealt with the control of the astral body and its numerous forms of desire, and in the section on discrimination He spoke much about truth, which involves the purification of the mental body. Now He deals further with control of the mind, and also of the emotions; an emotion is a combination of thought and desire. Emotions are desires which are penetrated by the thought-element. In other words, emotion is desire mingled with thought. When the Master speaks here of control of temper, He is speaking of emotion, because impatience and similar feelings proceed partly from the desire-body and partly from the mental body. The would-be occultist must certainly not let himself be carried away by temper, for until the control of that is gained, so that his emotions cannot be upset, he will not be able to see definitely or clearly. The vibrations of emotion will arouse corresponding excitement in purely mental matter, and all the man's thoughts will be disturbed and distorted, so that he will not be able to see things correctly.

The Master then says that the thought itself must be calm and unruffled; this is necessary because only in such conditions can influences be thrown down into the lower mind from the higher. I think it is in *The Occult World* that Mr. Sinnett quoted a letter from the same Teacher in which He told him that if he wanted to write usefully he must keep the mind calm, and then thoughts from the higher mind would reflect themselves in it, as mountains in a calm lake.

It is a good plan, if you want to write a letter on a serious subject—about Theosophy, for instance—or to produce an article, to sit quiet for some minutes, steadying yourself before you begin to work. This is not a waste of time, for when you begin writing you will then find that your thought will flow quietly and without effort, and you will not have to pause in the middle and consider how you are to go on. This will be so because the higher mind is being reflected in the mirror of the lower. This practice is especially important for those who cannot yet shut off the outer things at will.

One may make use of outer disturbances to practise concentration. As a child I was made to learn my lessons in a room where other children were being taught different things, so gradually I acquired the power to work at a task of my own while all sorts of other activities were going on around me. In consequence I have now the power to work undisturbed by what may be happening near by, though I must admit that I find it difficult to perform calculations under those circumstances. I have always felt grateful to my teacher, Miss Marryat, for this. The power comes with practice, and is then useful in a variety of ways. I found, for example, that I could also use it when partly out of my body, as when I was writing one of the lives of Alcyone.

In the Indian household this faculty is developed as a matter of course, because there it is customary for people to do different things in the same room, and there are generally children running about and numerous other small happenings. In the village school, and in the home too, a number of children are taught a variety of things at the same time, all reading aloud, each his own special subject, while their teacher follows it all, and corrects their mistakes as they are made. I do not think it is an ideal method of teaching any particular subject, but the children are learning how to concentrate, and that will be very useful to them afterwards.

If you can get that power of concentration so much the better; hence, if you have to live amid noise, do not complain of it but profit by it. That is the way in which the student of occultism works. I mention this especially, because it is by such means that occultists are made. To learn to work under difficult conditions means progress. That is one of the reasons why some of us have made progress, and others not so much. I personally have always tried to take everything as it came, instead of complaining. By this means one seizes every opportunity.

This last is difficult, because when you try to prepare yourself for the Path, you cannot help making your body more sensitive, so that its nerves are easily disturbed by a sound or a shock,

and feel any pressure acutely; but you must do your best.

A.B.—The Master says that it is difficult to control the nerves. That is so because the physical body is that over which thought has the least power. You can affect your astral and mental bodies comparatively easily, because they are made of finer matter, more affected by thought; but the heavier physical matter is much less responsive and therefore harder to control. Yet it must be mastered in time.

The pupil must be sensitive, and yet have the body and nerves completely under control. The greater the sensitiveness becomes, the more difficult is the task; there are many noises which pass unheeded by an ordidary person which are torture to one who is sensitive. There are certain diseases which produce excessive sensibility of the nerves; in such a case the bark of a dog may throw a person into convulsions. That example is sufficient to show how acutely sensitive the nerves may become.

The nerves of an occult student are not diseased—if they were, he would not be under training—but he is like a tense string, vibrating to the least touch. His nerves thus become so sensitive that he has to use great force of will in order to prevent irritability. The strain on the body under these circumstances may become so great that in some cases, like Madame Blavatsky's, it may sometimes be wiser to let go, to allow the body to go on as it likes at times, lest it should go to pieces altogether. It was necessary that she should keep her body for the work that she had to do, so she could not allow the strain on it to reach the breaking point. This, however, was an exceptional case; the aspirant who wants to follow the Master's teaching must do as He says here, and try as hard as he can to gain control over his nerves. He may fail again and again—that does not matter. The Master's last words on the subject are: "You must do your best." That is all that He asks, so do not let failures discourage you, but go on doing your best.

Sometimes a similar disturbed condition is set up from within, because of an exaggeration of scrupulousness and conscientiousness, into which the most earnest students are liable to fall. There are two tendencies among aspirants; one is to be careless, the other to torment oneself. In the second case conscience may reach a point when its condition is like that of the overstrained nerve. Thus it often happens to the best class of students to make too much fuss over little failures. Do not sit down and brood over such things till they have grown to the dimensions of a serious crime. Make your path between these two extremes. You cannot be too scrupulous before the event, but you may easily make yourself too unhappy afterwards. Do not brood over your faults and failures. Only look at them to see the reason why you failed, and then try again. So doing, you will starve out the tendencies which led you into them; whereas thinking about them only gives them new strength.

C.W.L.—The physical body is that over which the will has the least power. People say, "Oh yes, you can learn to do a thing with your physical body, you may even control your feelings but it is a much harder thing to control your thoughts." I know it is a popular idea that of all things that is the most difficult. In one way it is; because the mental matter is finer and more active, there is much more to control in the way of motion and of initiative. On the other hand, the mental body is much nearer to the ego within, and therefore more under his control: he has greater forces with which to grasp the mental matter and deal with it, than he has down here in the physical plane; and also the physical matter is less responsive. People think it easier, because they are in the habit of controlling the physical body, but not the mental body.

It is often said that you can control pain on the physical plane, but cannot ignore mental suffering. Really, exactly the contrary is true. The mental or emotional suffering ceases to exist if one grasps it and just puts it away from oneself, but actual severe physical pain is most difficult to ignore, though it can be very largely diminished by removing from it the mental element. The Christian Scientist does that by declaring that there is no pain; he leaves only the physical side of it, and that is comparatively small.

We should learn to control the mind so that the mental part of physical suffering is eliminated, because as pupils of the Masters we have to make ourselves exceedingly sensitive. Then it becomes painful to sit near a man who drinks alcohol, smokes tobacco and eats meat. It is positive torture to go about in a city, along a business street, with its tremendous roar of all sorts of hideous noises. It goes all through the physical body and makes it shiver, but if one thinks about it, that makes it much worse; whereas if no notice is taken at least one feels it less. The pupil who is trying to reach the higher planes, has to learn to eliminate the mental part of it, and not import into it any thought that makes it stronger.

Those who are practising meditation will find that they are more sensitive than the people who do not meditate, and because of that the strain on the physical body is sometimes enormous. One frequently hears it said that Madame Blavatsky used sometimes to have outbursts of temper. There was a very good reason for that, certainly, as she had a very unfortunate physical body; there was probably never an hour when she had not some acute physical suffering. The body was old, broken down and worn out, but it was the only body available for the particular work she had to do, and she had to keep it; she could not throw it away, as many of us might do. The opportunity was once offered to her to do that, but she said: "No, I will hold it till I have finished *The Secret Doctrine*"—the work in which she was engaged. That meant that the physical body was in a condition of terrible strain, and sometimes for relief she let it do what it liked. Of course, many people did not understand, but we around her came to know that these things did not mean much. We had many curious instances of that. For example, she would be in a wild tirade, apparently quite angry about some trifling thing, but while the newer people who did not know shrank away from her in fear, we discovered that if in the middle of that excitement some one suddenly asked her a philosophical question, the whole thing dropped away, was cut off as you might cut a thread with a pair of scissors; immediately the rage disappeared and she proceeded to answer the question. A person in an ordinary rage could not have done that. Many people misunderstood her and turned away, but I know quite well that she had sometimes to let go or her body would have gone to pieces.

The calm mind means also courage, so that you may face without fear the trials and difficulties of the Path.

A.B.—Courage is a quality upon which immense stress is laid in the Hindu Scriptures. It has its root in a recognition of the unity of the Self. " What fear, what delusion is there for one who has seen the Self ? " it is asked ; and the phrase is used : " the fearless Brahman." In *In the Outer Court* I recommended students to meditate upon the ideal character, using the list of qualities given by Shrī Krishna at the beginning of the sixteenth chapter of the *Gītā*. The first quality that He mentions there is *abhayam*, fearlessness or courage.

Courage grows out of the realization that you are the divine Self within, and not your outer vehicles, which are the only part of you that can be hurt. All differences of power between people arise from the degrees of strength which the Self within has unfolded. Essentially we are all equally strong, but there are stages of evolution. When you realize that you are yourself divine, you know that your weakness or power depends upon the amount of unfolded strength of the Self within you; so your refuge, when you feel fear, is to call out the power from within.

This realization of yourself as the Self is one of the things that ought to come to you through your meditation. Those who do morning meditation should include in it an effort to realize the Self; some of the strength they gain through that effort should then remain with them throughout the day. That will help to give them the courage that is needed for progress upon the Path. On it there are many difficulties which call for fortitude and endurance, if they are to be met and overcome, and these qualities are forms of courage. There is a novelty in things on the Path which also calls for courage. I know of no way of acquiring this quality except by realizing the Self.

C.W.L.—Much stress is laid upon the necessity of courage in all systems of occult training. If a man enters upon the Path he will have to face misrepresentation, calumny and misunderstanding. That has always been the lot of those who try to raise themselves above their fellows. Moral strength is necessary to meet that, and to enable a man to maintain his position and do what he thinks right, whatever those around him may think or say or do. Such strength is required to carry out the teaching as given in this book—and plenty of fortitude and determination as well.

Actual physical courage is needed, too. There are many dangers and difficulties on the Path not by any means symbolical, or on higher planes only; tests of bravery and endurance do come to us in the course of our progress, and we must be prepared for them. A man who is faint-hearted will not make progress on this Path, where is required, not merely goodness, but strength of character that cannot be shaken by the unaccustomed or the alarming.

I knew an occult society in England which tried for many weeks with various invocations to raise certain kinds of spooks, and at last they did raise something; but nobody stayed long enough to see what it was. Similarly, people try to obtain results on higher planes, but as soon as they get them they are afraid. The first time a man goes out of his body in waking consciousness, he may feel a little alarmed and may have a passing wonder whether he will get back again or not. He must realize that it does not much matter whether he does or not. He is used to certain limitations, and when those suddenly drop away, he is quite likely to feel that there is no certain base left to stand upon. We shall find as we go further on, that courage—plain, straightforward bravery—is a thing which is very much needed. All sorts of forces have to be encountered; it is not child's play.

When we realize and remember that we are one with the Divine, we fear nothing; but sometimes when sudden danger arises, men forget that and shrink back. The Self within is utterly unaffected, utterly uninjured, by any of the passing things, so if we can realize that we are that Self and not the outer vehicles, we shall have no fear. If ever fear of any sort is felt, the thing to do is to call up more power from within, not to appeal for help from some one from without. The common Christian teaching on that subject has been very unfortunate. They tell people always to take refuge in prayer, which literally means asking, and should not be applied to the highest form of aspiration, as it so often is. The word prayer comes from the Latin *precari*, which means to ask—nothing but that. If we hold that God is all-good, we should follow the advice of the Lord Buddha: "Do not complain and cry and pray, but open your eyes and see. The light is all about you, if you will only take the bandages from your eyes and look. And it is so wonderful, so beautiful, so far beyond anything man could think of or pray for, and it is for ever and ever."

I know that many people have the habit of calling upon the Master for help when they find themselves in difficulties. We may be sure that the Master's thought is always near, and assuredly He can be reached; but why should we trouble Him for something that we ought to be able to do ourselves? It is true that we may call upon Him if we wish; but surely if we can call upon the God within, and bring out more of that, we shall thus draw nearer to the Master than we could by calling feebly on Him for help. One does not question a man's right to do that; but knowing how the Master is always occupied in work for the world, surely we should not wish to call upon Him while there was any possible resource left to us whereby we could, by any means, do the thing for ourselves. To fail in doing it is to fail in faith; it is a want of confidence not in ourselves only, but in the divine power.

The practice of meditation also ought to prepare one to meet emergencies, so as not to be upset by them. Those who have grasped the inner laws should remain calm and composed whatever may come, realizing that to do so is a necessary condition of real progress, and that the shock and upsetting which result from an hysterical outburst will leave their scars on the sensitive vehicles of a pupil for a long time afterwards.

> It means also steadiness, so that you may make light of the troubles which come into every one's life, and avoid the incessant worry over little things in which many people spend most of their time.

A.B.—Steadiness is the next requirement mentioned by the Master; it is the quality that is necessary so that the pupil may not be blown about by every wind that comes. Such a dependence upon outside things gives rise to endless worry because the man is then not in control of his own affairs, and so cannot decide upon a definite line of work. It is worry that wears people out, not work. Worry is the going over and over again of a certain painful sequence of thought. It is difficult for a timorous person to prevent himself from falling into this habit in one or other of its different forms.

In some cases there is a tendency of the mind to dramatize, and then to live in its self-created drama. It is a thing I used to do to some extent myself. I am mentioning this and similar personal experiences because I think they will make what I have to tell you more living and useful than merely abstract thought would be. Most aspirants have probably done some such mental dramatization, for we are all made up in much the same way. I used to imagine that some friend of mine must have been hurt by some word or action of mine; I then imagined my next meeting with that person—the first words, the whole ensuing conversation. When we actually did meet the whole thing failed to work out as I had anticipated, because the first remark of my friend was always something quite different from what I had imagined. Sometimes people conjure up in this way an unpleasant scene, and imagine how they will act in the trying conditions they have invented; and at last they arrive at a painful condition of mind upon which they expend much feeling and emotion. Nothing of all this has as yet taken place, and probably none of it ever will: it has all been a pure waste of force.

All this sort of thing is merely unnecessary trouble, and it weakens the mental and emotional nature. The only way to get rid of this habit is to make yourself stand outside the scene, and observe whether the first thought in the series is a thing over which you have any control or not. If you have, then control it; if you have not, it is of no use to think about it till it comes, and this, after all, it may never do. It is useless to let your mind brood over possible happenings in the future. It is equally useless to let it run over and over the things which have happened; you cannot alter past events, so it is palpably useless to worry about them.

Many good people make their lives a burden by brooding over the past, thinking; "Perhaps if I had, or had not, done so and so, this trouble would never have happened." Suppose that is true, the thing is done, and no thinking will change the past. People lie awake at night and worry all day over unalterable past things or possible future eventualities. This action of the mind is like the racing of an engine or of the heart when normal resistance is lacking, which injures both heart and engine much more than work does. Recognize the futility and the positive harmfulness of such mental racing, and you will stop it, and learn to put out your strength effectively instead. It is pure silliness; it comes down to that. It is a thing which nearly everybody does, but ought not to do, and the would-be disciple simply must not do it.

C.W.L.—Of all mental difficulties, worry is the worst to deal with. It is an absolute bar to anything like proper progress. It is impossible in that condition to bring oneself into the state of mind for meditation. Some people worry about the past, others about the future, and by the time they have dropped one worry they have picked up another to take its place, and so they are never in a state of calm, and cannot hope to meditate with any prospect of success.

The best cure for it is to replace the trouble by a thought of the Master, but it takes unusual strength to do that. Suddenly to try to impose calmness on an astral body or a mental body in that condition is like trying to press down with a board the waves of the sea during a storm. Often the best thing to do is to get up and do something physical—weed the garden or go for a bicycle ride. There can be no permanent calm until the vehicles move rhythmically together; then all these other practices may be undertaken with some reasonable chance of success.

Often people worry over their own defects. Everyone finds himself falling into faults and failings now and then; it would be better not to do so, but that is hardly to be expected yet, for if we had no faults and failings we should all be Adepts. It is, of course, wrong to be careless about these things and think they do not matter, but it is also equally wrong to worry unnecessarily about them. In worry the mind races madly round and round, to no purpose. If you have been on board a steamer in rough weather you may remember that now and then the screw rises out of the water and races madly in the air. It is just a matter of mechanics that that does far more harm to the machinery than a great amount of regular work. That is exactly like worry.

Periodically troubles arise in our Society. I have seen a good many of them in my time. I remember very well the excitement over the Coulomb affair in

1884, and how many Theosophists were greatly disturbed and worried over that, and their faith in Theosophy was in some cases quite destroyed, because they supposed that Madame Blavatsky had been playing tricks upon them. That really, had nothing to do with the case. Our faith in Theosophy does not rest upon the statements of Madame Blavatsky or anyone else, but upon the fact that it is a perfect and satisfactory system which has been given to us, and that remains true even if it had been the case that Madame Blavatsky had deceived them—which was not so, of course. If people rest their belief on personal grounds, it can easily be shaken, but if our belief is based upon principles which we understand, it would remain unshaken even if a trusted leader did suddenly fail us.

> **The Master teaches that it does not matter in the least what happens to a man from the outside: sorrows, troubles, sicknesses, losses—all these must be as nothing to him, and must not be allowed to affect the calmness of his mind. They are the result of past actions, and when they come you must bear them cheerfully, remembering that all evil is transitory, and that your duty is to remain always joyous and serene. They belong to your previous lives, not to this; you cannot alter them, so it is useless to trouble about them.**

A.B.—Here the Master gives a reason for not worrying which, I fear, many people will not appreciate. He says that it does not in the least matter what happens to a man from the outside. The things which come to us in this way are quite beyond our control, because we ourselves made them in the past; they are our karma.

This does not mean, however, that there is nothing that we can now do in the matter. On the contrary, we can do much; we can meet them in the right way, and thus enormously modify their effect upon us. To do this is like changing a direct blow, which has force enough to knock one down, into a glancing blow, which is comparatively unimportant. It all depends upon changing the angle at which you meet to blow. If you meet every affliction that comes to you with the feeling: "This is only the payment of a debt; it is well to clear it off," then the sorrow will weigh upon you but lightly. A man who knows how to meet life will be calm and happy in the midst of difficulties, while one who does not know may be crushed by troubles that are half imagination.

How much of the trouble and pain that you feel is really caused by the mind, you can test for yourself when you are suffering physically; if you will then stand outside it all, as it were, you will find that the suffering will diminish very much. This fact can be realized in another way, by considering the state of the animals. An animal that has broken its leg will eat quite comfortably, dragging its wounded leg behind it. Now, that is a thing which a man could not do, yet a horse will do it, and the horse, so physiologists tell us, has an even more delicate nervous system than man has, so that its nerves are more sensitive to pain than his. Do not misunderstand me, and think that I say that animals do not suffer, or that their sufferings do not matter. Quite the reverse. But man intensifies his own suffering and prolongs it, because of the way in which he dwells upon it in his mind.

If you learn to check the effects of pain on your astral body, you will know how to diminish the pain itself very greatly. Those who call themselves Christian Scientists thus reduce pain very much, because they take away the mental element that usually mingles with it and increases it. I have had also some experience of the same thing, when I have had to lecture while suffering acutely physically; the result has been that during the time of lecturing I did not feel the pain. Why? Simply because my mind was entirely engrossed by my lecture. If you could completely withdraw your mind from paying attention to the physical body, as you would do perforce were you lecturing, any physical hurt which you might have been feeling would disappear to a large extent. If you have complete control over your mind you can do that, and so leave the outside things to affect only the outside body. People often do it under sufficient stimulus. Sometimes the soldier on the battlefield does not feel his wound until the excitement of fighting is over; and certainly some of the religious martyrs did not feel the flames around them, on account of the ecstasy that they felt in suffering for their Lord. Similarly, if a child meets with an accident, its mother will forget all about any pain that she herself may be suffering, as she rushes forward to rescue and help her child.

It is possible to learn this sort of control without the stimulus, and then you can largely neutralize the effect of any pain upon your astral and mental bodies. I do not say that it is easy to do this, but that it can be done. Personally, I do not think it is worth while to use a great deal of force, or make a very special effort, to obtain so little result as the stopping of a mere physical pain. Instead of turning your mind to the service of the body, as most people do, it is better to turn it away and occupy it with something profitable. If you take up the right attitude to life you will see that these outside things do not matter, and you will leave them alone to have their effect only on the outside of yourself. They have to be gone through, and their only value lies in the strength which you gain through them. By looking at them in this way you will gain great peace of mind.

All evil is transitory. You will realize that this is so if you look at the larger cycle of your life, and realize your past, not in detail, for details do not matter, but in its general sweep and trend. If one realizes how often before one has been through these things that grieve and trouble one—friends taken away by death, sicknesses, losses, troubles of all sorts—they sink into something approaching their true relative insignificance. It is important to make this effort, because the present is so insistent that it blocks out with its petty anxieties the deeper knowledge. The realization of your own long past will make you stronger, and then when some misfortune occurs you will think, "Why trouble? It will pass!"

I feel sure that I could not lead my present life at all if I did not refuse to bother, and to react to circumstances. Troubles of all sorts come pouring in daily, and if I reacted to them I should be dead in a week. In the past I have come through many movements of the kind with which I am now connected, and have found that they are always accompanied by turmoil. It is better not to anticipate trouble, but to attend to it when it comes, and afterwards to put it aside and forget all about it.

Your duty, says the Master, is to remain always joyous and serene. A warning was once given against casting dross into the crucible of discipleship. The evil and danger of doing so is carried to an extreme point at a place such as Adyar, where any dross—any form of trouble, suspicion, anxiety, doubt, and the like—acquires much more force than that of the person who sent it out. If sometimes you cannot at once rid yourself of depression, vexation, or any other undesirable feeling that you may have, then at least keep it to yourself. Do not let it pour out and infect the atmosphere, and make things harder for others. After training yourself in this way you will look back with surprise at your former condition, and wonder how such trifles could ever have troubled you as they did.

C.W.L.—The man who knows remains calm and happy even in the midst of what would be very serious trouble to other people. The man who does not know is very often crushed by the trouble, because of his own attitude with regard to it. There is a vast deal of imagination at the back of our sufferings. The real amount of payment exacted by karma is often small; but by taking it wrongly people frequently double their necessary suffering or even multiply it by ten; it is not fair to charge that to ancient karma, for it is the karma of the present foolish action—what Mr. Sinnett called "ready-money karma."

The amount of the debt to be paid cannot be altered —the karma which comes calls for a certain amount of suffering on our part; but as it can be increased, so it can be decreased. By an effort of our own we can apply new force, and change what would be the effect of a direct blow into one that glances off, as our President has expressed it, so that it will be much less felt. Every such putting forth of strength is the introduction of a new force into the case; therefore there is in it no sort of injustice, or interference with karma. That force which otherwise would have been spent in some other way is now spent in modifying the blow.

All evil is necessarily transitory. There was a Persian king who took as his motto: "Even this will pass away." It is a good motto, because it applies equally to pleasure or to suffering, and to good or evil fortune, whichever may be dominant at the time. The only things that do not pass are the real progress and the bliss which come from within—those remain for ever. Whatever is our suffering now, it will pass; we have had suffering before in other lives and have passed through it. If this can be realized it will help very much. Things that troubled us early in life seem quite unimportant now. We say: "Dear me, those things were not of any importance; I wonder why I worried so much about them?" The wise man learns from looking back. He says: "Here are these other things which are worrying me now, surely they are just as unimportant." Of course they are, but it takes a wise man to make that deduction.

> Think rather of what you are doing now, which will make the events of your next life, for that you *can* alter.

C.W.L.—Your next life will depend very largely upon the karma you make in this. More than that—the World-Teacher will come soon; things are moving fast now; the force which is being outpoured is tremendous, and because all that plays round us to some extent, we who are trying to prepare for His coming may modify not only our next life but the remaining part of this.

The karma of the pupil engaged in this work is more intense than that of most other people. There are probably many things which the man of the world does constantly and may do without much harm resulting in any way; but if these things were done by those who are nearing the Path, they would be very decidedly harmful. In the case of a disciple, whatever happens to him happens to the Master, because He has made him part of Himself. "No man liveth to himself, and no man dieth to himself"; this is true of everyone, but those who are drawn to the feet of the great Masters must be doubly careful. Especially anything whatever which puts difficulties in the way of a fellow-student in occult matters is a thing which makes serious karma.

> Never allow yourself to feel sad or depressed. Depression is wrong, because it infects others and makes their lives harder, which you have no right to do. Therefore if ever it comes to you, throw it off at once.

C.W.L.—Anybody who suffers from serious depression will probably shake his head and say: "That is very good advice, if one could only take it." But, as I said before, a thought of its effect upon others will give a man strength to throw it off when nothing else would. Depression is wrong, because it affects one's fellow-students and other people, and makes their way harder. Nothing can affect us that does not come from ourselves—from our own past lives, through our own karma. One may learn from that to be very careful that no one else shall be hurt by us. If some one has said or done something not quite creditable, we should think; "I will not pass this on; I will not do or say anything myself which will make the day harder for some one else." We can also determine not to be the instrument whereby the bad karma of others works itself out. If one hurts or offends some one, it is true that one is only the instrument of that other's karma; but it is a very ungenerous rôle to play. We should be the instruments of the good karma, in helping people and bringing them blessing and comfort; the evil karma must work itself out through other channels, not through us.

> In yet another way you must control your thought; you must not let it wander. Whatever you are doing, fix your thought upon it, that it may be perfectly done.

C.W.L.—It ought to be a simple matter to fix our thought upon whatever we are doing, so that it may be perfectly done. If we are writing a letter, for example, we can concentrate on that and see that it is what the letter of an occultist should be. An ordinary man writes his letters in a rather careless or slipshod way; he says what he has to say without making any special effort to see that it is well done. It appears to be quite a new idea to some people that ordinary little matters like that ought to be well done. I receive a number of letters, and I must say that many of them are not such as I should think of sending out myself. Frequently they are faulty in expression, and often so badly written that they waste a good deal of my time.

This sort of carelessness matters very much for those who are occultists or endeavouring to become such. The letter of an occultist should be carefully expressed, and well written or typed, as the case may be. It should be a nice thing to look at; a pleasure to the person who receives it. Whatever we do, it is emphatically our duty to do it decently well. I do not mean to say that one can always spare the time to write everything like copper-plate, or to make of every letter a finished work of art; that cannot be done in these days. But even outside of occultism, as a matter of common politeness to a correspondent, one should write clearly and legibly. If you write hurriedly and badly to save a few moments of your own time, remember that it is done at the sacrifice of, perhaps, four times the amount of the other person's time. We have no right to do that sort of thing.

Every letter that we send out should be a messenger; we should make it a message of the Master. It may be about business or any ordinary subject, but it should be charged with good feeling. This can be done in a moment: as we are writing the letter we should have in mind strong kindly feeling; that will affect the letter without any further action on our part, but when we are signing it we should take a moment to send into it a current of good feeling of some sort. If one is writing to a friend, one should pour affection into the letter, so that when he opens it there shall rush out at him the feeling of brotherly affection. If the letter be to a brother Theosophist, put into it a thought of higher things and of the Master, so that it will recall to him the higher thought which Theosophists always desire to cherish. If we are writing to some person whom we know to be in want of a particular quality, we should pour that quality into the letter, taking the opportunity to give what is needed. So let us see that each letter is well written, and also that it has a soul.

The same service may be rendered when we meet others directly. Some of us come into contact with many people during the day; we have to speak to them, and sometimes to shake hands with them. We can take advantage of that direct physical contact to pour in a rush of vitality or nerve force or affection or higher thought, or whatever may seem most suitable. One should never shake hands with anybody without leaving something of that nature behind—it is an opportunity. Our business, if we aspire to become pupils of the Master, is to watch for such opportunities to serve. A man who is not in some way or other being useful to his fellow-men is not on the road to being accepted. I suppose it is doing no injustice to the average man to say that his idea in making a new acquaintance is very largely: "What shall I get out of this man in some way or other?" It may not be in money; it may be in amusement, or social benefits; but at any rate he thinks about getting something. Our attitude must be exactly the reverse: "Here is a new opportunity for me, what can I give?" If I am introduced to a stranger I look him over and throw out something or other in the shape of a good thought; it will stick there and penetrate when its time comes. The pupils of the Master do that as they are walking about the streets or riding on the trams and ferries. They watch for cases where they see a good thought is needed, and they give it—a hundred times perhaps in the course of a single morning's or afternoon's journey.

When a greeting is given to anyone it should be a reality, not merely a form of words. The greetings into which the name of God comes, and which invoke His blessing, such as are customary among the Muhammadans, for example, are sometimes only formal, but sometimes they are hearty good wishes, and the thought of God is really there. We say, "Good-bye." Few people know that this is a contraction of "God be with you," but we should know it and mean it. These seem small things, but it is the small things in everyday life that make the difference. They show character and they shape character, and if we do all these small everyday things carefully and well, we shall soon develop in ourselves a character which will be careful and self-controlled and accurate about all sorts of things, great as well as small. One cannot have a character that is careful in great things and careless in small things. It is inevitable in that case that we shall sometimes forget and be careless at the wrong time, but we must learn to be careful altogether. Again, many small things taken together mount up to a big thing, and with a little practice one may learn to give not a small, but a very large amount of help to a person by the touch of a hand or the writing of a letter.

The Master says: "Whatever you are doing, fix your mind upon it." This applies even to the things we do in order to rest our minds, such as the reading of novels or magazines. The best kind of rest, apart from deliberate relaxation and sleep, is generally some other form of exercise, so even when people are reading something for the sake of amusement or rest, the mind should be their servant, not they its slave. If you are reading a story, fix your mind upon it and try to understand it, to see what the author meant by it. Often people read so vaguely that by the time they reach the end of the story they have forgotten the beginning; they are so utterly vague that they could not give you a sketch of the plot, nor say what it is meant to teach. But if we want to train our minds when we are reading for pleasure or recreation we ought to do it well. Similarly, when we are resting. There are actually millions of people in the world who do not know how to lie down and rest themselves properly. They have not learned that ten minutes of relaxation is worth two hours of lying down in a tense and strained condition. Quiet control of the mind is necessary even for success in resting. Such control forms a habit like everything else, and those who practise it presently find that they cannot do things in the old slipshod way; if they rest, they must rest properly.

> Do not let your mind be idle, but keep good thoughts always in the background of it, ready to come forward the moment it is free.

A.B.—That ought to be a very easy thing for the ordinary Hindu to do, because he has been taught from childhood to repeat good sentences in unoccupied moments. Even the quite uneducated people in India do so. You may often hear some man who has finished his work suddenly begin to repeat, "Rām, Rām, Rām, Sītārām, Sītārām, Sītārām," over and over again—just the sacred name and nothing else. Some people may think that that is a senseless thing to do; but it is not, for it has a very real effect upon the person who is reciting; it steadies his unoccupied mind on a soothing and elevating thought. That is infinitely better than allowing the mind to roam as it will, occupying itself most likely with the affairs of its owner's neighbours, and so leading to gossip and all the untold harm that that does. Of course, if you can control your mind without any outward repetition, it is all the better; but many people do neither the one nor the other.

It is a good plan, which you will find recommended in many religions, to choose in the morning some phrase which you then learn by heart. It will come up of itself in the mind during the day, and will drive away other less worthy thoughts at times when the mind is unoccupied. You can select a phrase or sentence from any good book, and the repetition of it a few times in the morning (perhaps while you are dressing) with your thoughts fixed upon it, will make it come up of its own accord during the day. One can see how easy such automatic repetition becomes to the mind when one remembers how a chance piece of music, a catching tune, will impress itself upon the mind, will take possession of it and be repeated by it over and over again. For many years I have kept the thought of the Masters in the background of my mind, and now it is always there, so that the moment my mind is released from a piece of work it reverts naturally to Them.

C.W.L.—Thoughts of the Master should be always present in the background of our mind, so that they come forward when it is not occupied by other work. If one is reading or writing a letter or doing some physical work, one is not necessarily thinking actively about the Master; but the resolution is made at the beginning: "I will do this well for the sake of the Master." Having done that, one is thinking of the work, not of Him, but as soon as the work is finished, the thought of the Master returns into the foreground of the mind. Such a thought not only ensures that the mind shall be well occupied, but it also causes our thinking on other subjects to be clearer and stronger than it otherwise would be.

Sometimes people practise the repetition of the names of God, in order to form such a background for the mind. In India you often find people muttering to themselves as they stand waiting for a train or walk along the road, and sometimes you hear them saying a sacred name over and over again. One of the special criticisms which missionaries have always made against the "heathen" is that they are "given to vain repetitions". The Muhammadan goes about reciting texts; he always has the name of Allah upon his lips. It may be that sometimes he does not think much of Him, but often it does mean something to him. It is true that a man may say things of that sort merely as a matter of habit, and give no thought to it: a Christian may repeat his prayers, and his thoughts may be wandering somewhere else all the time. Even a priest may go through his hours of prayer without necessarily concentrating much thought on them, because he knows the whole thing by heart; he may utter his "Ave Marias" and "Paternosters" without ever thinking of Our Lady or our Father in heaven. In any religion it is possible to be a formalist, to retain the outer shell, having lost most of its inner spirit; but that is not done more in Hinduism and in Buddhism than it is in Christianity—I should be inclined to say not nearly so much. It is a fact that the repetition of names like "Rāma, Rāma, Rāma," does help to keep the thought of the Deity in the minds of people, and when it does that assuredly it is good. If we can think equally readily and fruitfully of the Master without needing the repetition of His name, that is a still better thing; but it is infinitely better to do the physical repetition than not to have the thought.

There is a certain rate of vibration in the mental body which is appropriate to these devotional feelings; in time that rate becomes a habit, so that devotion easily arises and is built into the character. This habit also serves to keep out evil thoughts. If the mind is vacant, any passing thought can enter and influence it, and such a thought is more likely to be bad, or at any rate useless, than useful. It comes from the vast quantities of thought floating round us, representing the average level of the country, but we are aiming at something higher. We want to be in a position to lift our average brother, and we cannot do that until we first attain a higher level ourselves.

Use your thought-power every day for good purposes; be a force in the direction of evolution.

C.W.L.—We have been educated on a namby-pamby sort of theory that the one thing necessary is to be good; but it is not enough to be pious and to abstain from doing evil things; we must go ahead and *do* something with our goodness and piety. Why are we on earth at all? Why should we encumber the ground, unless we can do something? To sit down and be good (though it is better than sitting down and being bad, of course!) is simply a negative state. We are here to be channels for the divine Force. We, the Monad, came forth from God long ago as a glowing spark of the divine Fire. Truly, as *The Secret Doctrine* says: "The spark burns low"—very low, in many cases—but we must rekindle it with the fervour of our enthusiasm and faith and love, and make that spark into a living flame that will warm other people.

> **Think each day of some one whom you know to be in sorrow, or suffering, or in need of help, and pour out loving thought upon him.**

C.W.L.—Thought-force is just as real and definite a thing as money, or as the water we pour out of a jug into a glass. If we send a definite stream of it to anybody, we may be absolutely certain that it will get there, though we may not see it. Most of us know somebody in sorrow and suffering, who could be greatly helped by the stream of thought that we may send. Even if it should happen at any time that we know of no one in particular who is in such need, we can send out our thought in a more general way, and it will find some one among the many who are in trouble.

If one knows of a person who is in touch (as is Dr. Besant, for example) with a great many people who are in need and sorrow, one may send thoughts of devotion and strength to her, so that she will have a little more to pour out. It is the same with the Masters. When anyone pours out a thought of devotion to Them, it calls down upon him the answering thought of the Master, which is in the nature of a blessing. But besides that, a little more is added to the Master's store of force, and He uses that for the good of others.

A.B.—I must say that until I read this it had not occurred to me to make such a definite and regular practice of this mental helping of others. It is certainly a very good thing. Decide in the morning upon some person whom you will help during the day in your odd moments—there are always plenty of people needing help, unfortunately. Then, whenever during the course of the day your mind is free, instead of letting it be used as a kind of hotel for the most casual visitors, engage it in sending the person thoughts of strength, comfort, happiness, or whatever it is that he most needs. This practice is a stage beyond that of the repetition of a good sentence.

In one way or another you should close your mind against undesirable thoughts, until it is so strong that these helps are not needed. The thought of the Master should always be in mind; it is one that always goes out in help, and it does not prevent any of the higher activities of the mind. It does not exclude other ways of helping, but throws greater force into them. After a time it will fill the whole of your mental horizon, and then all that you do will be better and more strongly done because of it.

Hold back your mind from pride, for pride comes only from ignorance.

C.W.L.—There is a great deal of subtle pride amongst students of occultism. They cannot help realizing that they know a little more of the real facts of life than do people who have not studied these things. It would be foolish not to recognize the fact, but they must take care lest they have a feeling of despising the ordinary man who does not know these things as yet. In this particular respect students of occultism are ahead of the ordinary man, but there may well be other matters in which the ordinary man is far ahead of them. The man who knows, literature, science, or art thoroughly, for example, has spent very much more time and trouble in learning that than many of us have in studying Theosophy, and surely he deserves credit for the work he has done, and the amount of selfless labour that he has put into it. It is not the mark of a wise man to despise the work of another, but to realize that all alike are progressing.

Many people have what is called a good conceit of themselves; they like to think of themselves as always right, as very good persons, and so on. But the points on which they admire themselves are generally not at all what the ego would acknowledge. In the ego, so far as any quality is developed, it is pure. If, for example, affection is there, it is utterly untainted with jealousy, envy, or selfishness. It is a mirror of the divine love in so far as he can reproduce it at his level. Sometimes we pride ourselves on progressing fairly well. That is very like a little child of four years priding himself on the fact that he is getting on very well. So he may be—for that age—but it will be different with the man of twenty-one. Our powers of intellect, devotion, affection, sympathy—exist in us but in a small degree, as compared with what they will be. Instead, therefore, of stopping to pat ourselves on the back, we must press on and try to gain more of such qualities.

In this work, meditation is a great help. If a man really sets himself to develop affection, meditates upon it and works to try to feel it, he will be surprised at the strength of the quality evoked in himself in a short time.

Pride, the Master says, comes always from ignorance. The more a man knows the less likely he is to be proud, because the more he is able to see that he does not know. Most especially is this true if it be his good fortune to come into touch with one of our great Masters. Such a man will never feel proud again, not even proud of that fact, because whenever he thinks he can do anything, or that he possesses any quality, it cannot but come into his mind: "But I have seen that quality in the Master, and what is mine beside His?"

The virtues in Them are so magnificently developed that to know one of Them is an absolute and instantaneous cure for anything like pride. Yet discouragement never comes from the Master. In ordinary life you think you can do a little bit of something, but when you come into the presence of an expert in that line, you see at once how little you can do compared with the great man, and you feel rather crushed and hopeless. But that is not the feeling one gets in the presence of the Master. You realize your own incompetence and insignificance acutely, but at the same time in His presence you realize your own potentiality. Instead of feeling that there is an abysmal gulf which can never be passed, one feels, "I can do this; I am going to set myself to imitate that"; that is the stimulus which any touch with the Master always gives. In His presence one feels very much what the Apostle says: "I can do all things through Christ which strengtheneth me."[1] Because of this strength of the Master, a person thinks at the time: "I shall never again be depressed; I can never again feel sorry; I can never again fall into the silly mistake of irritability which I committed yesterday. I look back and see that some things worried me. How ridiculous; why should anything ever worry me?" It may be that, later on, having passed out of the direct rays of that divine influence, we do fall back, forgetting that it can reach us just as well when the rays are not visible and direct, that we may live always in the Master's aura if we choose to do so.

The man who does not know thinks that he is great, that he has done this or that great thing; the wise man knows that only God is great, that all good work is done by God alone.

[1] Philippians, 4, 13.

A.B.—Here we have a great lesson of the *Gītā*. It is the one will that works through us all. All work is done by the whole, not by the parts; and the most that any of us can do is to make ourselves good organs for the one divine activity to work through. It is as foolish for us to boast as it would be for one of the fingers of our hands to do so. Make yourselves healthy organs of the divine will; then you will find that the one Actor is using you, because you are convenient for use.

We have come back to the point where we began. We saw that realization of the Self destroys all fear; we now see that it destroys all pride. That is the one great basic truth. It is good to see how these multifarious things all lead us back to the one truth—the one Life seated equally in all beings.

C.W.L.—God is in everyone, and whatever goodness or greatness there is in any man is the God in him shining through. All that we do He does through us. This may appear strange. You may say that it seems to destroy the feeling of individuality, but that is only because our physical brains cannot grasp the real relationship. Not without reason the mediæval Christians used to say: "To God be the glory." For one of us to be proud of anything that he has done is just as though, when one is playing a piece on the piano, one of his fingers should say: "How well I struck that note! It was I who made that tune so beautiful!" After all, all the other fingers did their part, and they all acted, not with separate volition, but as instruments of the brain behind. We are all fingers of His Hand, manifestations of His power. I know quite well that it is practically impossible for us fully to realize that; but the more we develop the higher consciousness the more acutely we feel it, and sometimes in meditation, in moments of high exaltation, we get a momentary grasp of that unity.

CHAPTER 2

SELF-CONTROL IN ACTION

Self-control in Action.—If your thought is what it should be, you will have little trouble with your action.

A.B.—This sentence emphasizes the fact, with which every occult student is familiar, that thought is more important than action. This is exactly the reverse of the ordinary point of view; but it is true, because thought always precedes action. There can be what is called spontaneous action; but that only means that to find the preceding thought you must go further back, perhaps even to a former life.

When sufficient thought-force has been accumulated in the mind in any given direction, and then an occasion presents itself for the expression of that particular kind of thought, it inevitably overflows into action. Every thought along a given line acts as a little added impulse, until at last the stored-up force of the impulses carries you over into action along that line. The Hindu quite rightly looks upon action, or karma, as made up of the three parts—thought, desire and act. It is true; so you may have in any life an act which is unpremeditated so far as the immediate past is concerned, an act committed on the spur of the moment. Those are cases in which the thinking having been completed, the act—that is the last part of the whole action—must follow, as being the net impulse along that line. Thus it may happen that on any line of thinking you may exhaust your power of selection, and then, even when you have exerted to the full your power of control, on the first occasion that presents itself your thought will manifest in action. It may lie latent for a long time, if opportunity for expression be lacking, but as soon as ever the circumstances permit the action will be done.

Hence the great importance of understanding the working of thought. Guard your thought and lead it along good lines, for you cannot tell when the moment will be reached and your next thought will be embodied in action. This is one reason for the stress laid on the importance of thought by all the great Teachers of the world, and here in this book the student is reminded of it again. It may be well to remember at this point that manas, the mind, is itself activity. You have in the Monad the three aspects of will, wisdom and activity, and these embody themselves in ātmā, buddhi and manas. Here you have the recognition that thought embodies itself in action.

C.W.L.—It is a truism to say that thought precedes action. There are occasions on which we act, as we say, without thinking, but even so it is the result of previous thought—we have a habit of thought on certain subjects or along a certain line, and we act instinctively in agreement with that. A man does a thing, and then explains: "I could not help doing it; I did not think." But the fact is that he is carrying out thought belonging, perhaps, to previous incarnations. Although a man has not usually the same mental body now as in his last incarnation, he has the same mental unit, which is the nucleus of that body and is to a great extent a kind of epitome of it, and that carries from life to life the impressions of the type of thought to which the man has been accustomed.

It has often been pointed out that a man can take over from life to life, in his causal body, only his good qualities. That is quite true. The causal body is constructed from the matter of the higher subplanes of the mental plane—the first, second and third—and matter of those levels cannot vibrate in response to any of the lower or less desirable qualities. Therefore a man can actually build into himself only good, which is very fortunate for us, because otherwise we should all have built in a great deal that is not good, which would retard our evolution instead of helping it. But he carries over with him the permanent atoms belonging to the different planes—mental, astral and physical—and so the vibrations which belong to them come up as inherent qualities in his new vehicles.

In this way one brings over the possibilities of qualities, rather than actual qualities. Madame Blavatsky used to call these, among other things, "privations of matter," that is, forces which would operate when the matter was there for them to work in, but were suspended until it gathered round the ego again. So when a man acts "without thinking" he does so according to the momentum of those old thoughts. That is one of the reasons why we should so carefully guard our thoughts; we never know when they will overflow into action. The man who yields himself to some evil thought, thinking that he will never allow himself to act upon it, may some time find it translated into action almost before he is aware of it.

Great use can be made of this knowledge for the helping of children. When the ego takes up his new vehicles, parents and friends can do very much to help him by encouraging the good qualities as they show themselves, and giving the bad ones no opportunities to manifest. We give the greatest help to the child when we get the good qualities into action, and make them into a habit before those which are bad can assert themselves. The latter will sooner or later manifest, probably because the outer world will stir them up, but if there is already a strong momentum in favour of the good qualities, those which are evil will find it very difficult to make any impression. The whole will of the ego is then acting through his vehicles against their impacts, and in such a case they will probably be entirely weeded out in the course of that life-period, so that in the following incarnation the ego will come in without any trace of them at all.

Yet remember that, to be useful to mankind, thought must result in action. There must be no laziness, but constant activity in good work.

A.B.—Here is a very important reminder—thought to be useful must result in action. That is a point on which many of us are defective; we have in our minds thoughts which do not result in action, and all such are sources of weakness. The Master Morya once said that a good thought not acted upon acts like a cancer in the mind. That is a graphic simile, which should help us to realize that such a thought is not merely negative, but positively harmful. We should not enfeeble our moral fibre by good resolutions not carried out, which act as an obstacle and make it more difficult to carry out the same thought into action when it arises again. Do not delay, therefore. Do not put things off; do not leave them undone. Many of us stultify our growth by good resolutions not put into practice. An English proverb says that the way to hell is paved with good intentions.

A good intention not carried out becomes a force for ill, as it acts like a drug which dulls the brain. Be careful to regulate your thinking, and when from the higher Self comes an impulse of service go and carry it out; do not leave it for to-morrow. This putting off is a reason why so many good people in the world are marking time. It is quite a common thing to meet a really good person after a lapse of about ten years, and find him just the same as he was when you knew him before. Thus people remain for years, having the same difficulties and temptations, the same weaknesses and strength. That ought never to be true of a member of the Theosophical Society, for all of us ought to know something of the way in which these laws work.

That it is sometimes true is very much due, I think, to the failure to understand that good impulses not carried out make barriers. If you put into effect those which you receive, more and more will come. No favourable outer circumstances or additions of outer knowledge can make up for the want of inner effort and resolution, and for failure to carry out into action what you already know. Your thought ought always to result in action. Make that a rule. I do not mean that you will always be able to carry out your thought at once, because circumstances may not permit it: but presently opportunities will come. In such cases put your thought by, not losing it. It will then be like fruit that is ripening. If you do that, the unembodied thought will not harm you, and as soon as the time is ripe you will carry it out.

> But it must be your *own* duty that you do—not another man's, unless with his permission and by way of helping him. Leave every man to do his own work in his own way; be always ready to offer help where it is needed, but *never* interfere. For many people the most difficult thing in the world to learn is to mind their own business; but that is exactly what you must do.

A.B.—A warning is now given which is needed by those who have a very active—a rājasic—nature. We have to consider now the other side of the razor-path; laziness must be shunned on the one hand, but interference must be avoided on the other. Very active people are prone to want, as the saying is, a finger in every pie. But other people's pies are their own pies, and you ought not to put your fingers into them. You may remember how often in the *Bhagavad-Gītā*, which is a gospel of activity—for its constant burden is, "act! act!"—the warning is given against wrong activity. The duty of another, it says, is full of danger.

The reason is clear. If you, with your own line of thought-activity behind you, mix yourself in the action of another person, who similarly has his own line of thought-activity behind him—which is a different one from yours—you are sure to spoil what he is doing. His action is the logical outcome of his thought-activity; it is not, and could not be the right and proper outcome of yours. The energetic type of person must learn that he only creates confusion by mixing himself in another person's action. I used to want to set other people right, according to what was my view of what was right for them, which was my own right, of course; but I learned in the course of discipleship that that was not the way to work.

Even if another person's way is not the best way from the abstract standpoint, it may yet be the best for him. It has the force of both his faults and his virtues behind it, and it marks the line of evolution proper for him. Suppose that a man holds his pen in some particular way that is not the best one, when he is writing: if you interfere and induce him to hold it in a different way, you will make him write worse, not better. He will lose all the advantage of his long practice in the old method, and it will cost him a great deal of time and trouble to make that good. Of course, if he himself wants to change his way of writing because he is convinced that another way is better, and he asks your help in this, the case is different; he has a right to do as he pleases, and he will then have the force of his own will behind his action.

It is clear that a strong person can easily dominate another for a time. History affords many examples of great men who dominated all around them while they lived, but whose work fell to pieces when they died. They forgot that they were mortal and should therefore have provided for the gap that their death would leave; the unfortunate karma of their error, their self-centredness, lay in that result of things tumbling to pieces as soon as they were gone. That shows at once that those men did not understand the conditions of successful activity. They did not realize that a worker and leader should gather fit people together and trust them, and leave them independent in their own part of the work, independent along their own lines—that one should not try to look after every detail oneself; moreover, it cannot be done.

The world is made up of a great variety with an underlying unity. The lower types in the world obey law, because, unknowing of the fact themselves, they are compelled to do so. But man is left comparatively free—free within a great circle of laws outside which he cannot get, but inside which he may do as he pleases. In doing his work in his own way lies his development.

The divine plan is such that more and more liberty is bestowed on man as he progresses and can be trusted to use it wisely; so that bit by bit, step by step, we come to perfect freedom. The animal, at the lower end of the scale, obeys perfectly, unconsciously; the Master at the upper end of it obeys perfectly, consciously; and we all stand somewhere between those two.

We must remember too, that interference extends to the mind, and non-interference has also to do with the previous qualification, that of self-control as to the mind. Interference by thought is very potent. Take for example such a case as the following. One of us has a particular difficulty which he is trying to overcome; perhaps it arises from some weakness in his character, perhaps it is an undesirable way of thinking or acting, along which from force of old habit he is inclined to go. Whatever it is, he is doing his best to overcome it. Then some one comes along and suspects him of that particular line of weakness or difficulty—suspects, and goes on his way, never thinking that he has done any particular harm.

That second person does not realize that he has given a little push to his brother, which may just determine the latter's action and send it along the wrong line. The two forces of habit and effort were perhaps trembling in the balance, and the suspicious thought turned the scale. That is why suspicion is so wrong. It is always wrong. If unfortunately it is true, it only gives the man suspected an additional push in the wrong direction; if it be untrue, it may make it a little easier for him to go wrong in that particular way at some other time. In any case it is sending out an evil thought against him; so it is wrong either way. We ought always to think well of people, even if our thought of them is better than their practice; thus we throw out to them a thought which will work only for their good.

It is also important to remember these facts, because a mass of evil thought is sooner or later directed by the dark forces against every person who is advancing rapidly on the Path. Because you are having a mass of evil thrown against yourself, tending to push you into wrong actions, you should realize the harmful way in which suspicion works, and should be extra careful of your own thoughts and actions. You should think of what is happening to yourself merely with a dry recognition of the facts, without any feeling of anger or resentment, and whenever you come across a great outburst of hatred, remember that you ought, to use the Biblical phrase, to gird up the loins of your mind, and simply bring to bear upon the situation an added force of a contrary nature to neutralize the evil one. Do that, and the mass of evil thought directed against you will not harm you; on the contrary, you will draw advantage from it, as it will help you to see what are your weak points; it will bring them into the light when otherwise they might have remained hidden from you. Also your very resolution in the face of attack will strengthen you, and lead you onwards to the time when all these things will beat against you with small effect.

Therefore you should do your own work perfectly, and leave the work of other people alone unless they ask you for help. Do your own work to the utmost of your ability, and leave other people's work alone to the extent of your ability..

C.W.L.—A good deal of interference with others is due to religious misconceptions. Orthodox Christianity makes it its business to interfere with everybody. It starts out to save other peoples' souls, instead of recognizing that each man's business is to let his soul save him. Most assuredly no one has a right to interfere between the lower and the higher self of another under any circumstances whatever. The torturers of the Inquisition thought it right to do any frightful thing with a man's body in order to save his soul, by making the body say this or that. It was never even suggested, so far as I can understand, that you could make him *believe* it, but if you could make his body *say* that it believed a certain thing, that statement, even if false, somehow or other saved the soul. If those people *really* believed that (I wonder whether *anybody* ever *did* really believe so monstrous a lie!) they could actually justify all the horrible things they did; for whatever the horrors to which you subjected the unfortunate body for a few hours or days, they would be as nothing compared with the frightful pain lasting for all eternity from which you were saving his soul. The torture of your neighbour under those circumstances becomes quite a laudable action. It is difficult for us to believe that anyone could take up this position, yet it appears to have been held by great numbers of people—even after allowing for those who were using the power of the Church for political purposes.

> Because you try to take up higher work, you must not forget your ordinary duties, for until they are done you are not free for other service. You should undertake no new worldly duties; but those which you have already taken upon you, you must perfectly fulfil—all clear and reasonable duties which you yourself recognize, that is—not imaginary duties which others try to impose upon you. If you are to be His, you must do ordinary work better than others, not worse; because you must do that also for His sake.

A.B.—We sometimes find that when a person comes into occultism he begins to do his ordinary work worse, not better than before. That is altogether wrong. His great outburst of enthusiasm for his new studies and his effort to reach the higher things have their danger as well as their advantage; and the danger is precisely that the worldly duty appears unimportant. There is truth in the idea, and it is in the truth that the danger lies; all errors are dangerous only on account of the truth that lies at the base of them. It is the little bit of truth in an error that gives it its strength, not the great wrapping of falsehood that overlies the scrap of truth.

The perfect carrying out of the duties that have to be done in the world is what shows that the force coming down from the higher planes is being turned in the right direction. "Yoga is skill in action."[1] If a man is disciplined on the higher planes his lower plane activities will be good; but if he is undisciplined they will not be good. Even this last, however, is very much better than not to care about the higher things at all. The unwise activities of a man in this plight may work much temporary harm, but not permanent harm, because the motive power behind them is good.

The disciple must try to carry out physical plane duties better than other people. Very often, when he acts unwisely, a Master may have to step in in order to balance up his unwise activities. That is one reason why a Master puts a chela on probation, and the long time that the probation often lasts is sometimes due to this. Generally people need a fairly long time to balance up their enthusiasm and activity with wise moderation and forethought.

The first test of discipleship is usefulness to others. The aspirant should never think that his esoteric work is more important than his exoteric work. If, being a Theosophist, he neglects his Lodge and his work for the Society for the sake of his own progress in esoteric matters, he is blundering. If he neglects outside work for the sake of study, to take another example, he is doing quite wrong. Study is good, but it should subserve usefulness; you should study in order to be more useful, not cease to be useful for the sake of studying. And whenever a conflict arises between outer duties and such studies, the outer ought to take precedence.

[1] *Bhagavad-Gita*, II, 50.

In all such matters as these, we must never forget that the path of occultism is narrow as the edge of a razor. It would be quite possible to give almost every moment of one's waking time to small services for others, but in such case many of them could not be well chosen, and most of them would not be well done. Just as one must spend time in sleeping and eating, in order to have strength to work the rest of the time, so must one spend time in meditation and study, and in considering what work should be done and how it should be done. This aspect of the matter was dealt with by the Master in the section on discrimination. Every portion of His teaching directs the pupil back into the middle path; if he follows any piece of advice to excess, he will only fall over again. It has been said that the track of the best ship is not a straight line, but is made up of thousands of tracks, now to one side, now to the other. The life of the disciple is similar to that; the captain on the bridge is the Master, who points out the stars by which he can guide himself, and assists him to keep as close as possible to the direct line. One meets so many people who fasten on to one good idea, and then let it ride them to death.

The master tells his pupil that he should undertake no new worldly duties. The man who has pledged himself to the Master's work should know the importance of being always ready to serve Him in any way and anywhere that He needs him. I can give you a striking example of this out of my own experience. When I was young my children were taken away from me against my will. I fought against the separation by every means that the law allowed, but lost my case; the law broke the tie, took away from me the duty of protection which a mother has to her children. My daughter came back to me as soon as she was free to do so; for ten years I had not seen or written to her, but my influence held and she came straight back to me. I was then living with Madame Blavatsky, and she warned me: "Take care that you do not re-knit the ties which karma broke for you." If I had taken up my old life again then, after I had taken my pledge to the Master, I should have done wrong. It did not mean, of course, that I was to neglect the girl—she came and lived with us, and stayed with us till she married, but she had to come second, not first.

You are responsible for the duties which you have to fulfil, not anybody else; you are responsible to your Master and not to anybody else. If people try to force upon you what they imagine to be your duty, and you see that it is not so, you must simply disagree with them—good-temperedly, but firmly. *You* must decide. You may do so rightly or wrongly, and if wrongly you will suffer, but the decision must be yours. That responsibility of an individual to himself and to his Master must not be interfered with by anyone. To your own Master you are responsible, and you must do your ordinary work better than other people do, for His sake.

C.W.L.—This principle that the occultist should do ordinary work well was understood in the old religions. In the story of the youth of Prince Siddhārtha, who afterwards became the Lord Buddha, for example, it is related that he devoted himself very much to study and meditation, but when it became necessary that he should win his bride by skill in various manly sports, he showed that when he wished he could excel in those as well as the higher things. In the *Bhagavad-Gītā* it is said that yoga is skill in action; it is doing the right thing carefully, tactfully and courteously. Disciples of the Masters have therefore to learn balance in their lives, to know when the lower may safely be put aside and when it should not be put aside.

A man who has pledged himself and his time and strength to the Master's service ought not to undertake anything new which is not actually His work. He must not let people force upon him duties which he does not recognize as his. I can quite imagine, for example, that people might sometimes expect members of the Theosophical Society to attend various social functions. A member might say, "I am willing to give up a reasonable amount of time for the sake of friendliness," but he is quite justified in reserving most of his time for any work that he has taken up for the Society.

This instruction concerning duties had special reference to Alcyone's life at Adyar, while the Master was teaching him. In one special case, for example, he was being pressed to devote a whole day to some ceremony in connection with a distant relation. The matter was submitted to his Master, and He said: "Yes, for the sake of the rest of the family who might be shocked or troubled, you may go down for an hour at such and such a time, but be very careful that, during that time, you repeat nothing whatever which you do not understand, that you in no case repeat things blindly after the priest, and that you do not allow anything to be done for you that you can do for yourself—that is, in the way of ceremonies and blessings."

CHAPTER 3

TOLERANCE

3. *Tolerance.*—You must feel perfect tolerance for all, and a hearty interest in the beliefs of those of another religion, just as much as in your own. For their religion is a path to the highest, just as yours is. And to help all, you must understand all.

A.B.—I suppose tolerance is one of the virtues most talked about at the present day, but one of the least practised. It is one of the most difficult virtues to acquire, for where a belief is strongly held and highly valued people not unnaturally tend to try to push it on others. Out of that aggressiveness all religious persecutions and wars, both public and private, have grown; but even that aggressiveness is better than indifference, which is so often confused with tolerance. Indifference is not tolerance, and should never be mistaken for it.

Nowadays there is very little State persecution, but there is still much social and family persecution. Some State persecution of religion does still exist in certain countries, where the free-thought party has the upper hand. Free-thinkers were so much persecuted that the temptation to retaliate has been too strong, though of course they are acting in direct violation of their own principles. I hope it is only the reaction of the persecution that the religious party meted out to them, and that it will soon cease.

There still exists in the world much of the spirit out of which all persecution grows, and sometimes the State finds it necessary to impose forbearance, as in India, for fear of disturbances and troubles arising. The sufferance that we find existing between members of different creeds in countries where various religions are more or less evenly balanced is largely due to mutual fear. Thus what tolerance there is springs generally from some motive that is more or less unworthy.

The occult student must aim at the kindly feeling which grows out of the recognition that the Self in each finds his own road. This is the only right attitude, and nothing less than recognition of it will make tolerance a widespread virtue. We must recognize that each man has his own way of searching for the highest, and must be left absolutely free to follow it. This implies not only that you will not try to draw a person into your own religion, but that you will not try to force arguments and opinions upon him, will not try to shake his beliefs which he finds helpful. Such perfect forbearance is the object at which you have to aim. It is far as the poles are apart from what men of the world often think to be tolerance—semi-contemptuous feeling that religious things do not very much matter, but are useful merely as a kind of police force to keep people in order. But a man's religion must be sacred to you, because it is sacred to him. The White Lodge will not allow anyone to come into its Brotherhood who has not developed this attitude to a considerable extent.

C.W.L.—There is perhaps in the present day more tolerance than there has been since the time of the great Roman Empire, and it is very much like that which then existed. We hear curious things of the way in which the Romans are supposed to have treated the early Christians. Careful research shows that the greatest of the persecutions about which so much has been said never happened at all; but it is true that the Christians frequently got themselves into trouble. I do not mean to say that the conditions were not in some ways barbarous; but the early Christians seem to have been an anarchical set of people, and when they came into collision with the authorities it was not on account of their religion, but because of the things they said and did. The Romans did not welcome the kind of brotherhood that the early Christians preached. It was far too much like: "*Sois mon frère ou je te tuerai.*"[1] In some cases they would not perform small ceremonies which were considered matters of loyalty; they would not throw a pinch of incense on the altar or pour out a drop of wine to the Emperor—actions more or less equivalent to taking off one's hat in London when the King passes. The Roman Empire was the most tolerant in the world about other religions. They did not care in the very least what god anybody worshipped, because they did

[1] "Be my brother or I will kill you."

not believe there were any gods. They had a huge pantheon, where they set up temples to all the gods, and when they realized that the Christ was being worshipped they promptly set up a statue to Him. Their tolerance really amounted to indifference.

Many of those ancient Romans are incarnated in the English race. There are many people now who are tolerant to all forms of belief, just because they themselves do not believe in anything. They look on religion as a pleasant fable to amuse the ladies, but of course for a man it is not a serious matter. That is not the kind of tolerance at which we are aiming. Ours must come from a recognition that the beliefs of others are also ways to the highest. When one goes into a temple or church of some form of religion which is not one's own, one who is really tolerant conforms to the customs of the place, not simply because it is the custom, but because he respects those people who are different from himself, and that religion which is different from his own. There are people who go into a church and then refuse to bow to the altar and even make a point of turning their backs upon it. I have known people who tried to go into a mosque without taking off their shoes. One has no business in the church or the temple of another faith if one is not prepared to behave so as not to hurt the feelings of the worshippers. If you think it is wrong to genuflect before the altar of a Catholic church you can always stay outside, and if you feel it would be wicked to take your shoes off you need not go inside the mosque.

All men are manifestations of the One Self, so the form another's aspiration takes is to be respected. Often childish manifestations appear, but no good man would make fun of them, or try to turn people against them, for the less developed intellect cannot be expected to take the view that appeals to one much more advanced. Tolerance will always direct us to say, with the old Romans, "Since I am a man, nothing human is foreign to me," and try to understand the other man's point of view; even as an exercise for oneself that method would soon show us at how many different angles the rays of truth may be reflected by the human mind. The world would be monotonous if all things were done in one way only. It would be like a prison, where everything is done at the same time each day, and in the same way.

There are certain broad divisions, such as you find, for example, in the minds of the Catholic and the Protestant. Each of them approaches Christianity from his own point of view, and many on both sides are quite incapable of understanding the other. The Catholic takes the view that a great deal of ceremony should appear in his ritual, that it should be made in every way as beautiful as it can be, in order that it may glorify the God whom he worships, and that it may appeal to the people. He feels keenly that the ritual and the ceremony and all these beautiful surroundings are of the greatest help to him in his devotions. The Protestant, on the other hand, thinks all that to be very wicked and dreadful, because it distracts the mind from the inner meaning. The Protestant's mind is, perhaps, such that if he had to attend to all these ceremonies he would not at the same time be able to keep before him the inner things. What appeals so strongly to the Catholic type of man would be to him rather a nuisance, a disturbance —something which interferes with his inner devotion.

There are many people who feel their devotion and aspiration to be vague and uncertain when only subjective methods of worship are employed. To them the outer form gives great comfort and help; why should they not have it? Those who find the ceremony, the statue, the picture, the physical-plane manifestation, an intense satisfaction and inspiration, belong definitely to one of the seven great rays of life, one of the seven great lines of human endeavour that lead to the throne of God. Those who wish for none of these things, who find them rather troublesome and distracting, are also following their own different line; let them enjoy it; why should we trouble them?

As each one of us has his own language, in which he was born, so he has what might be called his religious language—a way in which his thoughts and feelings and aspirations most readily express themselves. It would be in the highest degree foolish to despise a Frenchman because his language is different from our own, and equally so to despise anyone because his religion is different from ours. A Frenchman says *maison* instead of "house": it means exactly the same thing; it would be absurd to argue that one is a better word than the other. One recalls the celebrated Mr. Lillyvick, a character in *Nicolas Nickelby*, who, after hearing that *l'eau* meant "water" in French, decided that it was a poor language. There is also a story about an old woman in the time of the Napoleonic wars who prayed to God that the English might be successful, and when some one reminded her that probably people on the other side were praying for the success of the French, she replied, "What does that matter; how can God understand them when they speak such nonsense?"

There can be no possible reason why each man should not follow the way which he finds to be best for himself, in the path to God which seems to him the most direct. All that is needed for peace and harmony is that both should recognize that fact. Each should say, "I prefer my path, but I am perfectly willing that every other man should have the same privilege, that he also should take the path which seems best to him." That does not seem much to ask, yet few will concede it. Each feels that what is best for him must be best for others. The larger mind sees that there are many paths, that they all lead equally to the summit of the mountain, and that each man should be left to take that which can most inspire him.

I confess that there is one disposition I personally find it hard to understand—the very gushing type of religious devotion, which applies to the Deity all sorts of endearing terms collected out of love-poetry and novels. It gives me a shock, and an impression of irreverence, though I know perfectly well that it is sincere and well-meant. Probably those who like it think me cold and expressionless, because my disposition is to take a common-sense view of everything and try to reason about it and understand it.

The devotional books written for the higher type of people in every religion are remarkably similar. If one compares, for example, those familiar to the Roman Catholic with those used by the followers of Shrī Rāmanujāchārya, one finds the closest resemblance. The life, too, of a good Christian is the same as that of a good Hindu, or Buddhist, or Muhammadan, or indeed a good man of any religion. The same virtues are practised by all; the same objects are striven for; the same evils are shunned.

But in order to gain this perfect tolerance you must yourself first be free from bigotry and superstition.

A.B.—The bigot is the man who considers only his own opinions, and not those of anyone else. I was once told by a very good lady—but also a very bigoted one, of the straitest sect of the evangelicals—that I ought never to read a book which was not written exactly from my own religious standpoint. That is the position of the bigot—never read another view lest it may shake your own. It is the very opposite of that of the seeker after truth, the man who wants to lead the higher life. He tries to read all round a subject, in order to see at how many different angles the rays of truth have struck the human mind and been refracted by it. If you would reach the truth you must study all these different views and opinions, and then assimilate what little, or great, truth they may contain.

It is well also to study people's superstitions; for, as the great phrase in the Upanishad says: "Truth alone conquers, not falsehood." Superstitions derive their strength from the little bit of truth which they contain. You should find that fragment of truth. The bigot, of course, will see only the falsehood in them, but you ought to know something of all religions; not studying them in the spirit of the missionary, but sympathetically. And the same plan should also be followed in political and social questions.

You must also destroy superstition, which is characterized later in this book as one of the three great sins which do most harm in the world, because it is a sin against love. Religion and superstition have been so muddled together in the world that it is necessary to separate them in our minds by careful definition. My favourite definition of superstition—though it does not cover the whole ground—is the taking of the unessential for the essential, the mistaking of a side issue for one of importance. In religious controversies people fight over some unessential matter, and each side as a rule represents a different misunderstanding of the truth.

Another definition of superstition—which also does not cover the whole ground—is that it is a belief which has no rational foundation. Thus, many truths are superstitions to the people who hold them, because they have no good and sound reason for doing so. The Lord Buddha said that the only right ground for believing a thing is that it commends itself to your reason and common sense, so that you may be said to know it yourself. If we apply that test, the greater part of most people's religion comes under the heading of superstition. For them that does not really matter, but for those who are trying to reach the Path all that cannot justify itself to the intuition and reason should be put aside for a time. As that higher sense in you which knows truth at sight gradually unfolds, you will be able to take in more and more of the truth. Then there will grow up in you a deep inner conviction, and when a truth is presented to you, you will know it is true. This sense corresponds to eyesight on the physical plane. It is the faculty of buddhi, pure reason. We should all try our beliefs by this test, for we inherit a great many of them which are only superstitions to us. As we do so, and to the degree that this attitude of mind becomes habitual to us, shall we get rid of superstition and develop tolerance.

C.W.L.—Superstition has often a very strong hold indeed on the minds of men, so that sometimes it has been said that it is impossible to have religion without it. It is true that there is much confusion in religious thought, and much of it is unreasonable, but whenever there is a belief that has a very wide hold, there is probably a fragment of truth somewhere behind it. Generally speaking, superstitions are not mere inventions, but distortions or exaggerations of facts. Our President once cited a celebrated Indian instance of superstition. There was once a holy man who had a pet cat which was so fond of him that when he wanted to perform his religious ceremonies he found it necessary to keep it quiet by tethering it to the leg of his bed. People seeing this thought the tying up of the cat was a necessary part of the ceremony, and in course of time the rest of the ceremony fell away, and the only part that remained of the devotion was the tradition that a cat should be tethered to the leg of a bed.

The scribes and Pharisees, whom Christ denounced as hypocrites, and likened unto whitened sepulchres, showed a similar form of superstition. They paid tithes, He said, of mint and anise and cummin ; because they were ordered to pay a tithe of all they had, they took into account most punctiliously the little things corresponding to our pepper and salt; but they entirely forgot the weightier matters of the law—justice, mercy and faith.

The superstition of Sunday is a serious trouble in some parts of Great Britain, especially in Scotland, where the day is made unutterably tedious. The idea was to minimize the amount of ordinary work that must be done on that day, and make it a day that could be devoted to spiritual things. However, the divine service aspect has dropped very much into the background, and there is more drunkenness and general looseness in other ways on Sunday than on other days—certainly an instance of taking the non-essential for the essential. Because there is one day at least on which people are supposed to be religious, men often seem to have the feeling that on other days it does not matter seriously if one fails to observe religious precepts and ideals. I have noticed that the people who do not keep Sunday—

Hindus, Buddhists and others—have religion permeating their lives in a way that is not found among Christians. I do not say that they are all good people, any more than the Christians are, but religion means more to them than it does to the average Christian, who often thinks that if he attends service one day a week he has discharged all his religious obligations.

Superstition has also been defined by our President as the holding of any belief without a reasonable foundation. It is quite rational to believe in the rotation of the earth, in the existence of foreign countries which we have not seen, in the reality of atoms and electrons which are beyond physical sight altogether, because we have good reason to believe all these things. But many popular beliefs are not in this class. The ordinary belief of the Christian in eternal fire and everlasting punishment is nothing but a peculiarly pernicious superstition. There is no rational basis whatever for it, yet if you told that to the average Christian he would say that you were an atheist and that you were making a mock of his religion. The first man who taught it may or may not have believed it, but millions of people have done so since, thereby most assuredly yielding themselves to superstition.

The only thing which from the Christian point of view ought to be of importance in connection with it is what the Christ Himself said on the subject. There are, I think, eight passages in which He is supposed to mention this eternal punishment: and every one of those can be quite plainly shown to have nothing to do with the popular idea which is attributed to them. There is a very valuable book on this subject called ***Salvator Mundi***, written by a Christian clergyman, the Rev. Samuel Cox; he very carefully goes into the original Greek of what the Christ is alleged to have said, and shows at once and conclusively that there is no scriptural basis for the belief in everlasting punishment. There certainly is no rational basis, for if God is a loving Father it is absolutely impossible.

One would have expected modern Christians to have outgrown that horrible superstition, which works enormous evil in this world, but millions of them have not done so, and it is still being taught. I saw not long ago a Roman Catholic catechism for children, and in that the old ideas of hell as a place of everlasting torment were set forth in the same old foolish way. We might be still living in the most brutal part of the Middle Ages as far as the teaching given to little children is concerned. It is a very sad thing. There are many Christian sects which have risen above that, but the oldest and largest of them still clings to its mediæval teachings. There are individual priests who explain the whole thing away very much as we might do, but the printed word which they teach to little children is an utterly horrible and blasphemous thing, because it starts them in life with an altogether wrong idea of God, filling their lives and minds with fear and cruelty, to the serious detriment of their character and evolution.

The teaching of the Lord Buddha about belief and reason, which I have already quoted, was very fine. At the council called after His death to determine which of the many reports current should be accepted as His sayings, the very first rule they laid down was: "That which is contrary to reason and common sense is not the teaching of the Buddha." They ruled out everything that did not satisfy them from that point of view, saying: "This is obviously not common sense; He could not have said it." They may perhaps have cast aside one or two good things which they did not understand, but they saved their religion from a vast amount of superstition. The Founders of the great religions, with the exception of Muhammad, did not give Their teachings to the world in written form. It is said, however, that the Lord Buddha wrote a book, which is kept by the Adepts, not published to the world. Usually, three or four generations have elapsed before the teachings have taken written form, and then those writings have been compounded from many sources. For example, in the Book of Isaiah, scholars have found eight different layers of tradition—three Isaiahs, one after another, then a committee, and so on. There is deterioration in the religion when people write down not what they know but that they have been told, and then quarrel about minutiæ.

There is also another source of confusion in the fact that when a new religion is launched it spreads like a wave of conquest over the existing ones, but does not obliterate them. A wise general, conquering a new country, tries to adapt his rules to the people, so as to minimize trouble; so have the religions become adapted to the various communities who adopted them. Thus the Chinese and Japanese still reverence their ancestors, and follow the ancient way, the Shinto, but they have added thereto the Buddhist ethics; while in Ceylon, they hold a materialistic form of the religion, and will tell you that nothing of a man passes on from life to life but his karma, yet they speak of their previous lives and their hope to reach nirvāna in a future life. The Christians also adopted the festivals of the nations among which the religion spread, but conveniently found names of Christian saints by which to call those days.

Traces of the old traditions are thus found everywhere —devil-dancing in Ceylon, the Kālī cult in India, and so on—and these are sometimes taken for the real thing, and thus form a prolific source of superstition.

One may sometimes know a thing to be true without being able to reason it out—that is the other side of the question. The ego knows, and has good reason for his knowledge; but sometimes he cannot impress his reasons on the physical brain, though the fact comes through that he knows. So, when a new truth is presented to us, we know at once whether we can accept it or not. That is not superstition, but an intense inner conviction. I do not think anybody will ever be found with that intense inner conviction about hell. They believe that they will be burnt for ever because they have been so taught. This sounds, perhaps, a little like abandoning reason in favour of intuition, but then it must be remembered that that very buddhi which we translate "intuition" is known in India as "pure reason". It is the reason of the ego, which is of a higher type than that which we have in lower planes.

The Master goes on to give instances with regard to this question of superstition :

> You must learn that no ceremonies are necessary ; else you will think yourself somehow better than those who do not perform them. Yet you must not condemn others who still cling to ceremonies. Let them do as they will ; only they must not interfere with you who know the truth—they must not try to force upon you that which you have outgrown. Make allowance for everything ; be kindly towards everything.

C.W.L.—The Master spoke so strongly about ceremonies perhaps because the life of the youth of the high Brāhmana caste to which Alcyone belonged begins to be very full of them at about the age which he had then reached. There is a tendency at that time for a boy to consider himself very important on account of them, for he is quite the centre of a great deal of attention which surrounds the *upanayana* or initiation of a boy into his full caste privileges. The life of an orthodox Brāhmana is full of ceremonial ; there are gestures to be made and texts to be recited at the time of rising, bathing, eating and almost every other action. Some people round Alcyone were probably trying to make him do these very fully, because they feared that modern education and the European friends he had made might possibly divert him from the old cult of his people ; so the Master guarded His pupil by saying that they were not absolutely necessary and that when doing them or when giving them up he must take care not to fall into the error and folly of thinking himself superior on that account.

Christian ceremonials differ from those of the Hindus and Buddhists in being generally done by a number of people together. Worship is nearly always individual among the latter, but in Christendom it is mainly collective. Though all these ceremonials are not necessary (except for the people whose temperament is so strongly in favour of them that they cannot really be happy without them), they are nevertheless a form of science, dealing with natural forces of the inner planes in perfectly definite ways.

There are many ways in which spiritual force can be poured out upon the world. That which we find in the ceremony of the Mass, the Holy Communion or the Holy Eucharist, is one instituted by the Founder of Christianity Himself, for the distribution through His Church of what is commonly called the divine grace—certain spiritual forces of the higher planes, which are, of course, not supernatural, but superphysical. He arranged it so that the priest, whatever his nature might be, doing the ceremony would be a channel for the distribution of this force. It would be all the better that the priest should be a really good man, full of thoughts of devotion and service, but it has been arranged that the ceremonial shall be effective in any case, for the benefit of the people. The general Christian scheme is that there shall be Churches dotted over the land, so that the outpouring may radiate out and reach everybody. This ceremony does enormous good to millions of people, but to say that it is necessary for salvation would be superstition.

Various forces are tapped by different ceremonies. They all, no matter how spiritual, work under the laws of nature, and if, therefore, the benefit of them is to be felt in the physical world there must be a physical mechanism through which they can work. It is the same in the case of electricity; the force exists all about us all the time and is always in activity, but if you want it to perform a particular work in a particular way in a particular place you must provide certain physical machinery through which it can operate.

A.B.—The Master says that no ceremonies are necessary, and all the religions recognize this truth. In India, the man who is highest and most respected of all is the sannyāsī, who performs no ceremonies at all. He breaks and throws away the sacred thread, which was his most important possession, put upon him when as a boy he was initiated into his caste, and worn throughout life as his most sacred symbol, until he became a sannyāsī.

Ceremonies are only necessary so long as a man has not reached realization and true knowledge, so long as they help to give him right emotions, quiet thoughts and noble aspirations. The great majority of people are still undeveloped and need all the help that can be given them in any way. Therefore no wise man will condemn ceremonies, though they are not necessary for him. The *Bhagavad Gītā* is the gospel of the sannyāsī, yet it is there written: "Let no wise man unsettle the minds of the ignorant, attached to action, but acting in harmony with Me, let him render all action attractive."[1] The child who is learning to walk catches hold of any thing that is firm enough to help him to sustain himself on his feet—chairs, table-legs and walls. So ceremonies are supports, intended for the man who is not strong enough to support himself. As a man develops, his ceremonies become more refined, more beautiful and symbolical, and at last he arrives at a stage when they are no longer of any use to him and he lets them go. There are two kinds of people who do not perform ceremonies—those who are above them, and those who are beneath them.

The responsibility of choosing the point when he shall abandon ceremonies rests entirely with the man concerned; each must decide for himself. None can take the responsibility of saying when a man should become a yogī. So also with ceremonies; none must criticize when a man decides to give them up, or chooses to retain them. Sometimes a man may still feel bound to attend them after he feels that he no longer needs them himself, on account of his position in the community. He alone is responsible for his choice, so we must not condemn those who perform ceremonies, nor those who do not perform them.

Ceremonies may be dangerous as well as helpful. In ancient Hinduism there was a strict rule forbidding the utterance of certain formulæ in a crowd; it was not made in order to withhold any benefit from the people, as nowadays is sometimes ignorantly supposed, but to avoid the harm that certain vibrations might do to some

[1] *Op. cit.*, III, 26.

people. It was on this account that Manu laid down the law that only Brāhmanas who were learned and of good life should be invited to the *shrāddha* ceremonies. A person who has some power but does not understand when he should use it and when he should withhold it might possibly, if he assisted at certain ceremonies, put strength into the formulæ which might injure the people present; for that reason one who has begun to gain such power might do well to keep away. I found, for example, when I attended some *shrāddha* ceremonies at Gayā, that had I added my force to them, I might have injured the priests, for some of the mantras which they were reciting were exceedingly powerful. They, however, did not bring out the power, since they were ignorant and not very clean-living men. Madame Blavatsky advised students of occultism not to go into a crowd unless they were in perfect sympathy with it, not merely because of any effect it might have on their own auras, but because their force might do more harm than good. In such cases, a man with knowledge might find it better sometimes not to take part in certain ceremonies, while another who did not understand how to say the formula in such a way as to bring out the power which is really in it might attend with perfect safety to the people around him, no matter what kind of people they might be.

Now that your eyes are opened, some of your old beliefs, your old ceremonies, may seem to you absurd; perhaps, indeed, they really are so. Yet

though you can no longer take part in them, respect them for the sake of those good souls to whom they are still important. They have their place, they have their use; they are like those double lines which guided you as a child to write straight and evenly, until you learnt to write far better and more freely without them. There was a time when you needed them; but now that time is past.

A.B.—Inevitably, as we grow older and wiser, some things in which we used to believe take on an aspect of non-reality and even absurdity; yet we can look at them kindly and sympathetically, as we can look on a child nursing a bundle of rags which she makes believe to be a doll. From one point of view the child's action is somewhat grotesque, but it is doing her a real service, for it develops the mother instinct in the little girl—she does not see the rags; she sees a child; and as she fondles and comforts her imaginary child she practises maternal tenderness and protection, and care of the weak and helpless. So, when we smile at that little child, our smile is a very tender and gentle one. It is the same with our old beliefs and ceremonies; they had their place; they had their use.

If one finds a savage tribe performing ceremonies which to us seem quite absurd, or when we see, as we frequently do in India, a rag tied to a village tree as an offering, we should not despise the poor outer expression of the savage's or villager's devotion—we ought to look at the feeling underlying it. Their humble offerings may mean as much to them as the costliest one could mean to us; the same spirit is underneath.

All outer offerings are unnecessary; the only acceptable one is the offering of the heart, and where that accompanies the gift the poorest gift becomes acceptable. Therefore it says in the *Gītā* that even a leaf, a flower, a fruit or a little water, if offered with devotion, is acceptable to the Supreme.[1] It would be a hard and unbrotherly act to discourage these things—to tear away the rag from the tree, for instance, as has sometimes been done—it would show a complete lack of the feeling of unity.

C.W.L.—Always be gentle and kindly towards childhood—that of the children, and the general childhood of the human race at its present stage as well. Our President has spoken of a little child nursing a bundle of rags and pretending that it is a doll. That is a superstition, of course, but at the same time it does not occur to anyone indignantly to scold the child for it. On the physical plane it is a bundle of rags, but in the child's imagination it is perhaps almost a living thing, with all sorts of qualities. One cannot disturb the idea in the child's mind without injuring the development of good feelings that are being aroused.

She has also mentioned the practice of the common people of India, who sometimes tie a piece of rag on a tree as an offering to the deity. The average Christian missionary would come along and be very angry about

[1] *Op. cit.*, IX, 26.

it, thereby showing his own ignorance, because the offering is made in all good faith. The comparatively primitive and childlike soul meant it well, and the thing should be taken like the child's rag doll, for what it means. They pour out a little water as a libation, or they offer a flower—a very small offering truly, but why should it be despised? The Christ Himself said that those who gave even a cup of cold water in His Name and for His sake should by no means lose their reward. It must be remembered, too, that probably no people, not even the most primitive, think of the statue or the form as a reality, but all have some sense of the Deity behind it.

> A great Teacher once wrote: "When I was a child, I spake as a child, I understood as a child, I thought as a child; but when I became a man I put away childish things." Yet he who has forgotten his childhood and lost sympathy with the children is not the man who can teach them or help them. So look kindly, gently, tolerantly upon all; but upon all alike, Buddhist or Hindu, Jain or Jew, Christian or Muhammadan.

A.B.—You have there an exact description of the occultist; he is the man who has not forgotten his childhood. He has grown to manhood, but he remembers what he has passed through, and so he can help all. *In order to train ourselves in this power of sympathy for* all and help towards all, it is a good practice to translate your religious thoughts into the language of some particular exoteric religion, to put your thought into its formulæ. We all have one particular language of our own, in which we express things to ourselves, until we reach the stage when we have a common language in which we can speak to anybody. The student will do well to study some language or form other than his own. Those who have been brought up as Christians might practise speaking and thinking in terms of Hinduism; then they would learn to see things from the Hindu standpoint, and would be quite astonished to see how different they looked from what they had imagined them to be. Hindus might similarly learn to speak and think in terms used in Christianity.

Shrī Rāmakrishna Paramahamsa, the guru of Swāmī Vivekānanda, trained himself in that way. He took several religions in turn, and for the time being followed their methods and practices. He took up Christianity: prayed in the Christian way, thought in Christian terms, and even dressed in Christian dress; and thus he went through one religion after another, learning to identify himself with each. He used every outside help that he could contrive in order to help himself in this effort. When he was trying to realize the mother side of nature, that which is represented by the Virgin Mary in the West, by the Shaktis in Hinduism, he dressed himself as a woman and thought of himself as a woman. Certainly the result of these practices in his case was very beautiful, for all outer religious differences ceased entirely to affect him.

How different is this line from that which most people pursue! Yet it is only by learning to identify oneself with all around that one can fit oneself for discipleship. Shri Rāmakrishna was fundamentally a bhakta, a devotee, and he learned through emotion in this way.

The aspirant should try for a time, then, to think of himself as a Hindu, or a Buddhist, or a woman—something which he is not. How few men ever try to think or feel as a woman does, to see things as she sees them! I suppose, too, that not many women really try to see things from a man's standpoint; but it is more marked in men—a man always wants to feel himself "he". Even among Theosophists it seems to me that the fact of our brotherhood being without distinction of sex is sometimes overlooked.

Learn also to understand how things would appear to you if coming to you through some particular atmosphere to which you are not accustomed. You have to cure yourself of the habit of looking at things exclusively from your own standpoint—that is contrary to occultism. Do this, and in the world you will be blamed; your impartiality and sympathy will be called indifference. That does not in the least matter. I have been accused of being "too Hindu" in the West, and of being "too Christian" in the East; because in the West I speak in Western terms and the people in India do not like it, and in the East I speak in Eastern terms and the people in the West do not like it. My answer to such complaints always is that I speak to the people in the language which they understand.

Such complaints and such blame rise from looking at things from the lower pole instead of from the higher. To learn to speak many religious languages is one of the lessons necessary for the man who is to carry the message to many lands. This is no new truth, and the blame which follows such action is also not new. The great reproach made against S. Paul was that he was all things to all men. He wrote: "For though I be free from all men, yet have I made myself servant unto all, that I might gain the more. And unto the Jews I became as a Jew, that I might gain the Jews; to them that are under the law, as under the law, that I might gain them that are under the law; to them that are without law, as without law, (being not without law to God, but under the law to Christ,) that I might gain them that are without law. To the weak I became as weak, that I might gain the weak; I am made all things to all men, that I might by all means save some."[1] From being one of the straitest, he became one of the most liberal of men; he belonged to one of the strictest sects of the Jews, yet became the apostle of the Gentiles—a remarkable transformation.

The occultist belongs to no religion or to all religions, according to the way you like to put it—to none exclusively, to all inclusively. Nothing less than that is tolerance. The reason why it is good to keep out of controversies is that for the time one may become intolerant; it is difficult to be quite impartial, if one is to be effective, when controverting a one-sided presentment.

[1] I Corinthians, 9, 19-22.

Always put the truth from the standpoint of unity, not from that of difference; then only will you be able to help all, and all alike. Then only will you be able to see the good in each and all, overlooking and looking through that which is defective.

C.W.L.—The Theosophist aims at brotherhood without distinction of race, creed, caste, sex or colour. That brotherhood can best be lived when we are able to enter into the feelings and thoughts of those of other races and creeds, and of the other sex. A man forgets the fact that he has had many births in feminine form; a woman also forgets that she has had many incarnations in masculine bodies. Though not easy to do, it is an exceedingly good exercise for the man to try to put himself in thought in the woman's place and to understand her way of looking on life; and so also for a woman to try to see how a man envisages things. The two points of view are surprisingly different in various ways. One who can identify his consciousness with that of the opposite sex has already taken a step towards a brotherhood which transcends the idea of sex. Having tried to understand the point of view of his sisters or mother or wife, a man may then extend this practice to people of other religions and races than his own. It is a most helpful exercise, because when anyone can really understand and thoroughly sympathize with another person's point of view, he has widened his own outlook by just that much.

Concerning tolerance there is a good story in the Talmud, about Abraham, when once a traveller came to him, and he was about to give him food and drink, as is the custom of the desert. Abraham called upon his visitor to praise God before eating, but when he refused and said he did not know anything about God, Abraham rose in anger and turned him out of his tent, and would not give him anything at all. Then the Lord came along, as apparently He used to do in those days, and said: "Why did you send him away?" Abraham replied, with great indignation, "Lord, He refused to recognize Thy Name; he is an infidel of the worst type." "Yes," God said, "but I have borne with Him for sixty years; surely you might bear with him for one hour."

Some of us who are Theosophists still have an outward religion to which we cling, yet I think we ought to be able to say that we belong to no religion exclusively, but to all of them inclusively. I myself, for example, am a Christian Bishop, but I am also a Buddhist, because I took the vows and obligations by which I accepted the Lord Buddha as my guide. In that, I was not asked to renounce any other religion. Buddhism is perhaps the widest of all religions in that respect—they do not ask you what you believe, but whether you will follow the teaching of the Lord Buddha and live so far as you can the life He commends. A Christian, Muhammadan or follower of any other religion might say, "The teaching is good teaching, I will undertake to follow it", and thereby become a Buddhist, without leaving his previous religion. Theosophy is the truth which lies behind all these religions. We study comparative religion, not merely to see that the Theosophical truths do appear in all religions, but also that we may understand the different presentations of truth and be able to help along all these lines.

Our President shows us the value of this. She speaks as a Hindu to the Hindus; she quotes from their Scriptures in support of what she says, using some of their own Sanskrit terms—and that appeals to them just as the sonorous Latin appeals to a Roman Catholic. When she speaks to the Buddhists she says exactly the same things, but quotes the sayings of the Lord Budhha, and uses the terminology of Buddhism. In the Western world you will hear her speak to Christians in their own terms, not in the least changing her own belief or religion, but simply speaking their language. She is, of course, learned in all those religions. When we know the truth behind all religions, even though we cannot begin to compare with her in knowledge and skill of utterance, many of us can by a little study of a primer of any particular religion, understand it well and become able to present the truth in its terms, and to explain the meaning of much that is obscure to others. I have heard Colonel Olcott do it again and again. He was not a man of the student or scholar-type, but he was an exceedingly good practical lecturer. He would speak effectively to audiences of Hindus, Parsis and Buddhists, and learned men of all those faiths agreed in saying that he had given them new light on their respective religions. That shows how Theosophy is the master key to all the religions. At the great conventions of our Society at Adyar the same fact appears in another way, for people of many different religions and races, gather together, and no one who attends can fail to be deeply impressed with not merely the tolerance, but the active affectionate brotherhood that is shown there.

CHAPTER 4

CHEERFULNESS

4. *Cheerfulness.*—You must bear your karma cheerfully, whatever it may be, taking it as an honour that suffering comes to you, because it shows that the Lords of Karma think you worth helping.

A.B.—This is the qualification which, as I have already explained, was formerly frequently translated endurance. Endurance may be a somewhat negative virtue; but what you have to do is not so much to endure things which you cannot help as to take them cheerfully and brightly, facing all trouble with a smile. The word cheerfulnees gives you the whole idea of what is required by the great Teachers with regard to this particular endowment. Many people can endure, but they do so sadly; you must take all your trials and troubles brightly. On that point a great deal of stress is laid in some of the Hindu books; things are to be taken gladly.

That karma is very much quickened for people who come forward and offer themselves as candidates for the Path is a fact that been much emphasized; this is done first in order to warn people beforehand of what they have to expect, and secondly, in order to cheer them up and when the experience comes to them practically, instead of only theoretically—for that makes a great difference.

Karma, being a law of nature, can be avoided for a while or else can be brought immediately into effect, that is to say, you can put yourself into conditions where it will affect you or into others where you will be sheltered from it for the time being. It is necessary to repeat very often that the laws of nature are not enactments; they do not command us to do anything. To take a common illustration: electrical forces are always in activity about us, but if we want them to produce certain effects at a given place and time, we require a special apparatus in order to bring them into manifestation. Similarly, karma is a law of nature, and the apparatus which may start its forces working in the life of an individual may be his appearance on the stage of physical life through the process we call birth. Some changes in an individual's life may very much intensify and quicken the working of the law of karma upon him. When, for example, you offer yourself as a candidate for rapid progress, Those who administer the laws of karma may, by your consent, which you have given, modify the apparatus, so to speak, and let the force which is there show itself more strongly, exhaust itself upon you in a shorter time. Your will is the real cause of the alteration in the apparatus.

If the expressed desire to grow more rapidly, and therefore to get rid quickly of his evil karma, is a real wish on the man's part, so that his soul is set in that direction, then his wish reaches the Lords of Karma, and They put in motion the karma he has made in the past and let it descend upon him. The karma was there; it is not that the man is creating anything new, but he begins to clear off what he has stored up.

If you realize what is taking place, you will not be surprised at anything that may happen to you. Consider the lives of Alcyone, and see how many terrible things occurred in them. In one life his child was murdered; in another he was executed for a crime he had not committed, and so on. You scarcely realize these things when you read them like a story; but you would think them very dreadful if any of them were to happen to you in this life. All those misfortunes and sorrows were so much clearing off of bad karma.

When troubles fall quickly on you it shows that the Lords of Karma have taken notice of your prayer, and that is a very good sign. If things were to go on very smoothly it would mean that They had not yet taken notice. So in this matter again the occult view reverses the judgment of the world: the things which the world calls evil are, from the occult standpoint good.

When to the pain and loss which fall upon you there is added the censure and ungenerous criticism of those around you, then you have the best karma of all. Some misfortunes at once awaken sympathy in others, and all the sympathy poured out on the man who is suffering helps him a great deal. But other misfortunes may excite blame; you may have done your best but acute suffering has fallen upon you, and in addition the world turns against you and blames you. When this happens one is clearing off a great amount of past karma; that additional disagreeable factor enables one to work it off quickly and thoroughly.

It is easy to see that these things are true theoretically, as you hear or read them; but what you have to do is to remember them at the right moment. What people generally do is to admit them till the time comes for their practical realization, and then promptly to forget them. Try to get these facts so thoroughly into your mind that you cannot forget them, so that the thought of them shall strengthen you when suffering and enable you to help others when they are suffering. It may help a little towards the clear understanding that is needed if you look around you and see how constantly troubles come to very good people, who have done, as so often one hears it said, nothing to deserve them—that is, nothing in their present lives, which are noble and useful ones. Our tendency is to compare ourselves with those who are more fortunate than we are; it is well sometimes to do so with those who are less fortunate, that we may feel gratitude for all the good that we have received. We are liable to forget how much there is for which we should feel grateful, because we think always of whatever pain and loss fall to our share; but we ought not to do this.

C.W.L.—No one who really understands and believes in the law of karma can fail to be cheerful. It should be made quite clear that karma is a law, like gravitation, and it is always acting. People sometimes think of it and speak of it as though it came into operation occasionally when they do something. This is not true; we are under its operation every moment. A man provides conditions in which the law of karma can act upon him when he does or thinks or speaks some definite thing. The law of karma for each of us at this moment has an account with us, the sum total of our good and our bad deeds. Because we have all come up through savage states when we did all sorts of uncontrolled things, there is likely to be a certain amount of evil karma waiting for all of us, unless we have spent many lives working it out. When we find suffering coming upon us, we should assume that we are working out, perhaps, the last part of that karma. If we read the stories of some of the greatest of the saints we shall find that they passed through an immense amount of suffering. All the people who have tried to help the world have suffered terribly. It is part of the training for Initiation, but it is absolute justice always, for not even for the purposes of training can any injustice take place.

The Lords of Karma are simply the Administrators of that Law. In some ways perhaps the word Lords is a little indefinite, because it rather suggests that They direct and rule karma. You cannot direct or rule gravitation; but you can make arrangements to use it at certain points and in certain ways. So with the law of karma; those who are working in connection with it are its administrators. One function of the Lords of Karma is to select a certain part of a man's store of karma and give it to him to work out in his forthcoming incarnation.

They cannot take more of good or more of evil than there is in the man's karma, but They do select from that what They think he can work through. Still, the man's will is free, and if the selected karma is worked through sooner than They had expected, if one may put it that way, They may give some more. "Whom the Lord loveth He chasteneth"—that is the meaning of that extraordinary statement. People also make much trouble from themselves which is not within their karma from the past, by taking things hardly instead of philosophically, and also by downright folly—but the Lords of Karma are not responsible for this.

However hard it is, be thankful that it is no worse.

C.W.L.—The tendency of almost everyone who suffers is to say how hard it is and to think of other times when things were better. We may take it the other way and say, "Things might have been much worse than this," and also, "I am very glad to be working off all this karma; I might have had much more to work out; at least let me make the best of it."

Remember that you are of but little use to the Master until your evil karma is worked out, and you are free.

A.B.—From the Master's standpoint it is a very good thing for a man to get rid of a piece of bad Karma which is hanging over him in the background; for we have to remember that the Master is hampered by the bad karma of those who wish to serve Him; it prevents His using them as freely as He otherwise could do. Madame Blavatsky, who always spoke very openly about herself, being truthful through and through, said of the Coulomb trouble: "I have not deserved it now, but for my past." It was a vital thing for her to get rid of this karma, and so the scandalous and shameful way she was treated throughout that affair was the greatest blessing for her; she recognized this when she looked at the matter philosophically, but at times she was disturbed by it on the surface.

All aspirants ought to be helped by that thought, helped to look away from themselves to Him and to think: "These troubles that I am going through make me more useful to Him."

If you have asked that your karma shall be quickened it is unreasonable to complain when your request is granted. Keep the inspiring idea always in your thoughts: "I shall be of more use to the Master the freer I become." A gift, once given, must not be taken back. This idea is very common in some of the old Indian books, recurring over and over again in the stories told in them; a gift once given, or a word once spoken, cannot be taken back. If a gift that you have once given should be put back into your hands by circumstances you must give it again; it is not yours, and to keep it would be theft. So, when there is this gift of yourself—the highest and noblest gift of all—you must never take it back. People continually give themselves verbally to the Master, but keep a finger on the gift in order to be able to pull it back if the Master goes too far—that is really what it comes to. They draw back, if the Master takes them at their word; as sometimes He might do, in order to let them see that they had been deceiving themselves, and had promised more than they were prepared to fulfil.

C.W.L.—If all one's bad karma were exhausted one would have the whole of one's time and strength free for the Master's work. It has been explained that the Master is hampered by our bad karma, and therefore in getting rid of it quickly we are making ourselves more fit to serve Him. Madame Blavatsky took that view very strongly with regard to the attacks made upon her by Madame Coulomb and others in Madras about the year 1884. While she was indignant that the attacks should be made, and sad at the ingratitude which they showed, and also disturbed lest they should reflect upon her Society and injure it, yet she said: "At least there is this to remember, that all these troubles make me more fit to serve Him."

We can apply that idea to the Society's troubles as well as to our own. Think always of the service of the Master when the Society is getting rid of what is evil; it goes forward the moment it has passed through some particular trouble, for it has got rid of some bad karma and so become more useful, a better instrument for its true owners.

Having disposed of that portion of its karma the Society could move onward to greater things. Such karma shakes out the dead material, the people who have reached their "saturation-point for truth", as

Madame Blavatsky used to express it, and cannot go further. They may previously have been a great help, but they have become a hindrance to future progress. Yet the rest of us are often very sorry to lose those friends. In the last trouble, it seemed to me that I was somewhat of a storm-centre, and that there was very good excuse for many of the people who misunderstood, so I ventured to represent to the Mahāchohan that the test was very hard for them, and to ask for an act of grace for them. Naturally, He smiled kindly at my presumption, and said: "Will you be satisfied if the same people throw aside Mrs. Besant?" "Oh, yes," I said, "of course." I felt they would not do *that*, but a few months later they did turn against her, and the Mahāchohan said, with the same gentle smile: "You see; for this life their sun has set. But there are other lives, and the sun will rise again to-morrow."

No one is indispensable, though it does sometimes happen in India that a Lodge grows up round some influential member, and fades away again when he removes to some other town. When Madame Blavatsky went, many of us, accustomed to daily inspiration from her, felt that all would be dark. Another great individuality arose in the person of our present President. Yet I am sure that she would be the first to say that we need not be anxious for the Society when her turn comes to leave us. The instruments change their bodies—"In the sight of the unwise they seem to die." But the Masters who stand behind do not die, and while They are there some one will always be found to continue Their work.

By offering yourself to Him, you have asked that your karma may be hurried, and so now in one or two lives you work through what otherwise might have been spread over a hundred. But in order to make the best out of it you must bear it cheerfully, gladly.

A.B.—According to the way in which an old debt is paid, a new cause is started. That should never be forgotten. If you make the best of what looks like bad karma you set in motion new forces for good, whereas if you take bad karma unwillingly and pay your debts grudgingly, the reverse happens. Remember how the Christ said in the sermon on the Mount: "Agree with thine adversary quickly, whiles thou art in the way with him."[1] That is good counsel to follow in the adverse circumstances that come to you. Your troubles and losses appear to you to come as adversaries; meet them bravely, agree with them quickly, and then they will be done with. We should rid ourselves of our bad karma very much more rapidly if we did not sow new while reaping the old.

C.W.L.—People sometimes talk of giving themselves to the Master, and are then afraid that the Master will ask too much. That is the spirit of Ananias and Sapphira. That unfortunate couple had assuredly the most perfect right to retain part of their goods for themselves if they wished to do so, but they made a mistake when they pretended that they were giving everything. To say,

[1] S. Matthew, 5, 25.

"I can give this; I can do this much for Him, but I cannot give myself unreservedly", marks a stage through which we pass. But when one offers himself to the Master it ought to be in the same whole-hearted spirit that he would give any other gift. It should be offered without reservation as to how it should be used, and one should not want to take any of it back. No one need fear that He will want too much. If we offer ourselves to the Master we must not be surprised and hurt if suffering comes suddenly upon us. That shows that the offering has been partially accepted. Many things that the world calls evil and suffering may therefore be taken as signs of swift progress. Instead of sympathizing with us people often blame us, but generally that is the best karma of all. To be misunderstood, so that our good shall be evil spoken of, as Ruysbroek put it, seems to come always when people are drawing near to their final goal. It has happened to every great occult or mystical teacher all through history. To bear it all cheerfully in itself makes good karma and develops in us various valuable qualities—patience, perseverance, endurance, long-suffering, determination. So, out of evil long past, we may bring good.

Yet another point. You must give up all feeling of possession. Karma may take from you the things which you like best—even the people whom you love most. Even then you must be cheerful—ready to part with anything and everything.

A.B.—We come now to a thing that is enormously more difficult than the preceding. The bearing of past karma is far easier than this. You must eliminate of all feeling of ownership—first of all for things, and then for persons. The latter is a more subtle task; have you given up all sense of possession with regard to the people you love best? Even when people think they have done so, circumstances arise to test them, and often show that they have not. Can you let a life go out of your own, which is more to you than your own life? You may call this the last and most difficult test of your real devotion to the Master. It is a point on which all aspirants should try to test themselves, before the test comes upon them by circumstances, because they can lessen the blow by practising beforehand. Do not try to kill out the love you feel towards anyone—that is the way of the dark powers. You might practise by loving a person all the time, but withdrawing yourself for a time from that person's society, by doing some work which has to be done away from the person who makes life happy for you, or in some such way as that. If you can do that cheerfully and gladly, you are well on the way to answer the call when it comes—the call to leave all and follow the Master.

Remember how much stress is laid upon that in the accounts that have come down to us of what took place when the Lord Maitreya was in Palestine. Not everyone who was called rose to the height of his opportunity, but some did so. Those who forsook all and followed Him became teachers after He went away; the others never heard of Him again. Remember the case of the rich young man who went away sorrowing, although it was only riches he was asked to abandon. People think that they would have obeyed the call at once, had they been in that young man's place, yet I am not sure that there are many people who would leave great possessions to follow a vagrant preacher—for that was how the Christ appeared, as a wandering teacher surrounded by some half-educated people. Yet this is the test of discipleship, to forsake everything—the things you most like and the people you love best—and follow the Master.

C.W.L.—We must realize that nothing is ours in the personal sense, that whatever we have is given to us in trust for the work of evolution. If one has money or is in a position of influence, that is because it gives the opportunity of doing more for the work. Nothing is our own, in the sense that we may make a separate use of it; one is always in the position of the trusted manager or employee who is using the firm's money, but is in every respect just as careful with every penny of it as he would be if it were his own. That ought to be the attitude of every rich man, and every man in a position of power.

The attitude of living as a representative of humanity is very wonderfully and beautifully expressed by the Masters. They regard Themselves merely as stewards of all the mighty powers which They possess. That is why the Master makes no karma, either good or ill, to bind Him to the human condition. Those who are the greatest actors and performers make no karma that binds Them, because They do all impersonally, utterly without personal desire. They do it all as a soldier fights in battle, with no thought of the particular enemy whom he happens to kill, but with the feeling that he is working for a cause, as part of a mighty machine. So They work as part of the Great Brotherhood, as part of the Hierarchy, part of humanity, and all the good they do comes back to humanity and helps to uplift it.

First we must have no feeling of possession about things, and then about people, which is harder still; they may be taken from us by death, as it is called, and also perhaps for service to humanity. Of many thousands that was true during the Great War; the wife gave her husband, the mother her son, to go forth and fight for the right. Surely it is not for us ever to hesitate to do as well in the Master's service as so many thousands of others have done in the service of their nations. It is difficult to let a life go out of ours which is more to us than our own life, and yet many have had to do that—some under very sad circumstances, others in conditions which made the sacrifice holy and beautiful.

It is the way of those who follow the darker magic to kill out love and so escape all this suffering. But those who would be of the Great White Brotherhood must make their love ever stronger, yet kill out the selfishness that so often mars it. Remember how a sword pierced the heart of our Lady Herself, the Blessed Virgin Mary. She might have escaped that sword if she had chosen to tear out from her heart all remembrance of her Son and forget Him altogether. In many cases it is as Christ said of Himself, "Think not that I am come to send peace on earth: I came not to send peace, but a sword."[1] He meant that His new teaching would be taken up here and there by one in a family, and that the others would object and so cause division, or that one might have to leave his old home and friends for the sake of some special work that he could do. Similarly there have been cases where one member of a family has seen the Theosophical truth and the rest have not, and that has led to suffering and division. Often, in modern days, one will leave the family to go to the other side of the earth in order to make money, and no one objects to that; but if one should propose to do it for the good of humanity there is immediate protest—so unevolved is the spirit of our time.

Remember the difficulties that King Suddhodana created when Prince Siddhārtha wished to devote himself to the religious life. He spent vast sums of money and a great part of his life in endeavouring to keep his son back from the high destiny that opened before him—endeavouring to make him, instead of the greatest religious teacher the world had ever known, the greatest king in India—an alternative future that the astrologers had foretold for him. The king knew that to become a religious teacher would mean poverty and self-abnegation for his son, and he did not realize that it would be in reality a higher position than that of any king. It is not the great king whose name goes down longest and

[1] S. Matthew, 10, 34.

furthest in history, but the great religious teacher. King Suddhodana wished enormous power and fame without parallel for his son, and it came, but not in the way for which he had hoped and planned. The power of Lord Buddha is greater than that of any earthly monarch, and his renown has spread all over the world.

The Christ said to the people: "Forsake all and follow Me." When our Christian friends read this in the Gospel they feel that they would have done it at once. That is not so certain. Let us try to put ourselves into the place of the people of that time. Remember the young man with great possessions and great riches who came to Him; those possessions probably brought their duties which he felt he had to fulfil, and therefore he could not forsake them. All the public opinion of the time, all the respectability, and all the orthodox powers were arrayed against the Christ; He was only a poor wandering Teacher who had nowhere to lay His head. Would we have followed Him in the face of all that? Is it so certain that we would have forsaken everything to follow Him whom all the elders and the high priests and the orthodox people stigmatized as a fanatic? Would we not have felt a doubt as to whether, after all, we might not be throwing away the substance and grasping at the shadow? It is not so certain. In the present day, perhaps, it looks like that still, and yet those of us who have thrown away other things for the sake of following Them have never for one moment regretted it.

Often the Master needs to pour out His strength upon others through His servant; He cannot do that if the servant yields to depression. So cheerfulness must be the rule.

C.W.L.—Constantly all through this book the same reason is brought forward for everything that is to be done, that it is for the sake of the service of the Master. We might expect many other reasons to be given against depression—that it is bad for the person and it has an unpleasant effect upon others; but the one point which is emphasized here is that the Master cannot use us as a channel for His force if we yield to it.

A.B.—Here the reason why cheerfulness must be the rule is given, for again that inspiring idea is presented, that the Master needs your help, that you can be of use to Him! His force is all joyous because it is part of the force of the Logos; it cannot therefore pour out through a pipe that is choked with depression.

It may sound strange to say that the Master is unable to do this or that, yet the fact is so. Now and again one will hear the Master say of something: "I could not succeed in doing it." Their power is limited when They work down here, by the conditions that exist on the physical plane. Often They cannot reach a person on the physical plane except through an intermediary; therefore They need the help which perhaps you can give Them. Without that help, things have to remain undone, and later on, in consequence, obstacles have to be removed which need never have been there.

CHAPTER 5

ONE-POINTEDNESS

5. *One-pointedness.*—The one thing that you must set before you is to do the Master's work. Whatever else may come in your way to do, that at least you must never forget.

C.W.L.—In ordinary life one-pointedness is necessary for real success. The one-pointed man always wins in the end, because all his powers are working together, while other people have a variety of aims, and are constantly changing them. The man who sets himself to make money, for example, and uses all his thought and will for that purpose, and watches and plans for it all the time, is almost sure to gain his object. If one determines all the time to serve the Master with constantly increasing power, and is willing to put aside *all* other things for that, his progress will be swift indeed.

Yet nothing else *can* come in your way, for all helpful, unselfish work is the Master's work, and you must do it for His sake. And you must give all your attention to each piece as you do it, so that it may be your very best.

C.W.L.—A good deal of a pupil's work consists in preparing himself for more responsible work for the Master in the future. Some of it is not directly useful in the Master's present plans, but may be compared to much of the work of a boy at school, who in learning, for example, Latin, is not doing any particular good, but is or ought to be developing powers of mind and qualities of character which will be useful in later life. The duties of common life often combine something of both these things, for they provide a splendid training and education for those who do them well, and also offer many occasions for helping other people to progress in character and ideals, which is most emphatically the Master's work. All the varied activities of daily life will come within our one-pointed endeavour to serve the Master, when we learn to do them all in His name and for Him. The Master's work for us is not something peculiar and apart from our fellows. To raise a good family who will serve Him in turn, to make money to use in His service, to win power in order to help Him, with it, are all part of it; yet in doing these things we must be ever on guard against self-deception, that we are not cloaking with the holiness of the Master's name what is, underneath, a selfish desire to wield power or handle money.

That same Teacher also wrote: "Whatsoever ye do, do it *heartily*, as to the Lord, and not unto men." Think how you would do a piece of work if you knew that the Master was coming at once

to look at it ; just in that way you must do all your work. Those who know most will most know all that that verse means. And there is another like it, much older : "Whatsoever thy hand findeth to do, do it with thy might."

C.W.L.—The whole world exists within the consciousness of the Lord of the World, the One Initiator, and therefore everything that we do is being done in His Presence. From that is derived the old Christian idea of the omniscience and omnipresence of God, of whom it is said, "In Him we live and move and have our being." It is not a poetic fancy, but a scientific fact, that we live within the aura of the great Spiritual King of the world. Of course, a consciousness that can grasp all the world simultaneously is to us inconceivably incomprehensible, yet one day we shall reach His stupendous level.

The old conception of God used to make His omnipresence a terrible thought; God was supposed to be one who was always watching to find fault, looking eagerly for any breach of His rules that He might come down in wrath upon the hapless offender. Many a child has suffered terribly because of that thought that God sees everything that he does; he feels it in a way unfair that there can be no privacy. This is especially so because a frightened child cannot tell how his mentor will take anything that he does. But if instead one realizes the mighty divine Love, then one begins to see that His omnipresence is our safety and our greatest blessing.

A.B.—The test that the Master gives here should be applied to all our work. Suppose you are writing a letter; if you knew that the Master would come and read it over, it would be very carefully written, both as to its contents and its form. Whatever your work is, it is His work, if it is the best you can do; whether it is something that the Master wants done for some immediate purpose, or something that prepares you for future work. Everything is for Him, if we are His; it cannot be for anybody else. Make this your normal and continual attitude of mind, and you make the atmosphere in which one-pointedness can grow.

If we had that real one-pointedness, how splendidly everything would go. That thought of doing all because of His service is one which I keep in my own mind, just as younger disciples can do, though I have more force of habit to help me than they have as yet. "Why should I answer this letter?" I sometimes ask myself; and the answer to my own question at once comes up in my mind: "It has come in my way to do, and so it is Master's work."

You will continue to hold this thought foremost in your minds all through the time that you are disciples; all have to make the habit, and when it is made they must go on strengthening it. That will help us to do with all our might whatever work we have. We must do it with our might because so it becomes part of the divine work, and because of the training of character that it gives. Make your work quite true, allowing nothing second-rate to pass.

One-pointedness means, too, that nothing shall ever turn you, even for a moment, from the Path upon which you have entered. No temptations, no worldly pleasures, no worldly affections even, must ever draw you aside. For you yourself must become one with the Path; it must be so much part of your nature that you follow it without needing to think of it, and cannot turn aside. You, the Monad, have decided it; to break away from it would be to break away from yourself.

C.W.L.—The statement that the individual must become one with the Path is made in other Scriptures besides this. The Christ said to His disciples, "I am the Way"[1]; Shrī Krishna made a very similar observation: "I am the way along which the traveller must walk." The same idea is put forward in *The Voice of the Silence*, where it said: "Thou canst not travel on the Path before thou hast become that Path itself." What is happening really is that one is becoming one's own true self. Patañjali, defining yoga, says that when a man has gained control of his mind he "resides in his own true state". The Monad is our true Self, the God in man, but he has put down a shadow of himself to form the ego, and that again has incarnated in a personality. Not until a man is considerably evolved can the ego manage the personality; before that, he looks down upon it without trying to do much in such a hopeless cause. Then comes the First Initiation, the

[1] S. John, 14, 6.

point when the personality has ceased to have a will of its own, and lives (except when it forgets) only to serve the higher. The ego is now active through it in the lower planes, and is beginning to realize the existence of the Monad, and to live according to its will. The Monad has determined the path for the ego's evolution; and he can choose no other, because he is becoming himself, gaining release from the bondage even of the spiritual planes. Constantly, while on the Path, the pupil will be swayed from side to side, but when he has achieved one-pointedness he will always swing back to the one right way.

A.B.—People often forget that they are the expression of the Monad. The real you is the Monad, and therefore whatever you do down here is done of your own true will, not through outer compulsion of another will. The Monad's will is your will; your desires are not your will at all, but you are drawn to outer things because one or other of your bodies wants to take a particular pleasure. It is not you who like the pleasure; it is the elemental material that wants to taste and experience it. Against this state of affairs you must oppose your true "I", which points undeviatingly to the highest. You must be like a strongly magnetized compass whose needle may indeed be drawn aside, but returns ever back. Until you are so strong that nothing can draw you aside, you must constantly practise bringing yourself back to the one will.

You are not matter; you must make matter your instrument. It is absurd that you should give way to the piece of material that you have picked up to fashion to your use. It is as though the hammer in the hand of the carpenter struck where *it* chose instead of where he chose, and crushed his finger instead of driving in the nail. It happens sometimes that a man crushes his own finger with his tool, but that is because he is a clumsy workman. Learn fidelity to your purpose, to your true will, and the time will come when you cannot turn aside from it.

One-pointedness can also be developed by concentration. Fix your attention on a small area at any given time; concentrate upon one thing at a time, so as to do it well. A quantity of water which is sufficient to make a strong current when penned into a channel, becomes a mere film when it is allowed to spread over a large surface. So is it with your energies. Take up one piece of work after another, and do each thing definitely and forcefully, instead of vaguely trying to do everything. If you follow this advice steadily you will soon begin to see some definite result, very small each week perhaps, but as the weeks pass the results accumulate and soon become very considerable in quantity of work done as well as in increase of power.

CHAPTER 6

CONFIDENCE

6. *Confidence.*—You must trust your master; you must trust yourself. If you have seen the Master, you will trust Him to the uttermost, through many lives and deaths. If you have not yet seen Him, you must still try to realize Him and trust Him, because if you do not, even He cannot help you.

C.W.L.—These are partly the words of Alcyone, who is speaking here of His Master; but the Master Himself spoke similarly of others greater than He, because just as we speak and think of the Masters so do They in turn speak and think of the Lord Buddha, of the Lord Maitreya, and others greater than Themselves.

It is practically impossible for us to realize a Master. We may try to do so; we may think of the highest ideals we know; but the Master embodies so many kinds of greatness that we cannot even imagine, that the highest ideal we can form of Him is still far too low. Such being the case, uttermost trust in His wisdom is but simple common sense.

Utter trust in the Master is largely a question of one's past. If we look at the lives of Alcyone we can see how that has been so in his case. He has been in close association with his Master through many past lives. From the same set of lives, I see, for example, that I myself have been in similar association with my Master, and so have others. I suppose I must take that as accounting for the fact that the moment I read of the Master I instantly felt the strongest possible attraction towards Him. When I had the privilege of seeing Him, it never for a moment occurred to me to distrust Him. In such cases it may be said that the ego knows, either by being aware of the Master's presence on the higher mental plane, or by memory of past lives in which the Master has been known. Sometimes the ego knows but cannot send that knowledge down into the personality, and sometimes it is transmitted imperfectly or incorrectly, or again, in other cases the ego simply does not know. The ego is never likely to be wrong; he is, apparently, not deceived about anything, but that he is ignorant of certain matters is quite clear, and indeed the very purpose of his incarnation is to remove that ignorance.

Those who have no proof of the existence of the Masters may well consider the reasonableness of the idea, the certainty that since man is evolving and many stages lie behind him, there must be other stages of evolution in front of him. We cannot regard ourselves as the crown of the ages. There is also much testimony to Their existence coming from those who have met and spoken with such Men.[1]

[1] This subject is dealt with at length in *The Masters and the Path*.

There are some who have actually seen the Masters and yet, incomprehensible though it may appear, have afterwards fallen away from full trust in Them. I remember very well, for example, a certain Mr. Brown of London; he has written a pamphlet describing his life, so there is no harm in referring to him. Many years ago he went to India, and there had the most unusual privilege of meeting in the physical body one of the two Masters who started the Theosophical Society. They come down very rarely from Their Tibetan home, but both of Them have been in India since I have been a member of the Society, in the earlier years of the movement. In *The Occult World* there is an account of the visit of the Master Kūthūmi to Amritsār, where the great Golden Temple of the Sikhs is. He said: "I saw our Sikhs drunk on the floor of their own temple, . . . I turn my face homeward to-morrow." More and more, I suppose, They find They can use Their energies to best advantage upon higher planes, and leave the work on the lower to those who are now gradually gathering round Them in the world. Young Mr. Brown had first seen the astral appearance of the Master Kūthūmi, and then he happened to be travelling in the far north of India as secretary to Colonel Olcott, when the Master came in His physical body to see the Colonel. Mr. Brown was sleeping in the same tent as the Colonel, but in a separate division of it. The Master spoke for some time with Colonel Olcott, and then came round into the other division of the tent. I do not understand why, but Mr. Brown wrapped his head up in the bed-sheet and was afraid to face the Master. Naturally, one would be highly conscious of one's faults, but to adopt the ostrich-like plan of putting one's head under the bedclothes does not seem to me to help much, because the bed-clothes, of course were also transparent to the higher sight. The Master, however, spoke to him patiently. "Take your head out of the bed-clothes," He said, "I want you to see if I am the same person you saw in your astral body." Eventually the Master gave up and left a little note for him, and only then Mr. Brown recovered his senses. He had there an opportunity for which many would give a very great deal. He had deserved it, of course, but he did not make the best use of it. And afterwards he doubted the existence of the Masters. There have been others also who have had the privilege of seeing Them, and yet have somehow fallen away.

Some people, owing to the experience of their past lives, have built up a sceptical nature; others are over-credulous. Neither of these extremes is good for a man's progress; both alike are unscientific. Each man has a general scheme of things in his mind. If new facts which are told him at once fit in with that, he is ready to accept them as probable without demanding exact proof. We say, "Yes, that seems very likely; that fits in very well; probably it is so." But if, on the other hand, the average person is told of something which does not in any way gear in with what he knew before, he altogether refuses to accept it. When one has had experience in the study of the inner side of things, one soon abandons the attitude which refuses to accept a statement because it does not gear in with what one already knows. One learns to suspend judgment, neither accepting nor declining to accept, but simply saying: "From what I have seen so far that does not seem to me very likely; but I do not deny it, I shall put it aside and wait for further light." It is futile to say that because a thing is not in one's experience therefore it cannot be. That is the tendency of ignorance.

Generally speaking, the less people know the more certain they are, down here on the physical plane. In ordinary science, those who dogmatize are the students. The great scientific men will usually say: "I have had experience of such-and-such things, but of course I cannot pretend to lay down the law." The Lord Chancellor once said: "I am as certain of that as the youngest barrister present." He is certain because he has not learnt that there are many possibilities, that you cannot lay down the law too definitely. Those who have been studying for years are much more thoughtful of the way in which they express themselves. There are vast numbers of realities before us all the time, which as yet we do not know. A generation ago many of what are commonplaces of our daily life now would have been derided by most people as utterly impossible. It is well to recognize that fact from the beginning and to be prepared for new discoveries, which may constantly be expected, as man evolves.

It is distinctly useful for us as students of these higher matters to try to get out of the attitude of being bound by our preconceptions. We must be sufficiently plastic to accept even revolutionary truths when they have good reason on their side. Failing that, we must simply put them aside and say we do not yet see, without condemning them or the people who hold them. Truth is many-sided, and to see it from all sides at once is not commonly given to any one man or set of men; consequently there may always be a modicum of truth in that which at present seems to us unreasonable.

One great trouble is that many people who know nothing whatever about a subject are persuaded that they know all about it; especially in matters of religion people who know little are nevertheless clamorously insistent that others should believe the particular delusion that happens to occupy their minds. Sometimes they say their conscience is thus directing them. Even if that be so in some cases, we cannot always depend upon the conscience, since the ego whose voice it is does not know everything. History records that people have burned and tortured others for conscience' sake. An ego who recommends such ideas is distinctly ignorant on very important points. One must, of course, give heed to one's conscience, when one is sure the voice is that, but always remember Bishop South's celebrated reply to a dissenter: "By all means follow thy conscience, but take heed that thy conscience is not the conscience of a fool."

While it is well to have confidence, one cannot make oneself believe, any more than one can make oneself love. But just as we can dwell upon a person's good points and so gradually acquire reason for loving him, so we can think over the reasons for belief, and perhaps gradually attain it thereby. Strictly, of course, one should not desire to believe anything in particular, but only whatever may be true; yet that truth may come to us only after considerable study of the matter, if we have no conviction arising from the past.

It is not the method of great spiritual teachers to make everything easy for us. I first came into touch with occultism through Madame Blavatsky. She gave occasional crumbs of knowledge to her people, but she constantly applied rigorous tests to them. It was a drastic method, but those who really meant business remained with her, while others very soon abandoned her. She cured us of conventionality, but there was much searching of hearts among her followers in the process. Many people said she did things which a great spiritual teacher ought not to do. My own feeling was always this: "Madame Blavatsky has this occult knowledge, and I am going to get that knowledge from her, if she will give it to me. Whatever else she does is her affair. I am not here to criticize her; to her own Master she stands or falls, and not to me. She may have her own reasons for what she does; I do not know anything about that. She has this knowledge, she speaks of these Masters. I intend to get this knowledge; I intend, if it is humanly possible, to reach the feet of those Masters." I gave up everything else to follow her lead, and I have never regretted the confidence I placed in Madame Blavatsky. If one is critical by nature it is his karma; he will learn much more slowly than the man who is prepared to accept things reasonably.

We have to remember that we cannot play with occultism. If we do, no benefit results from it and we are doing no good; if it is not the first interest in life it is of no value. We cannot give to it the second or the third or the seventeenth place in life as so many good people try to do. It must actually be the first thing in life and everything else must be subsidiary to it. Confidence in the Master does mean that we believe that He knows exactly what we ought to do, and that He says what He means; and so when, as in this book, He lays down certain definite rules we must do our very best to follow them. I know it seems difficult, and it is very hard to make people believe just that thing. They say: "Well, He means an approximation to that. He means something like it." But He means exactly what He says, and if we do not believe Him, and therefore we fail, we must blame ourselves. In occultism we have to pass from the insincerity of the world into the light of truth, out of our world into Theirs.

Unless there is perfect trust, there cannot be the perfect flow of love and power.

C.W.L.—If one is in a condition of doubt as to the existence of the Master, or doubt as to one's own power ever to reach Him or to make progress, then that very doubt sets all the vibrations going the wrong way, and the person having it will not be a channel which can be used. Therefore the pupil must have confidence in the Master and love for Him, and yet at the same time love for mankind which is quite impersonal. It is all the time the Master's one idea to do what has to be done with as little expenditure of spiritual force as possible, so that He may have the more to use in other work. If anyone is in any such condition as I have described he is not a good channel and so is useless to the Master. It would be indeed sad to fail Him just when He wanted our service—to have vibrations in our various vehicles that would repel His influence instead of transmitting it.

I remember a case of one who aspired very strongly to become a pupil of a certain Master. He had already served Him well in various ways, and his greatest desire was to see the Master. I was myself staying in that person's house when the Master came in His physical body to visit the city where he lived; but He did not come to the house. I met Him outside and spoke to Him for a long time, but He could not come to see the one who wished to be His pupil, because just at that time that person's astral body was very violently affected—it was all torn with ignoble passion along certain lines. Thus the opportunity of a lifetime was lost—perhaps the opportunity of many lifetimes. If that person could have known how near the Master was, I am sure that all his passion would have fallen away in a moment. Yet for the Master to use His power to drive that away in order to show Himself would have been a waste of His force.

It must not be thought that the Master resents want of trust or any attitude of that nature, or that He is hard when He does not spend his time in removing this or that state of passion from an aspirant. He will do only what will best serve the work, and He will not be swayed by sentimental reasons of any description. When there is real business to be done you must take the best man that offers, whether he be a friend or not, and to put him aside and take a less efficient one, because he was a friend, would be to fail in your duty. In the case of a great war, for example, you must take the best available man to lead your forces, to be at the head of this Ministry or that, or to carry on a particular department of the work. It is not a time for nepotism, to consider whether somebody's nephew could be found a certain post; you must have the man who can best do the work, because it is above all else important to everyone that the work should be well done.

The work of occultism is of that nature: it has to be done, and Those who direct it will employ the best man. Years of service to Them do not constitute any claim to office or to attention from the Master. It is the Master's duty to take the man who can do the work, whether he be one who has just come to Him or one who has been serving Him for many years.

Anyone who puts the work first cannot but rejoice at seeing another do it better than he himself could. Long ago Ruskin said of a certain piece of work: "Be it mine or yours or whose else it may, this also is well; it is well done." You should not hesitate to say that it is well done even though you did it yourself; you should not fail to recognize the better work of another, because it does not matter who did it. There are wonderful passages in Ruskin; he knew, so far as I am aware, nothing of occultism, nor did I when I knew him, yet there is very much in his writing which bears the true stamp of occultism.

> You must trust yourself. You say you know yourself too well? If you feel so, you do *not* know yourself; you only know the weak outer husk, which has fallen often into the mire. But *you*—the real you—you are a spark of God's own fire, and God, who is Almighty, is in you, and because of that there is nothing that you cannot do if you will. Say to yourself: "What man has done, man can do. I am a man, yet also God in man; I can do this thing, and I will." For your will must be like tempered steel, if you would tread the Path.

A.B.—When the various instructions that we have been considering are placed before some people, and they are advised to cease their old foolishness or wrongdoing, they sometimes say: "I cannot help it; it is my nature." Many people try to shelter under that excuse. But you are not really in earnest if you say that, and you must be earnest; you cannot afford to play with things that are so serious. You can do anything you set yourself to do, though perhaps not at once.

Of course, if you say, "I cannot help it", you cannot; for you paralyze yourself by the thought. It is a fatal fault; it prevents all progress, and leaves you where you are for months and years. It is as though a man tied his legs with a rope, and then said, "I cannot walk." Certainly he cannot, as he has been at pains to tie himself up; let him undo the rope if he does not wish to sit where he is, and then he will be able to walk well enough. You *can* do things! Get rid of the false idea that you allow to incapacitate you. Make up your mind that you can, and that you will; then you will be astonished at the rapidity of your progress. If you will not do this, you are not in earnest, or at least you are not in earnest in the way in which the Master wants you to be; you are merely playing at being in earnest. I do not say that you are not trying, but it is trying in a way that does not count for much.

See what I mean by applying it to worldly things, to the business by means of which you feed wife and children. You know quite well that if a thing stood in your way there, you would at once make up your mind to remove it, and would exert yourself to the utmost to do so. You would not sit down and say, "I cannot help it." Use some of that seriousness here. You have much of it for all the things which are not serious. It seems as if the one thing which matters is that in which earnestness is the most lacking.

It is of no use applying to the Master for help, if you make no effort to help yourselves. It is as though you held a cup which you carefully covered over with your hand, and prayed for water; when the water is poured down to you it flows over the covering hand and round the cup, and you are none the better for it. So long as a man is trying to do a thing with all his available strength, he is doing it in the occult manner. The results of his efforts may not show themselves in the outer world at once, but he is all the time gathering up his force which at last will pour out in successful action.

The things that you have to do have been done and can be done, but as long as you think that you cannot do them, you cannot. But if you say to yourself: "These things have to be done, and I will do them", then you can do them. Do that, and your thought will be a guardian angel, ever near you, enabling you to accomplish. Otherwise you have near you—as the Christian would put it—a devil, created by yourself with your own thought. You need not create such devils; make instead an angel, a great thought-form—"I *can* and I *will*."

C.W.L.—It is quite true that there is nothing a man cannot do, but it is not said that he can do it at once. That is where people sometimes make a mistake. I know this very well, because I receive scores of letters from people who are in some serious difficulty, fallen perhaps under the influence of drink or drugs or of some kind of obsession, and they often say, "We have no will left, it is all gone; we cannot overcome our difficulty; what can we do?" Those who have not met with any such cases have no idea how terrible the hold of such a thing is on the man, how entirely his will is sapped away and how he feels that he can do nothing at all.

Such people sometimes contemplate suicide. That would be fatal. Even if a man is maimed for life, he should take what opportunity he has to repair the harm, should gird up his loins and valiantly continue the struggle. Suicide would mean a return to conditions similar to those from which escape is sought, with the added bad karma of the act. Let the sufferer realize that the will is there, however much it may be hidden. If he had to create the will for himself, he might very well despair, but let him remember that the will is there; it is the will of God which shows forth in every man. It has yet to be unfolded and developed, but that can be done gradually. Sometimes the devotion of a relative or friend, endowed with great love and patience, proves a veritable godsend in such a case as this.

What has that man done to be in such a condition? Probably for the whole of this incarnation, perhaps for one or two previous lives, he has been deliberately yielding himself to the desire-elemental, to the temptations of the lower nature—deliberately letting it seize upon him. At first he could have struggled against it, but, since he did not check it, he has an accumulated momentum of the evil force—so much of it that he cannot all at once stem it. But he can begin to do so. We may use the example of a man pushing a railway truck or carriage. At a country station where they have plenty of time you will sometimes see a railway porter shunting a carriage from one line to another. See how he goes to work; there is a huge object weighing tons; he pushes against it steadily, and at first he makes no impression. Presently the thing begins slowly to move. He continues pushing, and it moves faster and faster. Then he goes to work to stop it. Now he cannot stop it all at once; if he stood in the way and refused to move, it would run over him and crush him; so he sets himself to oppose it steadily, giving way yet pressing all the time, until gradually he brings it to a standstill. He had put into it a certain amount of force; he cannot take it out again, but can neutralize it by a similar amount of energy.

The man who has yielded himself to the desire-elemental is in a similar position. He has put great force into the thing, and he must meet and face it. One may say: "But there is so much of it." Yes, but it is a limited amount. If only he could look at the matter not sentimentally, but abstractly, as a problem in mathematics, he would not say, "I am a degraded worm, and the force is too great for me", but would go to work and oppose it. He can be absolutely certain that he put into it only a limited amount of force. But now he has unlimited force at his disposal. Just because we are sparks of the Divine Fire we have all the power of God behind us. Only a very little can come through us at a given time, but it is coming all the while.

All this must be looked at from the point of view of the ego; he can do these things and he will. One can never do instantly anything that is worth doing in the work of occult development; just as it is not enough to have music in one's soul, but the ear and hands must be trained so that one can become a suitable channel for the power of the music. The ego has to train his vehicles patiently in a similar way.

People sometimes say: "If I cannot overcome this bad habit now, let me wait till I get another body." Such a person forgets that his next body will have the character and qualities of the present one, if he does nothing to change them, and the hopeless conditions will continue in the next life. But if he makes a determined fight against them now, even though they dominate him to the very end of his life, he will begin with a very much better body next time. It is the same way at higher levels. A man may so injure his mental body by debauchery that in this life it never can come back to its pristine condition. Nevertheless, if he makes a determined attempt against the evil he will get a good mental body next time, instead of having one which reproduces his present defects. In this, as in other cases, the chief struggle is at the beginning; confidence grows and becomes strong a little later on.

Just as many people want to introduce sentiment into their relations with the Master, so some people also want to obtain exemption from the working of the laws of nature; they want to be suddenly taken out of all their sin and sorrow. The emotional type of Christian says: "You will be saved by the blood of Jesus here and now. You will be taken right out of your trouble and be as though it never had been." That is in some ways attractive, but it is not true. What is true is that when you turn round and go the right way along with the divine Will, you at once become free from all the troubles and difficulties *within you* which have arisen from fighting against that; but it does not follow that the outer consequences of what you have already done will be wiped out. You have made the change; you are a converted man and you are going in the right way now, but you have still to deal with the results of having gone the wrong way.

You may change your attitude in one moment; and of course you are forgiven—there is nothing standing against you spiritually; you are absolved. But even an orthodox priest will tell you at once: "I do not profess to put right all the results of the wrong you have done. If you have lived a life of debauchery, if you have undermined your constitution, I cannot put that right—these results will remain and it will be part of your penance to try to undo them. What I can put right is the guilt—to use the ecclesiastical term. You have set yourself at odds with God; I can put you straight again. There my absolution will do something for you; it is the power of the higher will and not the lower. It will take you when once you want to be taken; it will help to keep you in the right line; but the physical results cannot be undone. You yourself can change your attitude; the priest can put you right on the higher planes where you lack the power. I do not say that a person could not do this for himself, but he would do it with great effort, clumsily, unscientifically. That is the power that lies behind the absolution; but it cannot take from a man the results of his sin—the laws of nature do not work that way.

There is another consideration to be added to what has been said: Until a person has developed his will and taken hold of himself he cannot really offer himself to the Master. People say, "I give myself entirely to the Master," but is it not obvious that one has not the entire self to give when part of it is in possession of evil qualities of various sorts? For this reason also we must develop the will. The Master said that that will must be like tempered steel. I remember the occasion very well because Alcyone did not understand what was meant by tempered steel, and a little materialization was necessary, to show him. It must be not simply a will of iron, but of tempered steel, a will that cannot be turned aside. The will is there; the divine power is in us; we have but to unfold it and so become masters of ourselves, and then we may make the glorious offering of that will at the feet of the Master.

PART V

LOVE

CHAPTER 1

LIBERATION, NIRVĀNA AND MOKSHA

Of all the Qualifications, Love is the most important, for if it is strong enough in a man, it forces him to acquire all the rest, and all the rest without it would never be sufficient. Often it is translated as an intense desire for liberation from the round of births and deaths, and for union with God. But to put it in that way sounds selfish, and gives only part of the meaning.

C.W.L.—We have said that in this book there are several departures from the ordinary translation of these qualifications. Of all those departures this one is the most daring—the presentation of *mumukshatva* as Love. The word is composed from the root *much*, " to release or set free ". In the desiderative stem the root is reduplicated, and other changes occur, to form *mumuksh*, " to desire release ". *Mumuksha* is the noun form, meaning " desire for release ", and *mumukshatwa* means " the state of desire for release ". The termination *twa* has somewhat the meaning of our *ness*, as in " eagerness ". From the same root comes also the word *moksha*, " deliverance ", " release ", or " liberation ".

The question has often been asked whether *moksha* is the same as nirvāna. The words mean different things, but they may be taken as attributes of the same state of being—or rather state beyond what we know as being. Nirvāna comes from the root *va* with the prefix *nis*, "to blow" or "to blow out", so it is translated "the blowing out". Moksha is release from the cycle of births and deaths, and nirvāna is the blowing out of that part of man which binds him to that cycle—which means all that men can usually think of as man. Some Hindus think of *moksha* as a negative condition, and work to destroy all personal desires and human interests, so that neither things nor persons can attract them back to rebirth, and so they win freedom from the wheel of births and deaths for long periods of time, but the conception of most of them is of an indescribable state of happiness, beyond the illusion of separateness, called *kaivalya*, independence, absolute oneness. Some Buddhists think of nirvāna as a complete blotting out of man, but others think of it as the attainment of wisdom and bliss that blots out all previous conceptions of self and experience, because it is superinenarrable. So we see that even in the same religion men hold different views.

We Theosophists sometimes apply the term nirvāna to the state of consciousness on the ātmic or spiritual plane, but we also speak of nirvāna as the condition of those supermen, or Adepts, who have taken the Fifth Initiation, who choose among the seven paths open to them that which resembles the true Buddhist nirvāna—not the "blowing-out" of the Southern Church of

Buddhism, but the indescribable rest and bliss of the Northern Church.

It is the Arhat, he who has passed the Fourth Initiation, who can raise his consciousness to the nirvānic plane, and there experience the flood of life that I have tried to describe in *The Inner Life* and *The Masters and the Path.* That consciousness is so much wider than anything that we know down here that one hesitates to call it his consciousness at all. He has become one with a very much greater consciousness; he has lost the sense of being separate. All efforts fail to put these ideas into words because we have not words to express them.

It is very difficult to get the right shades of meaning in translating Sanskrit books, but he who has had a touch of the nirvānic consciousness will best know what the old writers, who had themselves experienced it, meant by nirvāna; the mere lexicographer cannot be expected to give exact meanings to words of that kind. Suppose that a man who knew nothing about the Christian religion tried to understand such a word as "grace". If he looked it up in the dictionary he would become entangled with words like "graceful" and "gracious" and get quite another meaning. That is so also with "dispensation", in ecclesiastical language; it is quite a different thing from what it is in ordinary life. Every religion has a number of terms which in process of time come to have their special religious meaning, and unless one has been brought up in that faith, approaching it from the inside, it is not easy to realize the exact shade of thought. In the beginning of the Theosophical movement none of us knew Sanskrit. Madame Blavatsky understood something of the religions of India, but she did not know Pāli or Sanskrit. Her method was to describe as well as she could what she herself saw, and then say to any Indian friend who might be present, "What do you call that in your system?" He often did not fully understand her meaning, but he gave her the nearest term he could. The next time she wanted a word she would ask another man, but she never paid any attention to the fact that the first man might be a Hindu and the second a Buddhist—or that the various Hindus might belong to different schools of philosophy.

In addition to this, Madame Blavatsky was not in the position of a teacher of science, who is expounding a theory which he is illustrating with suitable experiments, brought forward as proofs as he goes along. She was not working with a plan or skeleton, into which one would try to fit every new piece of knowledge. She would make several statements which did not agree as far as words were concerned, and if asked for explanations would say, "Never mind the contradictions. Go and think over the statements." Her ideas were wonderfully clear, and her knowledge definite.

Hers was the opposite method of working to that of our day, when words are first defined very carefully and given fixed meanings. Often, it is to be feared, the result of that is that science and philosophy become a kind of game, like chess, where the moves that a piece can make are strictly prescribed. With her, words were living things—thought-forms on the physical plane, as it were—used as a means to awaken in the hearer's mind the knowledge already existing in her own.

If we wish to understand all the complicated relationship between the ego and the personality, we must first of all have a clear idea in our mind of what these things respectively are. This matter has been dealt with at great length in Theosophical literature both in the earlier days of the Society's teaching and also quite recently. I have said something about it in *The Masters and the Path.* Putting it very briefly and crudely, let it be understood that we can think of man as existing in the three divisions which S. Paul used long ago—body, soul and spirit. The corresponding Theosophical terms would be the personality, the individuality and the Monad. The Monad is definitely divine—a spark of the eternal flame—to all intents and purposes a part of God Himself. It is of course true in the highest sense that everything is a part of God—that there is nothing which is not He; and that is true of matter as well as of spirit. Nevertheless there is a very special sense in which the Monad may be thought of as a fragment of the Deity coming down into manifestation. I know quite well that is unphilosophical, unscientific, inaccurate to speak of a fragment of that which is indivisible; but there are no words to express the conditions of higher planes, so that whatever we say must be utterly inadequate and therefore to some extent misleading. Some writers who have tried to express these relations have spoken of the Monad as a reflection of the Logos, the ego in turn as a reflection of the Monad, and the personality as representing the ego in a similar way. There *is a sense in which that expression has its advantages, and yet it seems to me to give somewhat less of the true relation than this other suggestion—that the Monad may* be considered as a fragment of the Deity, the ego a fragment of the Monad, and the personality in its turn a fragment of the ego.

As part of the eternal unfoldment it has pleased the Logos of our system to project from Himself a vast host of these Monads. If we may use the simile with all reverence, they are thrown forth from Him as sparks in order that after their passage through various material planes they may return to Him as great and glorious suns, each capable of giving life and light to a magnificent system, through which and by means of which millions of other Monads may in turn develop.

The stupendous height from which this divine manifestation which we call a Monad originally comes cannot be measured in terms of any planes of which we know anything; but the lowest point which the Monad appears able to reach in his outrush is that which for that very reason we call the Monadic plane. It will be remembered that according to our great President's nomenclature the highest of the seven planes about which we are taught is called the divine, the second (coming downwards) being the monadic, the third the spiritual, and the fourth the intuitional. A still further descent into matter is necessary that the purposes of the Logos may be achieved. The Monad as a whole appears to be incapable of further descent, but it can and does put forth what we must call a part or fragment of himself which is capable of descending to the upper part of the mental plane. On the way down this fragment so put forth manifests itself on the spiritual or nirvānic plane as the triple ātmā. Of that triple spirit the first manifestation remains on that plane, while the second descends to the intuitional plane and clothes itself in buddhic matter. The third aspect or manifestation descends one plane more and resides in the higher part of the mental plane, where we call it the higher manas. Thus the ego (which is the name given to this fragment put down by the Monad) consists of ātma, buddhi and manas, which we represent somewhat inadequately in English by the terms spiritual will, intuitional wisdom and active intelligence.

The ego in his turn puts down a minute fragment of himself through the lower mental and the astral planes and eventually manifests himself in a physical body. Each of these successive descents is a quite indescribable limitation, so that the man whom we meet down here on the physical plane is at the best a fragment of a fragment, and as an expression of the real man is so inadequate as to furnish us with nothing even remotely resembling a conception of what that man will be at the end of his evolution.

The egos with whom we have to do in daily life are at different stages of this incredibly prolonged evolution. In all cases the ego exists primarily on his own plane, which as we have said is the higher part of our mental plane. At that level quite apart from his manifestation as a personality, he may be already wide awake, conscious of his surroundings and living an active life; or on the other hand he may be somnolent, almost entirely unconscious of his surroundings and therefore capable of experiencing anything like an active life only through his personality on much lower levels. As man raises his consciousness through the various planes he finds the vibrations on each one far more rapid than on that next below it. When we speak of the ego as developed on his own plane we mean that he is able fully to respond to all the vibrations of that plane; if he is not so conscious then these very rapid vibrations pass over him without affecting him, and in order to attain consciousness he must put himself down lower and draw round himself a vehicle of the matter of a grosser plane to whose vibrations he can already respond. By much practice in that lower plane he will gradually grow to be able to respond to its higher vibrations and then very slowly and by degrees to the vibrations of the plane next above it; so that the consciousness has to work its way up level by level.

His consciousness therefore in the personality should be reaching upwards all the while towards the ego; and when the consciousness of the ego is by this means fully developed, he in his turn will begin to reach upwards towards the Monad. The whole course of the movement downwards into matter is called in India the *pravritti marga* or the path of outgoing. When the lowest point necessary has been reached the man enters upon the *nivritti marga* or the path of return. He returns from his day's work of harvesting, bearing his sheaves with him in the shape of the fully awakened consciousness which enables him to be far more useful on those higher levels than he could have been before his descent into matter. On this path there is always the temptation for that lower part of the ego to forget its connection with the higher, and to identify itself entirely with the lower manifestation which is so much more vivid to it, and in that way to cut itself off from the higher and as it were to set up in business in the lower world on its own account. Presumably the ego himself as part of the Monad is liable to a similar temptation on his very much higher plane; but we are for the moment dealing with the relations between the ego and his personality; and furthermore we are viewing it from the point of view of the personality looking up towards the ego and trying to become one with him.

The ego has associated himself with the personality because he has a hunger, or thirst, for vivid experience. He is undeveloped on his own plane, unable to respond to the high vibrations of that region; the slower vibrations of the lower planes mean more to him, so he comes back again and again for them. As he develops, the hunger abates little by little, and sometimes when he is advanced and has become sensitive to the delights and activities of his own plane, he goes to the other extreme of neglecting his personality—caught as it is in the grip of karma, sunk in conditions which are now full of sorrow or of boredom for him because he feels he has outgrown them.

This diminution of his thirst for the lower planes has taken place as he developed his personality. When he gained full consciousness on the astral plane the physical life began to appear dull by comparison; reaching the lower mental world he found the astral dark and dismal; and all three of the lower levels lost their attraction when he began to be able to enjoy the still more vivid and luminous life of the causal body. Many people have reached the point of evolution at which they can travel about and do useful work on the astral plane during sleep. All students of occultism have their astral bodies well developed and ready for use, though many of them have not yet acquired the habit of using them. The lowest part of the mental vehicle is also in order, and is ready to come into activity; regular meditation develops this and brings it under control. At this stage the man may be taught to use that body, and he can then leave his astral with the physical vehicle during sleep. When this has been accomplished, the process is repeated at the causal level, and the ego is then awake and active on his own plane.

All the lower vehicles are temporary vestures which we put on in order to learn how to use the forces of their planes, and when we have done that completely, and the ego is working perfectly in his causal body, which happens at the Fourth Initiation, there is no need to incarnate again at those levels. Having triumphed over them, a man can at any moment materialize a temporary astral and mental body, show himself on those planes and do what he wants to do. One who has reached this stage need no longer go through the wearisome round of birth and death, which is so unpleasant. Perhaps we do not always think of it as so unpleasant, because we do get a little enjoyment out of life; true, but if we could look at it from the standpoint of the ego we should realize what an unspeakable bore it is to the eternal spirit to be down here "cribb'd, cabin'd and confin'd" in a body that cannot do this and will not do that. While we are in it we make the best of it, but it is only a temporary vehicle put on for the purpose of learning, and when we have learned the lesson we are very glad to get rid of the whole thing.

The man who has had some experience of the causal levels sometimes feels very deeply the oppressive limitations of the three lower worlds. He misses all the glorious freedom and love and truth of the ego's own regions. He realizes the cause of his descent into this state of darkness, and may then say to himself: "I will rid myself of this desire, which is the primary cause bringing me down into incarnation, and I will balance my karma by acting without attachment." The man who can say this is already a developed man, who has thought a good deal about these things; he is a metaphysician and a philosopher. He says deliberately: "I will shut off this desire; I will balance the karma accurately, and then there will be nothing to bring me back." That can be done. When he succeeds—and there have been many in India, all though its history, who have succeeded in doing it—the man escapes from this round of births and deaths. He lives in the heaven-world, or perhaps he may reach the causal level; but he does not, as a rule, rise any higher than that. He has attained what he would call *moksha.*

The man who can do that must be a man who has raised himself above all lower passions and desires, otherwise the thing would be impossible, but all the same he has forgotten one side of evolution. He has understood the action of the law of karma perfectly, and therefore he has been able to release himself from it. But he has not learned perfectly the law of evolution and he has not freed himself from that. He is like a clever boy at school, who might get far ahead of his companions and take several examinations in advance, and then do nothing for three or four years while the others were coming up to his level. That is precisely what happens to the man who attains *moksha*; he has not attained the goal which is set for humanity, because the evolution of humanity ends in Adeptship.

Now, an Adept is not only a man, free from birth and death, but he is also a living power; he has become one with the Monad, who is, in turn, a spark of the Deity. But the method of the Deity is to put Himself down, to pour Himself out in utter self-sacrifice into this whole plan. Therefore the man who becomes one with the Deity must be also filled with this spirit of self-sacrifice. The Adept does more good works than the greatest philanthrophist could possibly do, and is doing them all the time on higher planes, but He does them on behalf of the humanity of which He is a part. Therefore the karma resulting from them comes to humanity and not to Him, so there is nothing to bind Him to rebirth; but the whole of humanity gets a little uplift. It is not a great uplift; that amount of karma spread all over the world is not a very large amount for anyone, but it does mean a steady uplift for all. Therefore, in a sense, everyone gets just a little more than he may appear exactly to deserve. There is no injustice in this, however, because like the rain that falls on the just and the unjust, it is the same for everyone.

Therefore, after the lapse of thousands or even millions of years the man who has attained *moksha* finds that the tide of evolution has risen to his level and laps round him once more, and he has to come back and be reborn, and proceed with his development. He who seeks *moksha* generally knows that his liberation is not for ever, but he thinks that he will be called back in a remote future, and the world will probably be better by the time he has to return. He says: "I can afford to risk that; I shall gain thousands of years of freedom and be all that time in the heaven-world enjoying myself."

Our ideal is perfect consciousness on the highest level we can reach. We do not propose to rest satisfied at any level whatever. But on the other hand, we decline to give up our consciousness and go into trance, as some people do for the purpose of reaching a level beyond the scope of their waking consciousness. People talk sometimes about "passing into *samādhi*", and some who are fond of the rolling Sanskrit, talk of going into *samādhi* when they meditate. We were in much confusion as to the meaning of this word, until we realized that it was a relative term. *Samādhi* for anyone is the point which is just beyond that at which it is possible for him to retain his clear consciousness. If one is conscious on the astral and not on the mental, then for him *samādhi* would be the next level—the mental. It is to get just beyond the point where one can be conscious, to pass into a sort of trance from which one emerges with all sorts of glorified and beautiful feeling, but not generally with clear consciousness. People should not go into *samādhi* when they meditate; they should retain their consciousness, so that when they come back they can remember what they have seen. I know that many have passed into *samādhi* and have experienced a great feeling of happiness and beatitude. That, however, does not mean progress, because they lose hold and do not know clearly what they have been doing. There is always a certain danger in that—one does not know that he will be able to return.

Dr. Besant and I were once watching some tremendous outpourings of life from the higher planes, great waves that came pulsating forth from the Solar Deity. She said: "Let us throw ourselves into that wave, and see where it takes us." We should have plunged in had her Master not intervened, and told us not to do it. Afterwards Dr. Besant asked Him, "if we had thrown ourselves into that wave, where should we have found ourselves?" He said, "You might have washed up in a million years or so somewhere on Sirius or some other solar system." Manifestly it is not wise to throw ourselves into outpourings of that sort, when we do not know exactly what is happening. It is not a good plan to lose consciousness; it is much better to try to keep control of our vehicles and see a little bit where we are going—otherwise we may lose the physical body and end our temporary usefulness. Our method is to keep full consciousness on any plane that we can reach, and try to be of use on that plane. Our Masters never speak of mere passive contemplation. Our aim is not to sit down and enjoy ourselves anywhere, but to be active in the Master's work at all times.

This paraphrase that the Master has given of the fourth qualification, Love, is eminently characteristic of Him. He goes behind the word itself to the reason for it. He says: "What is your reason for wanting liberation? In order that you may be free to help better, you are trying to make yourself one with God. What is this God? God is Love. You must develop Love if you want to be one with Him. Therefore this qualification is in reality Love." Readers of *Man: Whence, How and Whither* will remember how it explains that different bodies of people came over from the other chains to this, and how certain of those groups of people were spoken of as boat-loads of servers. Practically all members of the Theosophical Society belong to one of those groups; so this idea of service is a very strong factor in our dispositions. We know how hard it is to get away from anything with which we are born.

Our nationality, for example, carries with it many little points of view, very difficult to avoid. That is the nationality of the personality; but this idea of service we may call the nationality of the ego, or perhaps of the Monad. He was born with that streak in him, and it has been cultivated ever since.

It is difficult for us to understand that there are other types which are just as good as this one under consideration. The solar Deity manifests Himself through three aspects: will, wisdom and love. That is the way they are given in this book. Men appoach Him along all these three lines. Each man's own way is the best for him, but he should remember that the other man's path is better for him and that, in the long run, they all merge. We must acquire the ability to look out simultaneously through all the aspects and know that in truth they are all one. We are told, in the Athanasian Creed, *that we must hold this doctrine of the Trinity* neither confounding the Persons nor dividing the Substance; we must learn that through all eternity there is only one God, although His manifestations are through Three Persons.

It was said in the beginning that if love is strong enough in a man it forces him to acquire all the other qualities. It makes people act, according to their power. Take one of the very best and most beautiful examples: mother love. Let us see how that operates among a savage race. The mother savage does not know much, but at least she is prepared to defend her child, and even if necessary to sacrifice her own life for him. The civilized mother among ourselves would do just the same thing in the same circumstances. Now and again you hear of a mother losing her life in saving her baby from a burning house, or more often as a result of attending to it when it has some infectious disease. In ordinary life among us that strong love makes the mother think. Her love for the child induces her to study hygiene, all about food and things of that sort. So love leads to both mental and physical activity.

A man must have this love, which is an intense desire for service, if he would reach the Master. S. John said: "We know that we have passed from death unto life because we love the brethren. He that loveth not his brother abideth in death,"[1] and: "He that loveth not knoweth not God."[2] All that is perfectly true. It is a very good thing to know the technical terms of Theosophy, and to understand its philosophy and science, and to be able to distinguish and employ the two thousand four hundred and one types of elemental essence is very useful for practical purposes—but love makes the true Theosophist.

I remember well, long ago, when Babu Mohini Mohun Chatterji, who was a disciple, came to London to instruct us, he told us for the first time about these qualifications, which were not expounded in Mr. Sinnett's books, or in *Isis Unveiled*, which were almost the only books we had. He told us quite plainly that without this fourth qualification, this intense desire for liberation

[1] I John, 3, 14.

[2] *Ibid.*, 4, 8.

(that is the way he put it), for union with God, the six points of good conduct "watered but the desert"; they would be really arid and all but valueless to us unless we had this intense desire to be one with God and to do as He does. We did not then realize that it meant service so fully as we do now, though the Masters had emphasized from the beginning Their love for "the teeming millions of humanity, the lowly and the despised". We were mainly occupied in trying to learn Theosophy. All was so new, so interesting, so exciting, that our time was mainly given to that—much more, perhaps, than it ought to have been, were it not that one must learn something before one can be of real service to others.

> It is not so much desire as *will*, resolve, determination.

C.W.L.—Will is pre-eminently the quality of the first ray, on which the Master Morya stands. The Master Kūthūmi is on the second ray, that of wisdom and love; but here He spoke as a first ray man would do. I remember one occasion on which Alcyone mentioned his desire to attain a certain quality. The Master said: "Do not desire a thing; desire is feeble. Will, because you are God. If you want to acquire a quality, will to do so, and go and do it." That emphatically is the standpoint of the Hierarchy. It is very important indeed for us to understand the Master's attitude and way of looking at things, which have brought Him where He is now, and can do the same for us.

To produce its results, this resolve must fill your whole nature, so as to leave no room for any other feeling. It is indeed the will to be one with God, not in order that you may escape from weariness and suffering, but in order that because of your deep love for Him you may act with Him and as He does. Because He is Love, you, if you would become one with Him, must be filled with perfect unselfishness and love also.

C.W.L.—The pupil of the Master has only one desire and that is to serve. For this, he is willing to give up all personal pleasure and ambition, and remain but a small wheel in the great machine. The ordinary man has not yet begun to think very seriously of anything higher. He takes life very much as he finds it, and his desire is not to get out of this kind of life into something higher and nobler, but rather to succeed in it. If you suggested that he should give up all that we call the lower self, he would ask: "But what will be left of me if I do that?" It is true that there would in such a case not be very much left, as far as he could see, although the whole of the reality would, in truth, remain.

It is difficult to explain to such a man what we mean by "becoming merged into the Divine Life". I knew a very good and clever man, who was making a considerable study of Northern Buddhism. He came to me one day and said: "I can't make anything out of this; it does not seem to me worth following up. It is quite interesting as a study in archæology, but the only object they put before you seems to be to become one with the Buddha. I can't see that that would be of any value to Buddha, and it would certainly be the end of me." That is the point of view the average man takes of these things. Yet there is a real, glowing, burning meaning to it all; if one can get hold of that it will revolutionize his whole conception. This widening of the consciousness does not take away any freedom, nor destroy individuality in the least degree. It is not that I am absorbed in the universe, but the universe becomes I. People say, "That Self am I." That is a delusion as applied to the lower self, but when one realizes "I am God", then the sense that God is God is not an illusion at all, and the sense that what I thought was I is in reality an expression of Him is not an illusion. It is the idea that anything can exist outside That or can be separated from the one Self that is illusion.

In every-day life there are some things that will serve as an example of this inclusion of the smaller in the greater. You have a great mercantile house, and some young man joins it as a junior clerk. At first he regards the house as a task-master, and it is a great trouble to him to have to come at regular hours and do all his work. But after he has been there for some years and has been raised to a more responsible position, he begins to say, "We do this," and "We do that," and then he is beginning to identify his interest with that of the house. So he goes on, until he becomes a manager, and at last a partner. Then he speaks always for the house; and when he considers any of the business, it is "the firm" he has always in his mind. He is just as free and as capable of taking the initiative along any line as ever, yet he is now certain to use his will along the right lines. The firm has not coerced him into that attitude, but he has grown into it. That is only a small illustration, but it gives an idea of the way in which a man may identify himself with a greater power, yet his will may be as much his own as ever.

There will come a time when we shall have become the Path itself, when we shall never fail in any of the qualifications because they will have grown into us and become part of our very nature. We are close to the living God all the time, because He is in us and about us and with us always, yet it is for us to learn to realize that, to raise our consciousness step by step, employing all the means that come in our way, until we can really grasp that idea. We are to become one with God in His highest manifestations, in the internal manifestations, not in the merely material form. The very matter in our bodies, and around us also, is His outer garment —but it is not the garment, it is He with whom we wish to become one. When we become one with Him, He on His side recognizes that and uses us as living channels through which His force can be outpoured. We are channels for the divine force on these lower planes, but we are effective channels only when we have reached the point where we have no separate personality in opposition to Him. He works through such means always, and His ministers, the great occult Hierarchy, do likewise. No doubt They could work miracles by direct action on people, but it would unnecessarily use up a great amount of Their force, so They work through the means which They have arranged.

There is a large class of people who never try to understand the principles of life. They think that nature must bow to them, and they will not accept things in the way that is ordained. They are, in their way, like those investigators at spiritualistic séances, who want to prescribe the conditions under which manifestations should take place. It is a very absurd attitude of mind, because there is no line of investigation in the world in which you can prescribe what the laws of nature shall do. One has heard of savages to whom electrical phenomena were shown, who declared that they were due to trickery. The savage chief would say, "I see all this is connected by wires; you are doing it with those wires. Cut them away and then I shall believe you." The electrician smiles and says in reply: "You do not understand the law. The wires conduct the electricity; without them the force could not come through." Then the man says: "I have exposed your trickery." People do the same thing at spiritualistic séances. They will not take the way ordained, but want to strike out another way. There is a certain amount of individuality about the idea of compelling God to do things in one's own way which, I suppose, recommends itself to some types of minds, but it does not appeal to mine any more than the idea of telling God in prayer what to do. I always feel profoundly that He knows infinitely better than I do, and if by any utterly inexplicable chance He should change His intention on account of my asking Him, I know I should be infinitely worse off under that scheme than I should have been under His.

The idea that one should will to be one with God may not have occurred to many of us, but it is very familiar to our brothers in India. The Master uses that sort of phrase several times in this book when He speaks of God. In an earlier life He was a prominent Buddhist teacher named Nāgārjuna, and in that incarnation He made many great speeches and wrote much. In His books which have been preserved, He is very strongly opposed to any idea of personality in the Deity. He objects even to the use of that word or that name, and goes deeply into metaphysical questions connected with it. Indians, knowing all that philosophy of Nāgārjuna, have often said, " How curious it is that, in this little book, our Master, who has spoken so strongly against personality in the Deity, should now use that word God. The Lord Buddha also spoke very strongly against anything like personality in the Deity." The answer to that objection is this: In this book the Master is not going into the question of the Absolute; He is not speaking of *That*—the Supreme, the Eternal; He is speaking primarily to an Indian boy, about *Īshwara*—that is, the solar Logos, the solar Deity—and it is in that sense undoubtedly that our Master uses the word God here. As Nāgārjuna he was speaking to students many of whom knew the systems of Indian philosophy, and so he spoke strongly against any endeavour to degrade the conception of the Deity by making it personal in the way in which many of our Christian brothers now do.

Then He says that you must make yourself like Him. This brings up the question: what do we know of Him? We know that He manifests Himself through three Aspects. Some approach Him through one of these Aspects and some through another. Our way is the way of active love, because that is the way of our Masters. There are seven great rays of the divine life, and therefore seven types of men. One is the line of devotion, another that of will, another that of wisdom. Men seek God in various ways, but as our Masters are on the line of active love, all who wish to follow Them must use the powers of his own special type in active service for love of God and man. Take, for example, the case of devotion, of which there may be three types or kinds. One person casts himself down before the object of his adoration and just longs to become one with it. I suppose this type is found in our Western races only among some few monks and nuns, whose desire is simply to spend themselves in perpetual adoration of the Deity. That is a splendid thing, but for the moment, at any rate, the man is not thinking of others, but only of becoming one with the Deity. If you ask him about others he will say: "Let them do what I am doing." I knew a man in India whose one idea was just precisely that—to sit in adoration before the image of his Deity, and try to become one with Him. That is the goal he set before himself, and it is the future he will gain. He will spend the whole of his heaven-life, probably a very long one—thousands of years—in a sort of swoon of adoration. Such pure devotion means the development of his various vehicles, and certain advance for himself.

A second kind of devotion scarcely deserves the name —that lower devotion which demands a *quid pro quo* of the Deity, and says: "If you repay me so much in the way of riches and promotion and general assistance, I will give you so much devotion."

A third devotee will say: "I love that Great One, or that Teacher so much that because of that I must be doing something to help others to know Him and understand Him as I do. I must do good works in His name." This is a very noble and practical kind of devotion. Those of us who are on the devotional ray will not be purely devotional, but will have this variant of activity which will make us want to do something on account of our devotion. So also if any of us be on the line that wishes above all things to know, we shall also have the same characteristic in our nature. There are those who desire to become wise merely in order to know and understand. That is a very wonderful quality in a man, and there are many who make great progress in that way. But those among them who are servers will find in themselves the complex resultant: "I want knowledge, but I want it only that I can be really useful to others." Such a person would see very clearly the mistakes made by other people who, though they desire with all their hearts to serve, yet, because of foolishness, do more harm than good. "Let me have perfect knowledge, then I shall be able to serve really well," such a man would say.

We wish to become one with God, not merely that we may be one with Him, and may bask in all that glory and joy, but that we may act as He does, and as His great action was to pour Himself out in utmost self-sacrifice into matter, in order that we might come into being, therefore he who will be one with God must himself show forth the same spirit of utter forgetfulness of himself for the sake of the work which is to be done for the God who is all Love. That one sentence: "You, if you would become one with Him, must be filled with perfect unselfishness and love also," really epitomizes the whole Path. Will, wisdom, love—each one of these carried to perfection and employed in service brings in all the others, so it is really true that "love is the fulfilling of the law." [1]

[1] Romans, 13, 10.

CHAPTER 2

LOVE IN DAILY LIFE

In daily life this means two things; first, that you shall be careful to do no hurt to any living thing; second, that you shall always be watching for an opportunity to help.

C.W.L.—Those are two sides of the same thing—the passive that you shall do no hurt, and the active that you shall do good. People sometimes say that the Oriental religions are negative, that the idea of service which we import into them is in reality a Christian idea. That is not so. Though the modern Christian has relegated it to a back seat, it is true that in original Christianity service was expressed and emphasized very strongly. "But he that is greatest among you shall be your servant."[1] The same idea appears in the old religions also.

In Buddhism—which has always been spoken of as the most negative of religions—it certainly does give you directions as to the things you must avoid. But its five precepts are not more negative than the Jewish ten commandments. The Buddhist religion does not say "Thou

[1] S. Matthew, 23, 11.

shalt not", though it asks its people to promise to avoid certain things. The wording is: "I observe the precept to refrain from taking life, to refrain from taking that which does not belong to me, to refrain from saying that which is not true, to refrain from taking intoxicating drinks or stupefying drugs, to refrain from unlawful sexual intercourse." That is the form; it is not a command but a promise.

In the summary of the religion in one *sutta* or verse, given by the Buddha Himself, we see its positive aspect:

> "Cease to do evil;
> Learn to do well;
> Cleanse your own heart:
> That is the religion of the Buddha."

The same thing comes out clearly in the Noble Eightfold Path, in which you have: "Right views, right aims, right words, right behaviour, right mode of livelihood, right exertion, right mindfulness and right meditation." Most of this is very positive indeed.

In the *Bhagavad-Gītā*, which is practically the gospel for millions of Hindus, you find taught the most positive activity. There God is described as the great Actor, and it is said that he who will not follow His example, and work for the welfare of the world, lives in vain. Inaction, it says, may be really an action in a deadly sin. It warns people, as Madame Blavatsky used frequently to do, that sins of omission are as much to be feared as sins of commission. And as to the sannyāsī, the man who has renounced the material life, it says that he must constantly perform acts of charity, sacrifice and austerity. The great historical Scriptures of the Hindus are full of accounts of men who devoted themselves to the public weal, and teachers, many of them considered to be divine incarnations, who taught the service of our fellow-man.

Nowhere could public service be more emphasized than it has been in those religions, yet they have always had their contemplative sides, as had Christianity all through the middle ages. It is only in recent years that, in the intensity of our activity in the fifth sub-race of the fifth root race, we have become secretly inclined to despise the monk and the nun and to magnify the man of action, the great commander in war, the great ruler or statesman in peace. The whole idea of the contemplative orders is, however, a very beautiful one. The plan was that the active orders of the monk and the friar would preach to the people and perform acts of charity, while the contemplative orders would shut themselves up and devote themselves wholly to meditation and supplication. Translating it into other terms, that would mean the formulation of good and high thought, and the sending of it out with a definite view to the helping of people. It was their business to make a speciality of prayer and meditation and to do it for their brethren who, for various reasons, were unable to do it so well and so thoroughly for themselves. The theory in every religion was that they were a part of humanity supplying a need of humanity; they were not merely lazy monks retiring from active work. They were doing very much harder work, which the others could not do, in connection with higher planes, and doing it generally under circumstances of self-abnegation and asceticism which would appal the ordinary man.

That the life of the monk, however, when it was not so definitely ascetic, attracted many who wanted a comfortable, lazy existence, is also true. Such people escaped physical work, but did not substitute for it the work of the higher planes. Among the Buddhist monks there are some of this kind, who are looked down upon and called "rice monks"—men who are monks for the sake of the assured living, which, though it is not a very luxurious one, will never fail while anyone in the country has any food at all. The same was true, perhaps to a somewhat greater degree, of the monastic orders of the middle ages in Europe. There were people who joined them for the sake of power and influence and did not mind, in many cases, the lack of possessions. Though the individual monk had no possessions, the monastery as a body did acquire a very great deal, which was at the disposal of the individual to a large extent.

First, to do no hurt. Three sins there are which work more harm than all else in the world—gossip, cruelty, and superstition—because they are sins against love.

C.W.L.—When one hears of sins which work more harm than all others one is apt to think of murder and robbery and such crimes, and perhaps is surprised to find such comparatively ordinary things as gossip, cruelty and superstition at the head of the list. The Master is taking into account the quantity of these sins, and their far-reaching effect. Murder and robbery are universally recognized as serious sins, and consequently respectable people avoid them, unless you dignify them by the name of war. But gossip is universal; and if one thinks of the harm it does in any individual case, of the great amount of mental suffering which it may cause, of the depreciation of ideals which it often brings about, then multiplies that by the millions of cases which are going on all the time, one will very soon see that it does vastly more harm than the other. It is a terrible thing to destroy a person's ideal, to cheapen it and lower it, and make him feel that after all it is not so good or high or noble as he had thought. Sometimes there is talk of the destruction of idols as a good thing. The destruction of a person's idol may be the most serious injury one can do him. If he idealizes something which to us is low and mean, we may, perhaps, be able to lead him to some higher ideal, but it is a most evil and wicked thing to take away his ideal without leaving him something higher and better to take its place. It is not for us to point out the flaws or to try to belittle anyone under any circumstances.

Many of us know, probably by personal experience, what a wonderful amount of good Dr. Besant has done. Tens of thousands have seen the light through her lectures and writings, but still the gossip that has been circulated about her has prevented thousands of others from listening to her and reading her books. They say: "I have heard so-and-so about Mrs. Besant. Why should I read a book by a person of that sort?" There have been many in that way turned aside from what would have meant their salvation in this particular incarnation. Thousands of people also write to her and ask her advice about all sorts of difficulties in which they find themselves involved. Many people have been prevented from applying for such advice by the evil and utterly false reports that have been circulated about her.

I think I know no one who has been more frequently and more fully attacked than our great President. Long before she became a Theosophist she was before the public as a teacher of free-thought. She was assailed and vilified first of all because she republished what is called the Knowlton pamphlet, dealing with sex problems which ought to be faced and studied, and not prudishly hidden. This pamphlet had been written long before she was born, but its publication had been discontinued on account of a threat of prosecution. Our President took the matter up partly because she believed that the question should be ventilated and that the poor should be put in possession of the information which the pamphlet gave, but still more, I think, as a matter of protest against the suppression of facts and in vindication of free speech and free publication in regard to everything that concerned the public health and public good generally. Her reissue of the pamphlet was fully intended as a challenge to what she considered a bad law; she announced beforehand to the police her intention of selling this work and invited them to come at a certain hour and officially buy a copy. They accepted the invitation, came and formally purchased the incriminating document and then proceeded to prosecute her, but the case ended in *nolle prosequi*. Then she wrote a more carefully worded pamphlet on the subject. Her reward for that—at any rate on the physical plane—was to have her personal character attacked in the most abominable manner. Later she withdrew the pamphlet, having come to the conclusion that it did not present the best way of dealing with this social difficulty; but I am sure she has never regretted that she did her best to deal with the facts as she then understood them. Such unselfishness and courage are rare in this world.

A great deal of gossip was also started by jealous people against Madame Blavatsky. Wild and mad accusations were brought against her; these appeared instantly and obviously ridiculous to all of us who knew her personally, yet many people have been deterred by them from a careful examination of Theosophical truths. She died in 1891, yet to this day it is quite a common experience, if you mention the Theosophical Society, to be met by the remark: "Oh, yes, that was founded by Madame Blavatsky, who was exposed as a charlatan. We do not want to spend our time and energy considering the teaching of a fraud. It is not likely to contain the truth." In this way many have missed the Theosophical knowledge that might have changed their lives.

From these instances alone we see that immeasurable harm may be done by spiteful and foolish gossip. This form of selfishness also very much hurts the feelings of the person at whom it is aimed. That the person can be hurt shows a weakness in his character, but that does not excuse the gossip, or relieve him from the evil karma which he has made. Our President is quite impervious to gossip about her, though if she is abused for more than the usual time along one particular line she does sometimes say: "This is getting very monotonous; I wish they would find something else to discuss." I also have been much abused, but it has never cost me a night's sleep. Thus karma falls back from us. But the harm done to others by the gossip brings its karma to those who started it and passed it on. It is more difficult not to care what is said about somebody else, and I confess I still find it hard not to be angry when some one speaks ill of our President, for example, or when unworthy thoughts, which to us who know Them are nothing less than blasphemous, are directed to the Masters.

Gossip is not real criticism. Unfortunately the very word criticism has come to mean picking holes. It is derived from the Greek *krinein*, to judge, and should mean a judicial attitude, but now it does not. Justice is one of the manifestations of God; therefore to judge a man's words or actions without their context is wrong and leads to evil. I suppose there is not a scripture in the world, no matter how holy and beautiful, which could not be made ridiculous by taking some words away from their context and putting them by themselves. We are always doing that with the thoughts of other people. We find a man to be irritable; he speaks sharply, perhaps roughly, and we at once assume that this indicates his character. But we do not know the reason for his irritability. Possibly he has been sitting up all night with a sick child; somebody else may have jarred him or annoyed him intensely in some way and we get the reflex action of that, although he is not really annoyed with us. If he were a great Adept he would not be annoyed, but we are not all great Adepts yet, and so these things happen.

I first learnt this as a small child, from an old coachman. I was near him one day when a man approached and spoke to him very roughly. The old coachman answered without seeming to pay any attention to the gruff tone of the other. After the man had gone, I said, "Why, John, what have you done to make that man so angry with you?" "Oh, nothing, sir; he's not angry with me," the old servant replied. "I haven't annoyed him; but probably his wife or somebody else has." And he explained to me that when once a man got thoroughly upset he was likely to vent his feelings on anyone who came in his way.

The grip of unkind judgment on a man's mind and the tenacity and virulence of its poison would be unbelievable, did we not have thrust upon us constant evidence of it. A man gets a wrong idea, and his whole outlook is coloured by it. We have seen that even in regard to this book. When I first heard this teaching about gossip given to Alcyone, long before the book was published, I was much impressed by its importance, so I repeated it on several occasions. When the book was issued some people immediately pounced upon the fact that these statements had been made months before it was published, and said that therefore part of it must have been my work.

I have mentioned that there were two periods in the development of Alcyone's memory of astral plane experiences; one during which he could not remember perfectly, when I would repeat to him the special precept given to him by the Master as applying to the next day; the other, in which he could bring through the memory. I found that in Bombay the story was being circulated that the whole book had been repeated to him by me in that way. But, as a matter of fact, the book was written in the second period, when he was able to remember what the Master had said to him, and he wrote it down by himself. When people get a little twist like that they distort everything. I have suffered from all sorts of injustice and misconception in consequence of such distortion of facts. I do not mind in the least, but it shows me very clearly how easy it is for people to misunderstand when they start with a wrong idea. I have seen the most ludicrous mistakes made, in which every event that occurred was made to bolster up some idea for which there was no foundation in fact, but which was simply imagination from beginning to end.

One of the experiments we have to make in the course of our occult training is to identify ourselves with the consciousness of certain animals. It is merely a question of practice; a pupil is set to do that in order that he may be able to learn later how to do the same thing with other and higher forms of consciousness. We consider ourselves far superior to any kind of animal, and rightly, since we belong to a higher kingdom. It should therefore be perfectly simple for us to understand the mind of that animal, yet from the experience I have had I imagine almost everybody who pays any attention to animals must be misrepresenting their ideas and motives all the time. When you really find out what an animal is thinking, you discover that it has reasons for what it does which never occurred to you. Since we are unable to understand the animal, whose lines of thought are few and simple, we are even less likely to understand our fellow-men. We are nearer to the human being, of course, but I doubt whether any human being ever understands another human being at all. Strange as it may sound, we are all isolated; each stands by himself. There is another way in which it is true that we are a mighty brotherhood, yet as far as our minds are concerned, each lives in a tower of his own. The circumference of his mind touches that of another man's only at a point, and even there only doubtfully and uncertainly.

Against these three the man who would fill his heart with the love of God must watch ceaselessly.

C.W.L.—One would think it fairly easy to avoid the three evils mentioned. It is not, because they are so painfully common and so much a matter of habit that few people realize their existence. They are our special difficulties because of the place where we stand in evolution. We have been developing the lower mind which looks first for points of difference. Because of that people notice first the points which they do not like in anything which comes before them; then comment and criticism almost invariably follow. The man who is devoting his energies to picking holes and finding differences is behind the times—a hopeless anachronism. We ought now to be studying synthesis and trying to find the divine and good in everything, because we should be beginning to develop buddhi. We are trying to live for to-morrow, not for yesterday; therefore we must not let ourselves be swept away by this tide of ignorant obscurantism; but we have constantly to remind ourselves not to give way, otherwise the stream will so surround and press upon us that we shall occasionally slip back.

CHAPTER 3

GOSSIP

See what gossip does. It begins with evil thought, and that in itself is a crime. For in everyone and in everything there is good; in everyone and in everything there is evil. Either of these we can strengthen by thinking of it, and in this way we can help or hinder evolution; we can do the will of the Logos or we can resist Him. If you think of the evil in another, you are doing at the same time three wicked things.

C.W.L.—The Master speaks of evil thought as a crime. When we remember how exceedingly careful and balanced is the speech of the Master always, we realize that that against which He speaks so strongly must be evil indeed.

An attempt to understand the motives of another man, to follow his line of reasoning, is very likely to be incorrect; *therefore the least we can do is to give him the* benefit of the doubt. Most people are on the whole quite respectable and well-meaning, therefore we should give them the credit of good intentions. If we are wrong, our slightly higher thought about the person will act upon him and actually do him good. When you hear something to the disadvantage of another, ask yourself whether you would repeat that piece of gossip and send it on to be magnified if it were about your own son or brother? No, emphatically you would not. You would combat it in the first place, and in any case you would not circulate it. Why should you act differently with regard to somebody else's son or brother?

(1) You are filling your neighbourhood with evil thought instead of with good thought, and so you are adding to the sorrow of the world.

C.W.L.—The world is very much to us what we make it and as we take it. If a man is pessimistic, bent upon finding evil and darkness, looking for a chance to be offended or hurt, he can find it. There is evil in the world and much sorrow in these lower planes, as the Lord Buddha pointed out. We can magnify these things into serious difficulties, or we can approach the world optimistically, in a cheery spirit of determination to make the best of everything. In the latter case we shall find that there is a great deal that is bright, and shall also be making the world more cheerful for others by our outer life and our thought-power.

There are many people who have been practising regular meditation for many years. They must inevitably have learnt to think a little more definitely than those who have made no such attempt; their thoughts are therefore more powerful. If these people should think evil of others, it is very much worse in a great number of ways than if the ordinary person did it. First, because they know better, they are, as it is expressed in the Church, "sinning against light". Secondly, their thought produces definite and relatively permanent forms, which often have considerable influence in the astral and mental atmosphere. Use your power, therefore, to make the world brighter and happier. You have no idea how much that can be done, simply by putting away all sorrowful and selfish thought, and filling yourself with love that will radiate all around you.

> (2) If there is in that man the evil which you think, you are strengthening it and feeding it; and so you are making your brother worse instead of better. But generally the evil is not there, and you have only fancied it; and then your wicked thought tempts your brother to do wrong, for if he is not yet perfect you may make him that which you have thought him.

C.W.L.—The clairvoyant can see the thoughts of one person going to another and buzzing round him like a crowd of mosquitos. They cannot get in while the man is busy with some other matter, but when his thoughts for the moment slacken, when he is meditative or tired, or absent-minded for a moment, they take their opportunity. The thought-form then fastens on his aura like a burr, and by its vibrations gradually colours the part on which it has impinged, and from there its influence spreads. Thus it suggests the bad or good idea, and if there be something in him that is akin to it, as is usually the case, it sets that in motion.

A little impetus given to another might not matter so much sometimes, but in some cases it makes all the difference in the world. School boys running about often push one another; cases have been known in which a boy has quite unintentionally pushed another over the edge of a precipice. You never know when a man's thought may be on the verge of some wrong course of action, and one evil thought about him may just push him over. On the other hand, when a man is in that way balanced between the good and the evil, one strong, helpful, good thought may push him definitely on the good side and set him going on a career which may mean for him rapid development.

I have seen cases in which an evil thought about a man led to a course of evil action on his part the result of which would last for many lives; it was near the surface, but it had not materialized itself in action; there came an evil thought from some one else, which gave just the push which sent him over from thought into action, and committed him to a course of crime. Till you see that clairvoyantly you will scarcely be able to realize it; but see it once, and you will be careful forever, with a care born of horror. It gives you a new sense of responsibility, sometimes rather overwhelming. Remember how the poet Schiller wrote about clairvoyance, how he desired the welcome blindness of the senses again; "Take back your cruel gift; take back this dreadful gift," was what he said.

(3) You fill your own mind with evil thoughts instead of good; and so you hinder your own growth, and make yourself, for those who can see, an ugly and painful object instead of a beautiful and lovable one.

C.W.L.—Many people take much trouble about their physical personal appearance, and the grace and gentleness of their manners, not merely because they are anxious to appear at their best and to be thought well of, but also because it is recognized to be a duty to society in general. In ancient days it was understood to be every man's duty to make himself as perfect and as beautiful as possible in every way; in attire, appearance, speech and action, he was to learn the right, the graceful, the proper way to do everything. Not only one's personality but one's surroundings also were to be not merely useful but also beautiful. If a man built a house it was his duty to his neighbours to put up something that would be graceful and beautiful, though not necessarily costly; and his pottery, as well as his statues and pictures, was to be good. In these days many think only of building as cheaply as they can, regardless of the hideous effect produced. A man builds a great ugly house or factory, and everybody who is sensitive shrinks back from it at once, and all who look at it are the worse for doing so. The man who is responsible for the building actually makes bad karma. Some think such things do not matter, but they do. Our surroundings are of very great importance. True, the strong soul can conquer, but why should we not have things which would help us instead of those which hinder us? Everybody who builds a beautiful house deserves well of his fellow-citizens, because he has put up something the sight of which will benefit everyone who sees it. The touch of pleasure that you get when you see something beautiful is no light thing. I always feel that our gratitude is due to anybody who wears a beautiful colour, because of the effect that colour produces in this terribly grey civilization of ours.

All that is true of beauty physically is even more evident on other planes. The man who makes for himself a radiant and beautiful astral body, full of love and devotion, which he pours out on all around him, deserves the gratitude of his fellows. The audience on the astral plane is generally larger than that on the physical. If we allow ourselves to appear badly in the astral world, a far greater number of people are scandalized by our appearance or annoyed by it, than could possibly be the case on the physical plane. Not only do the inhabitants of the astral world see the beauty of it, but everyone, even those who do not see, feels it. These vibrations act upon them, and the people are helped thereby. The man who yields himself to ugly, selfish, evil thoughts is spreading unpleasantness about him, besides being a horribly disagreeable and unpleasant sight. In the physical plane people hide their loathsome diseases, but the astral leper carries his sores in full view.

Not content with having done all this harm to himself and to his victim, the gossip tries with all his might to make other men partners in his crime. Eagerly he tells his wicked tale to them, hoping that they will believe it; and then they join with him in pouring evil thought upon the poor sufferer. And this goes on day after day, and is done not by one man but by thousands. Do you begin to see how base, how terrible a sin this is? You must avoid it altogether. Never speak ill of any one; refuse to listen when any one else speaks ill of another, but gently say: "Perhaps this is not true, and even if it is, it is kinder not to speak of it."

C.W.L.—It requires a certain amount of courage to say this, but it should be done, in kindness to the gossip, as well as to the person who is being criticized. One may do it gently by using the first person plural: "Perhaps we had better not say any more about it." Then you have not appeared to assume superiority, which is both unoccult and irritating, and probably the man will agree with you, and let the matter drop.

CHAPTER 4

CRUELTY

Then as to cruelty. This is of two kinds, intentional and unintentional. Intentional cruelty is purposely to give pain to another living being; and that is the greatest of all sins—the work of a devil rather than a man. You would say that no man could do such a thing; but men have done it often, and are daily doing it now. The inquisitors did it; many religious people did it in the name of their religion.

C.W.L.—Cruelty is the work of a devil rather than a man; that is how it looks to a Master. Very often in daily life a man does or says something in order to cause pain to somebody else. He comes under that condemnation; he is doing a thing which is worthy of a devil rather than a man. It seems incredible, but people can be found who do it.

Horrible things have been done in the name of religion. Read the oldest literature we know, the Vedas, and we find evidence of them cropping out very strongly there. We find the Aryans pouring down into the plains of India and proceeding to put to the sword the people who were there. Nothing is too dreadful to be done to these people; they must be wiped off the face of the earth! Why? For one all-sufficient reason: because their rites are different! The Muhammadans swept over a large part of the world offering their Koran or the sword to the people they conquered. Christians have been no better. The same spirit led to the persecutions by the Inquisitors, the atrocious treatment of the South American Indians, and all the rest of such things. We think we are becoming more civilized now, yet even to-day religious feeling is very strong and bitter in some quarters. It is the fashion to say that even if the law permitted such persecutions as used to take place, our higher civilization would prevent us from ever resorting to the horrors of the past. I am not so sure of it. I know places in England where a person of unorthodox religious views is regarded as to be excluded from social functions, and to be suspected of all sorts of bad things. We do not put people on the rack, and wrench out their teeth, as our forefathers did. *Autres temps, autres moeurs!* I do not think I should like to see absolute power given into the hands of any of the dogmatic sects.

Vivisectors do it.

C.W.L.—There is no excuse for practising deliberate cruelty to animals. They are our younger brothers, and though not yet men, they will become so after a greater or lesser number of incarnations. The practice of animal experimentation involving cruelty is abhorrent, and can never really benefit mankind, because the law of karma cannot be changed, and as man sows so shall he also reap. I have heard Dr. Besant say that no lives ought to be saved by such methods as that. We know that the instinct of self-preservation is strongly implanted in every man and every animal, so that the body which has been acquired at the cost of considerable effort and trouble may give service to the life within as long as possible, and that therefore human life must be saved when it can rightly be done. But that end cannot justify all possible means. We rightly admire the men who face death rather than dishonour ; surely it is great dishonour to human beings to have their lives saved by anything obtained in such a diabolical manner as this. Our President said she would rather die than be saved in this way.

There is very varied opinion on this subject among members of the Theosophical Society, in which everyone is free to have his own beliefs, but the Master's opinion, as quoted above, is definite. Whatever may be our abhorrence of the cruelty of vivisection, however, we must make allowances for the fact that many doctors and others who support and practise it do so regretfully—not for the pleasure of cruelty (though the existence of such things in our midst does give an opportunity for that to some ghouls in human form), but because they think it the only way to save human bodies from suffering and death, and they sincerely believe that the end justifies the means in this case. However much, therefore, we may disagree with them, let us condemn the sin but not the sinner. There can be no question but that karma will bring great suffering to those who practise vivisection. Many who view them with indignation approaching hatred would change their feeling to pity did they realize this fact.

All vivisectionists are not cruel to the same degree. I know, for example a member of our own Society, who is one of the leading surgeons, who has performed vivisections of a certain kind. There are certain tubes in the human body which sometimes become severed. They are so fine that when one tries to join the severed ends again the inevitable scar always blocks the tube. It was for a time impossible to save people in this condition until it occurred to this doctor that if one made a larger incision it might be possible for the wound to heal and yet at the same time to keep the tube open. He did this by making an incision in the tube near the end of one piece and on the side of the other, and let them overlap and heal in that way. In order to see whether this would work, he tried it upon a number of dogs. He told me that he tried this experiment on about half a dozen stray dogs. They were thoroughly well fed and brought into perfect health before the operation, some anasthetic was then administered, and the dogs were nursed very carefully until they had recovered, and it was found that the operation had been successful. The result was that this which before had been thought impossible became a recognized possibility. The operation is now a common one all over the world, and is known by the name of the doctor who invented it. The principle was wrong, but there was practically no cruelty to the animals concerned, and they were much better off, instead of worse, for the time being. This experiment was thus quite different from what usually occurs, and I think it would be entirely inappropriate to attack this doctor in the way in which anti-vivisectionists constantly attack the mass of the vivisectors.

Some of the experiments that one reads about are atrociously cruel, such as that of seeing to what degree of temperature an animal can be baked before certain functions disappear, and dozens of other ghastly and obviously useless horrors. And there are thousands of others performed needlessly for the general instruction of students, and to try all kinds of effects, many of which are quite useless, because the human constitution differs from those of different animals in a variety of ways. For example, a goat, among its other miscellaneous food, will eat freely of henbane, with no apparent injury; but if a human being takes it he will pass on to the astral plane. Again, when an animal is in frightful pain and terror, that must change the fluids of its body and render any observations with regard to them of very uncertain value.

The proper substitute for all this cruelty is, of course, clairvoyance. It is very far better for the doctor if he can see into the interior economy of the living man while the body is whole, than it is to deduce certain things about it by cutting into the living body of an animal which differs from the man. Those who feel that they *must* do vivisection had better form a society in which they will agree to practise on one another; in that way they will have human subjects giving reactions likely to be useful when those of an animal are not, and they will avoid horrible cruelty to defenceless creatures, which in God's world they have no right to inflict. This is unnecessary, however, for a tenth part of the trouble, and study and research that is put into these experiments would produce an army of reliable clairvoyants; indeed, the attention that is given by the average student to his long training would generally be quite enough to develop his clairvoyance.

There is serious danger of another form of cruelty rising out of the great authority claimed by the orthodox medical fraternity. We do not want to become slaves to them, as our forefathers were slaves to the Church. Though they have done good in various ways, that gives no authority for the establishment of scientific "inquisitions" with power to penalize the heretic who does not wish to submit to their creed of the moment. True, it would be only the civil law that would punish, but that was also the case with the Church—those who would not believe and submit, it handed over to the civil authorities, with the hypocritical prayer that there should be no shedding of blood, which prevented those in power from cutting off their heads and made them burn their victims instead. There has been trouble with the enforcement of vaccination, and it is still compulsory in some countries; though it is an arguable question as to whether the remedy is not worse than the disease which it is professed to prevent. There are very frequent changes in medical opinion, yet each fad is frantically supported while it lasts. The interests of a community in power have often in history given rise to terrible oppression and widespread misery. Let us have no scientific "inquisitions".

There are some people who try to excuse any cruelty to animals on the old Jewish theory that they exist only for the sake of man. We know better than that. They exist for the Logos; they are stages of evolution permeated by His life. It is, however, justifiable for us to make use of animals, so long as we promote their evolution. They benefit by being in contact with man. It is true that we interfere with the wild horse when we capture him, but in other ways, especially mentally, he gains much development.

Some even extend the old Jewish idea to children. There are parents who think that children exist for them —to be used as servants, to be a source of pride, to provide for their old age, and so on. And that leads on to the inhuman notion that a child should be forced to become what we think he ought to be, regardless of the special interests and aptitudes that are his because of his past lives. This leads to superfine cruelty.

> **Many schoolmasters do it habitually. All these people try to excuse their brutality by saying that *it is the custom; but a crime does not cease to be* a crime because many commit it.**

C.W.L.—The beating of children is a widely spread custom, but that is no excuse for it. It is not, however, a universal custom; I am happy to say that there are a few countries which in that respect have attained civilization. I believe that Japan is one of them. I know from my own experience that Italy is another. I lived for some considerable time in one of the Italian cities, in a house which overlooked the grounds of a large school, and I watched with very great interest the relations between the masters and the boys. Because of their more excitable and freer natures they did not treat discipline as we do. The boys, would all be drawn up in line and at any moment one of them would suddenly leave the ranks and rush up to the master, seize upon his arm and say something to him in quite an impassioned way. The master would smile and pat his head, evidently granting his request or saying something about it. They were all on the most friendly terms. I noticed, too, that whenever those boys met their master in the street, they immediately sprang upon him and pulled him about, and were the very greatest of friends out of school hours also. That was a very good sign, because the man whom children love is always a good man at bottom—their instinct is infallible. In Italy anything like the cruelty that exists in most English schools could not happen, because the customs are different. To lay a hand upon a person is the one unforgivable sin in that country; it involves knives and duels and things of that sort. So the children are perfectly safe.

Punishment has long been a custom, but that does not prevent it from being both cruel and futile. First of all, it is not our business to administer chastisement.

The law of karma will attend to all that, and it cannot make mistakes, as we often do. Frightful legal injustice has been committed again and again ; the severest penalties have been imposed upon quite innocent people. The criminal has done more wrong to himself than to anybody else, and vengeance may be left to the course of nature.

Apart from that, punishment is applied to inspire fear —in the offender for the future, and in the possible offender at large. The idea of beating a child is the same as that of punishing a criminal by law; these things have in them the elements of revenge. They seem to say: "You do such-and-such a thing, and I will make it very uncomfortable for you." Often a teacher gets angry, and his feelings are the cause of the punishments he applies—not any reasoned judgment as to what is best for the child. I know it is said that punishment by law is intended to prevent people from committing crimes. But it does not act in that way. A hundred years ago the punishments of the English law were very severe. For example, a person would be hanged for stealing anything to the value of one shilling and sixpence. I remember having seen it recorded at the entrance to Newgate prison—and in other places there is the same sort of thing—that such-and-such a person was hanged for stealing a pair of gloves, valued at two or three shillings. When such severe punishment was meted out, the proportion of crime was much greater than it is now. The amount of crime has little to do with the punishments meted out ; it is chiefly a question of general education and civilization.

Punishment by the law or by the school generally has no relation to the crime committed. A man steals something; then he is shut up in a prison for a certain time. What is the relation between the two things? He might reasonably be made to do some work which should return the value of the article stolen, to the person from whom it was taken. The punishment should fit the crime in some way. Merely to shut a man up because he has stolen something is a kind of nightmare. So also among us a child does not learn a certain lesson and they beat him. What is the connection between the two things? There would be some reason in saying: "You have not learnt the lesson; you will be behind the others in your class, therefore you must stay and learn it when otherwise you would be playing." There is no sense in this kind of thing, and it is radically wrong. The idea of giving intentional pain is always wrong, and no amount of custom can make it right. All sorts of eminently undesirable and foolish things have been the custom—foot-binding in China, for example, and some of our own fashions at different times. We must not get the idea that because a thing is the custom, even if it has been so for hundreds of years, it must be a good or necessary thing, because very often it is not.

A community might reasonably say to some habitual criminals, as they did to such people in ancient Peru: "We are a civilized race. With great trouble we have arranged our State upon a certain scheme, and it is intended for people who will keep its laws. If you do not intend to keep these laws, go out and live with some one else." There, exile was the only punishment; and to be cast out among the barbarian tribes was the greatest disgrace, as well as a discomfort. Society has the right to restrain a dangerous person. When you get a Malay running amuk you must stop that man, even though it should be at the cost of having to take his life. But except in emergencies, when it is unavoidable, we have no right to kill; and no one ever has the right to torture —that is absolutely certain. Capital punishment, if it is revenge, means that we become as brutal as the criminal who has aroused what we euphemistically call our righteous indignation. If it has the purpose of saving us further trouble with that man it is wrong in principle, since the State has a duty to every citizen, not only to those who are normal, and also it should think of the real man, not merely of the body. To seek the easiest way out of our difficulty by killing the man is thus positively criminal; and it does no good because much evil passion is aroused, and the man will reincarnate in unpleasant kārmic relations with us in the future. The real criminal—who is rare, because most offenders are products of unfortunate environment—is really a pathological case. What he requires is not torment and brutalization, which accentuate his anti-social tendencies, but the right treatment and training that will bring him physically and emotionally within the ranks of normal citizenship. The State cares for the physically and mentally defective; it must deal in the same way with the criminal, who is generally either mentally or emotionally defective. This would be the attitude of love, the standpoint of the Master.

These ideals are real, and quite clear and practical. Both the criminal and the child must be helped by education, not driven by fear. The system of terrifying children produces exceedingly evil results. It introduces into their lives fear and pain and deceit, and is generally disastrous to character and good citizenship. It is another form of the old Church idea of hell; but the hell is to be here, and it can be escaped by one with sufficient cunning. People thought they could make others good by frightening them. It is odd how that idea still holds. One of our principal living novelists wrote to me some time ago and said that once at the seaside he met a young man and gave him some Theosophical ideas, in the course of which he explained to him that the hell theory was all nonsense. Later on this youth's mother, full of anger, paid the novelist a visit. She said: "That is the only way I have been able to keep this boy in order—by the fear of hell, by threatening him with it every day and all day long. Now that you have persuaded him that there is no hell, what am I going to do?" Perhaps if she had known a little better, and had explained things to him from the first there would have been no need to adopt this very unpleasant form of terrorism.

Liberty and love are great factors in the development of the human soul. There are many people who are quite willing to give liberty to others, if they will do exactly what they prescribe! But true liberty means the freedom to try in one's own way. In general there is far too much interference; too much direction from the outside diminishes the very life-activity that it seeks to protect or assist. This is seen in school life, where quantities of unnecessary rules are made, when individual freedom would give more opportunity for growth. That is one of the great differences between the English scheme of government and that of some of the other nations. England tries on the whole to leave its people as free as possible. Some countries try to avoid trouble and danger and to assist the people by all kinds of restraints. I remember an official of a foreign state saying to me once: "Well, sir, in a really well-managed country everything would be forbidden!" In travelling about the world I have been much struck by the different forms in which the regulations are expressed. In one country you will find a stern prohibition; in another, a request. Some obviously adopt the military plan, which is good only for very young souls; but others appeal to the good sense and goodwill in a man. I remember, for example, reading one sign, forbidding certain unpleasant practices, which ran: "Gentlemen will not, and others must not" do so-and-so. That was in America, which is one of the newer countries. I thought it was rather well put.

There are cases where you must assert compulsion in the interests of the community; but it is always better when possible to have the wills of the people with you than to drive them along. I am afraid that is only very slightly understood with regard to education.

Everything is prescribed; all the time it is: "Do this, do not do that." Even in teaching the child his interest is not usually engaged, but he is told: "This is a lesson and it must be learned."

In the newer methods, such as that of Mme. Montessori, the lesson is made interesting, so that the child mind opens like a flower. There is only one way in which you can really and usefully teach a child anything, and that is by making him love you to begin with. You exercise a certain amount of moral suasion afterwards, because you look injured and pained if he does wrong. That is quite legitimate, because you really do feel the pain. If you start ruling by love you call out the love of the pupil, and get something done. To teach children one must have a clever mind, a heart full of love, and patience as wide as the sea; one must understand the mistakes that children make, and be able to show them how to do things properly, but in their own way. If you start with force and brutality you call out nothing but hostility, and then you do not get anything worth while done.

It is the same in ordinary life. If one business man wants to deal profitably with another, he speaks pleasantly to him, and tries to convince him that the business he proposes will be to their mutual advantage. It would not occur to him to start out by trying to drive the other man; it would only antagonize him and make anything like friendly relations between them impossible. Boys and girls are human beings, too, and you can get more out of them if you have them on your side than if you set them against you to start with. These are matters of experience to those who try to teach. No teacher, however skilful, however learned, is worthy of that highly honourable name unless he can interest the children and get them to love him. It is an absolute prerequisite. That is the way in which the Masters teach: never by force, never by issuing commands, but by showing the right way and encouraging us to try to imitate Them.

> Karma takes no account of custom; and the karma of cruelty is the most terrible of all. In India at least there can be no excuse for such customs, for the duty of harmlessness is well-known to all.

C.W.L.—The man who takes up the profession of a school-master does so in order to earn his living, just as he might enter any other profession. The Lords of Karma do not, however, regard the matter from that point of view. They put a man into such a position with the idea of giving him a magnificent opportunity. If he should take it, and carry his work through carefully, tactfully, lovingly, it will lead him to another life in which he will probably be a religious teacher. From that the way is open to become a great saint, a great benefactor of mankind. The teaching profession lies straight in the road to some of the highest prizes of life, from the point of view of the Lords of Karma.

The teacher should realize that each child is an ego; and should give all the help possible to the development of its character. He naturally has a vast opportunity, because the children are in his care to learn, and he can make of them very much what he will. As to the strength of this innuence, a well-known Jesuit once said: "Let me have a child up to the age of eleven, and after that he can go where he pleases." The teacher's influence upon the young operates quite as much by what he is and the way in which he acts, as by anything directly said to them. He who is what he ought to be radiates love in a strong and powerful influence. His position is also one of great responsibility, for if instead of rousing love and good qualities in his charges he awakens fear and deceit, he is hampering the progress of those egos, and thus doing serious positive harm.

Misuse of such an opportunity involves a terrible fall for the man. Cruelty in such cases produces very horrible results; on certain occasions we have found it to bring a sort of repayment in kind, but quite often it brings insanity as its result, and short of that, a great many conditions such as hysteria and neurasthenia. In many cases also it has resulted in a remarkable and cataclysmic descent in the social scale. A person who has been cruel in a reasonably good position finds himself thrown down among the drugs of the populace because of that cruelty. For example, I have seen cases of Brāhmanas reborn as pariahs, in consequence of cruelty to children. So it is evident that the Lords of Karma, demonstrating the great laws of the universe, take the same view of these things as the Master does.

An opportunity somewhat similar to that of the schoolmaster is given to a man who is the manager of a factory or the head of a large business of any kind. A man thinks of such a place as one to be desired because it gives him an opportunity of getting a good salary or of making a good deal of money and obtaining a certain amount of power. But the Lords of Karma would regard that, again, as an opportunity to help all those other men who came under his control. An employer often regards his men with a sort of scarcely veiled hostility; he thinks they want to get as much out of him as they can and to take advantage of him in various ways. On their part, the men usually think he wishes to grind them down, to get all he can out of them, paying them as little as possible in return. It is true, unfortunately, that in some cases both sides are right in thinking as they do. There are employers who have that attitude; and there are very many workmen who take that line towards their employers: but the man who understands will look at it not in the least from that point of view. That the position gives the man an opportunity of being a helpful influence in the life of a number of people is the only aspect of the matter which concerns the Lords of Karma. The Lords of Karma do not usually look at things from our point of view. Mankind generally, for example, regards death as a terrible thing and a heavy punishment: but it is often given as a kind of reward—as a release leading to better and more promising conditions.

The fate of the cruel must fall also upon all who go out intentionally to kill God's creatures, and call it 'sport'.

C.W.L.—As regards conditions in the country in England Punch's satire, "It is a fine day; let us go out and kill something" was not very far wrong. As a clergyman in a country parish in England I was in close relation with a typical set of the people who shoot and hunt and fish. They did all these things as their regular daily occupation, and that formed also the principal subject of their conversation. Yet, however hard one may find it to believe, these people were perfectly gentle and kindly towards their fellow-men; the men were good fathers and husbands, lenient judges and kind friends, but they did not see the wrong in this particular thing. One of those very men, who would kill deer and shoot as many pheasants as he could in the most reckless way, would nevertheless sit up all night with a dog that was sick, showing that he had a kind heart, and that even towards the animals he felt a certain brotherhood. The cruelty is all due to a kind of mental blindness. They do not lack intellect, but on this matter they have never thought, but have taken it for granted that all these creatures were created for their use, and for the enjoyment which they could derive from their skill in killing them. People eat meat with the same thoughtlessness. As a young man I did so, and it never dawned upon me that it was wrong until I found a book on the subject—that was long before the Theosophical Society was founded.

When we have once seen that such "sport" is a horrible thing, and that in following it we are taking part in the slaughter of God's creatures, we wonder why we never noticed it before. Thousands of people have not yet seen the evil. The glamour of custom is upon them, and they have never thought of the frightful harm that is being done. The same thing is true in connection with some articles of attire. There are certain kinds of feathers, for example, that can only be procured at terrible cost in animal life—not only the pain and death of the creature concerned, but generally of other young creatures depending upon it. People who wear these things are certainly criminally careless. They are not desperately cruel—not in the least: they are simply following the custom. Still, karma will operate. A man may be in a brown study and walk over a precipice; the fact that he did not know where he was going does not alter the result.

Such things as these you would not do, I know; and for the sake of the love of God, when opportunity offers, you will speak clearly against them.

C.W.L.—Here we must note the words "when opportunity offers". We do not want to thrust our ideas upon other people, so one speaks on such matters usually only when an opinion is asked, or when the subject comes forward in a natural way. To thrust forward one's own ideas, however excellent they may be, generally does more harm than good. The aggressive people who do this always arouse resentment. A man who accosts you in the street and wants to know whether you have found Jesus, or whether your soul is saved, does not impress you favourably, and most people are inclined to feel that since he is so tactless his religion cannot be of great practical value. If a suitable opportunity occurs one may lend a book or a pamphlet, or converse gently and quietly on the subject. But if you find yourself among a number of sportsmen, I should not advise you to start out by saying: "This is a very wicked thing" —although it is. If I were asked, I should say quietly: "I hold that all life is sacred, that these animals are really younger brothers of ours, and you have no more right to go out and kill them for pleasure than you would have to kill a man for your pleasure." They would be surprised, no doubt; perhaps they would sneer covertly at me; but they would not be so strongly set against the idea as they would if they were attacked.

We who are vegetarians often feel great disgust if we have to sit at the same table with people who are eating meat, yet it is frequently unavoidable when travelling. Still, it is not well to show our feelings; that is certainly not the way to convert other people, but if they ask about our views we can express our opinions temperately, forcefu y but quietly. If we do this it is quite probable, if the man begins to think about it, that he will come over to our point of view.

But there is a cruelty in speech as well as in act; and a man who says a word with the intention to wound another is guilty of this crime. That,

too, you would not do; but sometimes a careless word does as much harm as a malicious one. So you must be on your guard against unintentional cruelty.

C.W.L.—Some people pride themselves on speaking out just what they think, even if it hurts others, and they seem to regard this as a virtue. The Master, who never uses words carelessly, says it may be a crime, if the words are cruel. In debate or discussion we need not refrain from putting our side of the case, but we can put it carefully and courteously. The Apostle said: "Let every man be fully persuaded in his own mind."[1] That does not mean that he is to try to persuade other people, but that he himself should understand why he holds certain beliefs. When that is the case he will be able to state his views, when necessary, gently and temperately.

It is a curious fact that many people cannot differ in opinion from others without getting more or less angry, although they know that there are thousands upon thousands of questions in the world upon which there is so much to be said on several sides that one point of view is almost as defensible as another. A discussion between a Catholic and an Orange-man is exceedingly likely to end in blows, which, after all, do not constitute a form of argument which carries conviction with it. If a person differs from another's opinion it appears to be taken as a kind of slight; such a person is so sure that

[1] Romans, 14, 5.

his own idea is right that any other man who disagrees is wilfully of malice prepense declining to accept it ! We have therefore to be careful how we put our views before others.

There is a special temptation in regard to Theosophy, because we definitely base our belief on reason, and we only try to show people this; yet often the other man cannot see it. Reason, however perfect, however logical, does not necessarily impress the ordinary man at all; he does not live in his reason, but in his feelings, and if these are roused by what is said, no amount of reason will convince him, and the more we talk the angrier he will become.

It comes usually from thoughtlessness. A man is so filled with greed and avarice that he never even thinks of the suffering which he causes to others by paying too little, or by half-starving his wife and children. Another thinks only of his own lust, and cares little how many souls and bodies he ruins in satisfying it. Just to save himself a few minutes' trouble, a man does not pay his workmen on the proper day, thinking nothing of the difficulties he brings upon them. So much suffering is caused just by carelessness—by forgetting to think how an action will affect others. But Karma never forgets, and it takes no account of the fact that men forget. If you wish to enter the Path, you must think of the consequences of what you do, lest you should be guilty of thoughtless cruelty.

C.W.L.—By paying a little less than what a thing is worth one may be causing much suffering to the workman, and his wife and children. The reduction of a few pence from a day's wages may mean that the family has insufficient food. Business is business, I know, but it is better if necessary, to make less rather than fall into the sin of grinding down the poor. Employers are finding that it pays to give "good wages", as has been the experience of Mr. Henry Ford, who is said to be now the richest man in the world. As a priest, I used to go among the poor and see things from their standpoint, and often found people taking advantage of their helplessness. This was so also in India, where sometimes in the Pariah Schools children actually fainted from hunger, until we were in a position to give them food.

CHAPTER 5

SUPERSTITION

Superstition is another mighty evil, and has caused much terrible cruelty. The man who is a slave to it despises others who are wiser, tries to force them to do as he does.

C.W.L.—Superstition never takes into account the differences of temperament between people. It has some form of belief which it wishes to impress upon all alike, not realizing that you never can impress any belief, except, perhaps, some dry scientific fact, upon all people alike, because there are as many attitudes towards life as there are people. Even if you know a great number of people, you will rarely find two who are alike in the way in which circumstances affect them. You can predict certain general possibilities with regard to the great majority of men, but until you know them very well you cannot judge accurately how they will react to certain things. So superstition implies among other things a very great want of sympathy. The man who is subject to it does not understand that there are other ways than his own of looking at things.

Superstition is not only bad for the person himself, but when prominent it always leads to attempts to coerce other people. All through history, superstition in religion has led to frightful trouble. On its account the followers of Muhammad have at different times spread bloodshed and slaughter over vast tracts of Asia, Europe and Africa, offering "the Koran or the sword". The superstition which produced the Inquisition has been previously discussed. The massacres of St. Bartholomew and the Sicilian Vespers, when the Protestants and the Catholics respectively massacred each other were other terrible results of superstition. The last were partly political, but the former was a matter of "religion". The ill-feeling between the different sects of Christians was very largely responsible for the massacre, though no doubt political considerations also had their share in it, as they had also with Constantine when he became a Christian, thinking it a good card to play in the then state of affairs in the Byzantine Empire.

The Crusades were another mighty superstition. Because of a story which had little foundation in fact, as to the life and death of the teacher Jesus, twenty million men lost their lives in those Crusades, trying to get into Christian hands the country where His life story occurred. If they could have been brought to understand that it was the life story of every Initiate, and that that has been led in all countries of the world at one time or another, all that loss of life might have been avoided. Perhaps it was not all loss, however, because by going out to fight with the more enlightened Saracens the Christians brought back, some useful information into Europe, and that they were willing to die for an ideal counted to them for righteousness. There was something chivalrous and beautiful, no doubt, in the idea that the sacred places of a religion ought to belong to the people of that religion. Time has proved, however, that in this case it was fortunate that the Christians did not succeed. In that holy land the Muhammadan soldiers have had to keep peace between the rival Christian sects—the Latin and the Greek—because they always fight for precedence about the holy fire and at the sepulchre.

At the present day we have in India a similar problem, but no one dreams of trying to settle it by the method of the Crusades. The holy places of the Buddhists—the place where the Lord Buddha was born, the place where He attained His Buddhahood, the place where He died—are all in the hands of people of the Hindu faith, a religion which is as different from Buddhism as Christianity is different from Muhammadanism. The Buddhists earnestly desire to possess their holy places, but it has not occurred to the Buddhist nations to start upon a war of conquest. We may be very thankful for that, for the Buddhists number about five hundred million people. Their religion forbids them to do anything so irrational. Some Buddhists have tried to buy back the site, and they nearly succeeded in doing so. The Theosophical Society assisted them, but unfortunately a great part of the money was lost in a law suit, and the plan fell through.

There is no great religion except Buddhism which has never persecuted. It could not do so because of its inherent principles: it is bound to toleration by the very words of its Founder. Who is a Buddhist? He is a man who follows the teachings of the Lord Buddha; not a man who believes this or that, but a man who lives as the Lord Buddha said men should live. Ask a missionary what will become of the really good Buddhist, and he will usually answer, "If he does not believe in Christ, there is no hope for him", or at best he will leave him to the uncovenanted mercies of God, if he is a very good man. If you ask a Buddhist the same question about a good Christian, he will say, "He is quite a good Buddhist; he calls himself a Christian, but he is following the teachings of the Lord Buddha; all will be well with him." Such is the tolerance of Buddhism, as I have explained before. Of course, every religion really forbids intolerance and violence, but the level of ignorance and fanaticism in some of them has blinded their people to this simple fact.

The form of superstition called race hatred, in which one race instinctively dislikes another *en bloc*, is also foolish, because there is good and bad in every race. I remember that in remote villages in England the attitude of the peasantry towards a foreigner was always one of suspicion and ridicule. The fact that a man spoke a different language was something to laugh at, among those ignorant people. There are other peasantries who, in that particular respect, are less uncourteous than our common folk. I always feel that if a foreigner visits our country we are in the relation of host towards him, and it is our duty to make his path easy, and to give him as good an impression of our people and our country as we can.

In the Napoleonic era there was a superstition in England that all Frenchmen were practically devils, fighting against us with the full knowledge that they were on the wrong side and against the light. To-day you may get cases where a vast number of people are obsessed by one dominant idea, resulting in a kind of national monomania. Under the influence of such a temporary monomania dreadful atrocities occur, which the same people would never dream of committing at other times. In this case the individuals are responsible only to the extent to which they allow themselves to be swept off their feet in that way; the things that they do are done by the monomania more than by the individuals themselves. It is in much the same way that a man will sometimes lose his temper and say unpleasant things; it is the temper that speaks and not the man. He is to blame in that he allows the temper to get control of him, but we must take into consideration that in all probability he will afterwards very much regret what he has said.

Think of the awful slaughter produced by the superstition that animals should be sacrificed.

C.W.L.—Mention of animal and other sacrifices in connection with religion raises the whole question of the relation of God to man. There are only three fundamental views that we can take upon this subject: the first is that God started this scheme of things and left it to take care of itself afterwards, being quite indifferent as to what happened to it; the second is that He retains what must be called a malevolent interest in it, desiring to enjoy blood or other sacrifices; the third is that He remains always the all-loving Father of His creation.

The first theory is practically modern materialism plus the idea of an original creator. The second represents God as a monster full of blood-lust. Many of the old scriptures misrepresent Him in this way. In one case in the Old Testament the Jews boast of sacrificing a hundred and twenty-two thousand bullocks at one time. Probably they were exaggerating, as was their habit in those early days. Jehovah demanded sacrifices, and did not in the least care how much suffering he caused so long as he could get what he wanted. He was always clamouring for sacrifices, which must be made to him, and to no other deity. The Jews of the present day would recoil in horror from such a thing, but evidently they did not do so in the days of David and Solomon. It follows that the Jehovah whom they then worshipped was not what we call God, to which conception they could not then rise, but one of the great elemental deities coming over from Atlantean days. The Jews had before then contacted the civilization of Egypt, but its great ideas had made little impression upon them; but later, during the Babylonian captivity, they learned of a supreme God. They at once identified Him, characteristically, with their own Jehovah, and their later prophets wrote magnificently of Him, but still with frequent outcroppings of the old ideas.

Blood-sacrifices belong only to early stages of human evolution. They involve the primitive magic of elemental worship, and are always connected with elementals which live on the fumes of blood. The elemental wants the sacrifices because he absorbs the aroma of the blood and obtains from it the power to materialize himself. Among some hill tribes the people say that if they do not perform such sacrifices troubles come upon them—their crops are spoiled and their houses catch fire; the hill gods of India are therefore also probably great elemental deities of Atlantis.

We may be sure that the Great Ones have never countenanced such sacrifices. In India, for example, the original revelation of the Vedas certainly did not contain them, but they came from the aboriginal traditions, which still exist to some extent. The Lord Buddha spoke against animal sacrifices, and induced King Bimbisara to issue an edict abolishing them in his realm.

Clearly no Deity whom we could wish to worship would want offerings of blood, though there are elementals and nature-spirits who do. We must, therefore, regard those portions of Scripture which deal with such offerings as belonging to a period in human evolution long outgrown. Some people do not like to say this openly, because they reverence the Scriptures, but it is nothing but superstition to regard one particular set of words as sacred and sacrosanct for all time. We ought to be eclectic about the Scriptures, as about everything else. We take up a book, and value and remember those passages in it which we find especially beautiful and helpful. In the same way, we should take from any scripture what is noble and beautiful and grand for all time, and we may with advantage drop all those parts which do not come up to our standards. Although blood-sacrifices are mentioned in the Psalms and other parts of the Bible, we must face the fact that God could never have wanted them; they invariably belong to the type of religion that considers the Deity as an evil being, who must be bought off.

It has been the great tragedy of Christianity that this idea became mingled with the pure teaching of the Christ about God the loving Father. True, animal sacrifices to the Deity have not disgraced Christianity, but the idea of God as a being who will do harm unless bought off is still taught by the great Christian organizations. They invented the amazing theory that God sacrificed his own Son instead of all the other people who would otherwise have been sent to hell. I suppose most people never stop to think what kind of a god it could be who would require or permit such a sacrifice. You can imagine what would be said of any earthly king who condemned quite casually a number of people to horrible tortures and then released them because his own son came forward and said, "If you must kill somebody, kill me. I have not done anything wrong; but nevertheless, kill me, and let these people go free." That theory is not Christianity.

Colonel Ingersoll was right when he said that an honest God is the noblest work of man. It is true that only a nation which was already highly developed could rise to the conception of a really grand and glorious Deity. It is true that our remote forefathers, who ran about in the woods and painted themselves blue, and the ancient war-like Jews, and others, had crude conceptions of the Deity, but there is absolutely no reason why we should carry them on at the present day.

The third theory, which we hold in Theosophy, is that God is beneficent, that He has brought the whole scheme into existence for a purpose which He is steadily pursuing all the time, and that therefore everything that happens is part of His work. He allows a certain amount of free-will to His creatures and they do things which are clearly not in harmony with His great plan; yet as their will is part of His plan, all is ultimately His work.

When we say that God allows man some independence or freedom, we must make it clear that we understand it to be limited, and growing. If a man uses well the freedom and power that he has, more will be given to him. The method seems to be like that by which a little child is taught to walk. The teacher allows him to try, and tumble, and try again; if he were always carried in some one else's arms, so as to avoid all possible tumbles, he would end as a cripple. But what the teacher does not do is to let the child learn to take his first steps alone on a marble floor, at the head of a staircase or in other dangerous places. Later, when he has grown up, he may walk on the edge of a precipice to admire the view, if he so chooses. In some such manner the Logos guards us while He trains us, so that we cannot wreck our lives or hurt ourselves beyond repair.

This third theory is steadily gaining ground. For a long time now, Christianity has been much better than its creeds, and very many Christians have held wider views than their Churches have officially authorized. The Church of England, for instance, formulates what it supposes to be its theory of things in a certain predication called "The Articles of Religion". The clergy have to assent to them, but if one of them should ask, "How am I to accept these Articles; they are evidently contradictory?" he is told that at the time they were written there were two irreconcilable parties, and something had to be said to please them both. They say: "The Bishop and the rest of us have all signed them, we have all taken them in this philosophic way, and since we have done so, I think you may do so, too." The young man will probably say. "Well, I suppose if you assure me that it does not mean anything, I may as well accept it." But the position is not quite dignified.

I have no objection to the Christian Creeds; there is a far deeper meaning underlying them than the Christian usually suspects.[1] But I do object to the Thirty-nine Articles and the Confession of Faith, because with some most beautiful ideas they contrive to intermingle others which are absolutely impossible. If in the Catechism they had only stopped at the end of the first question and answer: "What is the chief end of man? To

[1] See *The Christian Creed*, by C. W. Leadbeater.

glorify God and enjoy Him forever", that would have been magnificent.

Christianity has gone very much ahead of its authorized pronouncements and beliefs. I came across a passage the other day which shows that rather clearly. There is a book by the Dean of Ripon, in which he says: "The development of Christ in man is the object of Christianity." Then he goes on to explain what the Christ in man is: "It is the wisdom of the man of science; it is the eloquence of the lawyer; it is the fairness of the judge; it is the love of beauty in the artist; it is the love of man in the philanthropist," and so on. That kind of Christianity we will all accept. There is very much the same idea in the *Gītā*. "Of rulers," says Shri Krishna, "I am the sceptre; of those who seek victory I am statesmanship; and of secrets I am also silence; the knowledge of knowers am I." "Whatsoever is glorious, good, beautiful, and mighty, understand thou that to go forth from a fragment of My splendour."[1] The Christian Dean is very nearly in agreement with the writer of the *Bhagavad Gītā*, a scripture of immense antiquity, very much older than the *Mahābhārata*, of which it became a part. Much of the glorious teaching incorporated in the *Gītā* existed among the Atlanteans residing on the plains of India long before the Aryan invaders entered the country. I know that that is not the generally accepted idea, but it represents certain facts which we have seen.

[1] *Bhagavad Gītā*, x, 38, 41.

Assuredly we may trust God utterly, because He knows and we do not know. We know, in a general way, what is expected of us in the helping forward of His scheme of evolution, but we do not know the details. Yet we know that those details are in competent hands. What our karma will be we do not know, but the great Powers who are managing the matter know it all, and will decide wisely how much of it can usefully be brought down upon us now, and how much should be reserved for the future. If it were possible for the Great Ones to listen to us, and to change our destiny in accordance with what we think we should like at any time, it would assuredly be the worse for us. I do not say that our own aspirations in the matter are useless—very much the reverse, for if we have good aspirations, those are new factors introduced into the case, and they may well enable the Great Lords to modify the working out of our karma, perhaps to bring down more so that we may the sooner be rid of it, perhaps to alter its incidence and bring it down in some other way. But whatever is done, is done for the best for every one and not for a few only, and so we surely should not try to alter God's will; we should thankfully accept whatever comes to us, and should always make the best of it, not the worst. We should take our difficulties as something to be dominated, yet be always glad because we know that God is behind it all, and He is utterly beneficent.

And by the still more cruel superstition that man needs flesh for food.

C.W.L.—That *is* a superstition, because, there are many millions of people who exist in perfect health without it. There are probably some few people who, owing to bad heredity and their own karma, are really unable to make their bodies digest the purer form of food, but they are very, very few. I have myself known of a few instances, among many hundreds of Theosophists, of people who after really trying for a long time to adopt a vegetarian diet, found that they were unable to do it; but all the rest, after a certain amount of difficulty just at first, were able to maintain and often improve their health on vegetarian food.

It has been proved unquestionably that most people can be perfectly strong without saddling themselves with the crime of taking part in the slaughter of animals. It is but a small percentage of physical bodies that cannot be adapted to vegetarian food. It is an unfortunate condition for these persons, but if one has really tried intelligently to reform one's diet in this way, and finds it impossible, one must accept it as karma. In such a case it is not always wise or right to say, "I will force my body to do what I will, or let it go. I will live on pure food or not at all." It may be that one has duties towards others, which cannot be fulfilled if the body is weak, duties which demand rude health. I know, of course, that advice of this kind may very easily be used as an excuse by those who do not like the higher form of food or who shrink from the trouble of adapting the body to a new diet, but it must be given because there are some few unfortunates who must needs continue in their old ways.

Flesh food is undesirable because it is cruel to kill animals, and also because it brings undesirable particles into our bodies, which coarsen them, and excite animal desires in the elementals of those bodies. There are many other reasons also, which I marshalled together once in a lecture which may be found in my book *Some Glimpses of Occultism.* This is one of the few subjects in which practically all the arguments are on one side, for there is nothing to be said for meat-eating, except that people follow the practice because they like it. I think we can make it abundantly clear to any enquirer that it is entirely in his interests to abstain from flesh food. It is not only a question of principle, although surely that is enough for us, but a vegetarian diet means better health, and the avoidance of certain fearful diseases; and definite facts show that the vegetarian has relatively greater endurance.

People sometimes object to this idea and say that in any case we must destroy life in order to live, that those who are vegetarians also destroy life. That is true, to a very limited extent. I suppose we may be said to be destroying the vegetable life, but that is much more primitive, and has not the acute sentiency of the animal.

The fundamental objection to killing is that it interferes with the course of evolution. If you kill a man, you really do no harm to that individual, so far as his pleasure and happiness are concerned; he goes usually to a plane where he will be far happier than he ever was on the physical plane; and the mere destruction of the body is not necessarily cruel, because a man killed suddenly does not feel it. The wrong you have done is to cut him off from the opportunity of evolution which he would otherwise have had in that body. He will have a further opportunity in another body later on, but you are delaying him, and giving the Lords of Karma the trouble of finding another place for that man's evolution, and of carrying him on again through babyhood and childhood before he has the opportunity for development that the conditions of mature manhood provide. That is also why it is so much more serious to kill a man than an animal; the man has to develop an entirely new personality, but the animal goes back into his group-soul, from which incarnation is a comparatively easy matter. Still, in the case of the more evolved animal, which is a more complicated manifestation, it causes, if we may reverently put it so, a great deal of trouble to the evolutionary Powers. The killing, say, of a mosquito is an infinitely smaller matter, because it flows back into its group-soul and comes out again in a very short time. The trouble caused by the destruction even of hundreds of thousands of those insects is as nothing compared to the killing of one horse, or cow, or cat, or dog.

There is no conceivable case in which it could be the right thing to kill a man for any purpose of one's own, except in emergencies in self-defence or the defence of another. The yogi does not even defend himself; he leaves the whole matter in the hands of karma. Still, I believe that we are justified in defending our lives when they are attacked, and I am quite certain we are justified in defending a friend or a child, even at the cost of killing the aggressor. The same thing holds good with regard to all kinds of animals. If an animal attacks you, endangering your life or your safety, you have, I think, the right to kill it if necessary. The whole question is : which will cause the greater harm ? If, for example, you are troubled by mosquitos, which have left their own natural food to attack you and poison your blood, and perhaps spoil some important work, it might very well be the lesser evil to kill the mosquitos. If you can take refuge behind a mosquito net, or drive them away, so much the better. The mosquito is vegetarian by nature and by instinct. There are millions upon millions of them which have never tasted blood. Bring them into contact with human beings and give them that vitiated taste and you know how it turns out. It is exactly the same with a variety of other small pests. They are good in their proper place, but that is not in close contact with human beings. Not only do we ourselves suffer if we permit them to overrun us, but we also subject other human beings to infection from which they would have been free if it had not been for us.

Though, with our imperfect knowledge, it gives us no special justification to kill or exterminate any creature offensive to us, it is a fact that some forms are now intended to die away, either because they have run their course, or because they are experiments that have been improved upon and are therefore no longer needed. It is not irreverent to think of the great evolutionary Powers as experimenting to some extent. The Lord Maitreya, when He succeeded the Lord Buddha as World-Teacher, tried some new methods in religion, which might conceivably have failed. Madame Blavatsky used sometimes to speak guardedly of certain plants and animals as failures, whose life-form was being permitted to flow on and die out gradually, being used sometimes for the indwelling of creatures lower than those originally intended to occupy them and sometimes even for those undergoing involution. She spoke of certain loathsome forms of insect and reptile life as "by-products", and considered that the killing of these was by no means the same thing as the destruction of evolving forms of life.

The theory of the non-destruction of life is carried to extremes in certain places, as for example, where people decline to kill vermin, and allow themselves to be eaten by them. That does not commend itself to any civilized person. Again, a person who has a library of useful books will sometimes find them attacked by little silver-fish. It would be preferable to drive them away, but it is better, certainly, to destroy those insects than to allow good books, which might be of use to others besides oneself, to be rendered useless. There are many small forms of life which if we permit them, would render our lives practically impossible. For the yogi, who never destroys life, food is always provided, but the agriculturist who provides it has to protect his crops from grubs and worms. In Australia he has particularly to deal with rabbits, which having been imported into the country, have increased in such millions that if left free to do so they would destroy every vestige of cultivation.

It is not only for the sake of food for man that one must destroy some of the pests, but also as a matter of protection, for if one cultivates plants, or trees or vegetables, one has a certain responsibility to the life that takes up its dwelling in those forms. I think we should use common sense in all these matters all the way through. In any case, to kill any animal in self-defence is surely a different thing from killing highly evolved creatures, such as cows and sheep, to gratify a low form of taste, when it is absolutely unnecessary.

> Think of the treatment which superstition has meted out to the depressed classes in our beloved India, and see in that how this evil quality can breed heartless cruelty even among those who know the duty of brotherhood.

C.W.L.—The depressed classes in India, sometimes called the panchama, or fifth caste, really the outcaste, the pariah—are the descendants of the original inhabitants of India, whom the Aryans found there when they came over the Himālayas. The caste rules ordained by the Manu, which were good eugenic and magnetic rules at the time, forbade the settlers to intermarry or mix or eat with them. Beyond that, however, they have been treated with great cruelty. For instance, the pariah is not allowed to approach the caste well to draw water, because he will contaminate it for the caste people; consequently he has to depend upon such inferior wells as he can make or find, and this often causes serious hardships, especially as in some parts of the country the outcaste villages have been driven to unfavourable plots of land, and often forced to move. Until quite recently a pariah could hardly attain a good position in life, except by the undesirable expedient of becoming a Christian or a Muhammadan, a course which removes some of their most serious social disabilities.

This, and even worse than this, has been the treatment which superstition has meted out to these depressed classes, even among people who make a speciality of brotherhood. In this case they have forgotten what brotherhood means, because of their superstition. One hopes that in time they will come to form a respectable and clean community. Modern conditions, such as the mingling that takes place on trains and tramcars, tend to facilitate this process.

It is the duty of the better classes of the Indian people, and also a kārmic obligation upon them, to uplift these outcastes whom their ancestors conquered. Their very nobility, their innate Aryan quality should urge them to this necessary task. If a child is not clean we do not recoil from him, but we take him to be washed; so must we not shrink from the pariah, but provide him with conditions in which he can acquire health, cleanliness and knowledge. It is not necessarily a question of eating together, but it is assuredly our duty to be kindly and compassionate to our younger brothers.

It is true that birth in a given caste or community always offers a man certain definite opportunities, but it does not follow that he is making the best of them. To be born into the family of a good man of lower caste would offer better opportunities in some ways than to belong to the family of an unworthy Brāhmana. Often men strive for some goal, and when they attain it they fail to make good use of opportunities which it brings; hence a bad Brāhmana may be one who is taking his first incarnation as such, or who has neglected or misused his opportunities in a former birth. It is true only in rare cases that:

> Who toiled a slave may come anew a Prince
> For gentle worthiness and merit won;
> Who ruled a King may wander earth in rags
> For things done and undone.[1]

As a general rule those who are in the great mass of the working classes will only gradually raise themselves into the bourgeoisie, and then higher. Most of a man's karma is made with the class of people among whom he is, and he needs similar conditions for working it out in a future life. The way of evolution is also by gradual advance in culture and refinement, so a sudden transition into a distinctly higher or lower class is somewhat in the nature of a surgical operation, necessitated by very exceptional karma. Still, mankind is one family, and the duty of brotherhood applies to all without exception.

Many crimes have been committed in the name of the God of Love, moved by this nightmare of superstition.

[1] *The Light of Asia*, Book VIII.

C.W.L.—One other point about superstition is that the man who does the most harm because of it is the one who has the best intentions, who is standing loyally to the letter of his law. A really selfish bad man—there are such people, though perhaps not very many—is concerned mostly with gratifying his own desires. He does not want to interfere with others unless they obstruct his way; so, after all, he does not do so much harm in the world. The stupid person with good intentions is really a far more serious danger, because he always wants to interfere with others. Missionaries, for example, are often a case in point. I do not doubt that the missionaries sent out from Europe and America have done much good among Central African savages and people of that type, but in India, where any common labourer in the street usually knows more than the missionary about the philosophy of religion, about all the greater and higher ideas, the missionary is ridiculously out of place. His intentions are good enough, but he does a great deal of harm. Many wars have been caused by the irrational methods of missionaries; their State has to step in and save them when they are in danger of what they call martyrdom. It has come to be a regular thing: first the missionaries, then those selling brandy and gin, and after them a conquering army. Poor old ladies in England and America even go without the necessities of life in order to help these missions, and think they are doing it for Christ's sake! They have absolutely no conception that thousands of years before Christ India had a profound religion and philosophy, and that their money could be better employed in converting the heathen in England itself.

Be very careful, therefore, that no slightest trace of it remains in you.

C.W.L.—The emphasis which is laid upon it clearly shows that there is a danger that we may be superstitious without knowing it, so it is well that we should carefully watch. There are always at least two sides to any question. No one sees the whole thing—not even the Theosophist. When we become consciously one with the Logos on His own high plane, then we shall see all round everything, and be able to say: "My view is right", but when that occurs our view will probably include all the others, because there is generally some germ of truth in all.

These three great crimes you must avoid, for they are fatal to all progress, because they sin against love.

C.W.L.—That love should govern our lives and vivify all our other powers is the special teaching of the line to which the Master Kūthūmi belongs. It is difficult for many to understand exactly how the Masters, who contain within Themselves all the highest and the noblest qualities which we can imagine, can yet somehow have one quality more than another. The Master Morya, who represents to us the First Ray, has for His greatest characteristic will and power, yet it would be a mistake to suppose that He has any less of love or of wisdom than any of the other Masters. So also should we be quite wrong in supposing the Master Kūthūmi to have any less power than Masters of the First Ray. These are differences beyond mere human knowledge.

In the same way there are distinctions of level among the Great Ones; the Bodhisattva stands far higher than our Masters. To us They all appear so great that we cannot venture to make any distinction between them. They are all suns of blinding light, and to us there seems no difference between a great Angel and a Devarāja; yet one is a whole kingdom, a whole evolution above the other. It must be that the Solar Logos has greater power than all these that are parts of Him; although it seems as though no being could have more than They. The knowledge and the power of the Master are so much greater than ours that for us the whole thing is one blinding glory; but the distinction exists.

CHAPTER 6

SERVICE

But not only must you thus refrain from evil; you must be active in doing good. You must be so filled with the intense desire of service that you are ever on the watch to render it to all around you—not to man alone, but even to animals and plants. You must render it in small things every day, that the habit may be formed, so that you may not miss the rare opportunity when the great thing offers itself to be done.

C.W.L.—We may very often miss a chance of helping some one if we have not formed the habit of watchfulness; but if we have that habit we are not likely to pass many opportunities, because it will assert itself, even in the most unusual surroundings or in the greatest emergencies. That is the whole reason of the long, rather painful drill through which soldiers are put; not only that they may know exactly what to do when certain orders are given, but that they may have certain habits instinctively part of them. In battle in the old days, if not to-day, the soldier found himself in absolutely novel surroundings, that might well try his courage, however brave' he might be, conditions such that a man might well be excused if he lost his head. But even in such an emergency habit would assert itself, and the man would obey orders and do what was required.

This remark about being active in doing good is not directed in any way against those whose activity is on other planes. Such a remark as that might easily be wrongly used against the contemplative orders of monks and nuns, or the Brāhmana caste in India. The theory in the old days was that the Brāhmana was the spiritual leader of the nation, and he was supposed to devote all his time to the performance of ceremonies and rites, and to study and teaching and giving advice, which would benefit all the community. The other people, whose lives were taken up in ordinary work, and in making money, supported him because he was doing this spiritual work for them. A similar idea in Catholic countries is behind those orders of monks and nuns whose time is taken up in praying for the dead. In the days when those arrangements were made it was recognized that the dead and the living were one community, and that this was a far higher service to the community than the growing of corn; therefore those people received their living in charity and were in nowise ashamed of it, and those who gave to them felt themselves highly honoured. The whole conception was entirely different from the modern one; there was no shame whatever attached to begging for a living; in fact, those who did it were the most spiritual of the people, bound by the vows of poverty, chastity and obedience. To condemn the people who lived in that way is to make exactly the same mistake as was made in the French Revolution, when they said that a philosopher or a writer was a man living an idle and useless life, and that he ought to be breaking stones upon the road.

> For if you yearn to be one with God, it is not for your own sake; it is that you may be a channel through which His love may flow to reach your fellow-men. He who is on the Path exists not for himself, but for others; he has forgotten himself, in order that he may serve them.

C.W.L.—The whole idea of this book is to get people into a certain attitude. What is aimed at is not nearly so much to know as to be; that is, to live the Theosophical life, to be filled with love for all and with an intense desire to help forward evolution, so that we forget ourselves in the service of others. If you ever saw a surgeon perform a big operation, you know how a man in the most intense activity and with the keenest use of brain and hand, can yet be absolutely absorbed in the work he is doing, with his whole life, as it were, in the ends of his fingers. In war, too, a man sometimes forgets himself utterly in the effort to save a wounded comrade or to perform some necessary but dangerous deed.

The Logos is omnipotent in His system; He pours out force at all levels in that system. We cannot but suppose that He could flood the whole system with that force at any level and to any extent that He chose. As a matter of fact He does not do that; the force poured out at each level seems to be a definite amount, and of a definite kind only, and so it remains that we, who are sparks of His fire can do certain things which the Great Flame of which we are a part does not do, except through us, who are parts of Him. We cannot say that He could not do it, but that He does not, apparently. It is within our power, with our intense devotion, setting our wills to work along with His will, to draw down more force from higher planes, to transmute it and send it out. That is work which would not be done, as far as we can see, unless we did it. It would seem that He counts on our co-operation. Yet that is also His, because there is no force that is not His.

I have several times used the simile of a channel or pipe to help in describing the fact that the force of the Master is distributed on lower planes by a pupil. One may use also the simile of the transformer of electricity; you have great quantities of electricity sent at high pressure, perhaps hundreds of miles from the generating station, to the transforming station in a city; there are there transformers which receive it at that high pressure, and convert it into huge volumes of current at lower pressure, suitable for lighting and other purposes. So a pupil in Sydney, for example, may receive the Master's force coming on higher planes from the Himālayas, and transform it into force of the lower planes, so that it may be distributed around him or directed to those for whom it is intended.

Every Initiate is thus a transformer of spiritual force; through him it can flow at a certain level, according to his stage or degree. The divine force is all round us, just as the sun is shining all the time. When the sunshine does not reach the earth it is the earth's doing, except during a solar eclipse, because it raises clouds which come between it and the sun; so also do men raise clouds of selfishness and ignorance between themselves and the Logos, who is raying out a great variety of His forces on every plane. The Initiate takes a definite step which enables him to be a better channel for these forces. It is not that the forces are themselves in the least affected—they are there all the time, but they pass us by when we are not ready to receive them.

Let us take the analogy of prāna on the physical plane. Every body draws in prāna, but sometimes when a man falls ill he is unable to specialize it for himself, and soon begins to feel a great lack of vitality. Although he is then unable to specialize prāna for himself, he can still use that which has been prepared by another; another man, abounding in vitality, may pour it upon him and give him the strength that he requires to enable him to recover his normal condition. Similarly, the Initiate takes up many of the higher forces and transforms them into a condition in which they become readily assimilable by others. As more and more of our mankind reach the stage at which they can do this work the evolution of men in general will increase in rapidity. Though it is true that there is a limit to the amount of sunlight that plants can bear, it is also true that it is impossible to pour upon any man too much of the spiritual light.

Do not, however, think of these channels as merely passive. They are living channels. The pupil is not sitting still and simply acting as a pipe. There are forces that do come through like that, and the pupil of the Master is often conscious of the nature of the force pouring through him and knows to whom it is going. But there is also a great amount of it which he can at any time employ as he will, which he can turn this way or that, as he sees it to be needed. His own adaptability and tact are thus called into play, and his life is very full indeed of positive activity of this kind. His is not, therefore, a life of blind obedience—on the contrary, he is busy when others are idly thinking about themselves.

Ordinary men cannot commonly be used in this way, because they are not sufficiently developed on the higher planes, and because even when the ego is somewhat advanced the thread of connection with the personality is very narrow. The Master can use the pupil because the channel is open; so also can the One Initiator use the Initiates for the force of the Hierarchy. In these cases the man is the higher self, and even when he is engaged in the duties of the physical plane there is the feeling always in the background of the mind: "I am I; a spark of the Divine; I can do nothing unworthy of That; *noblesse oblige.*"

Because of the importance of the work, the relation between Master and pupil is never based on sentiment, though it is full of the deepest affection that the world can know. The Master does not accept a man as a pupil because some other member of his family is a pupil or because He has known him in previous lives. Both Master and pupil think only of what was called in Egypt "the hidden work", the building up again of the riven body of Osiris, the reuniting of the scattered fragments. They know of "the hidden light" in every man, "the jewel in the lotus", through which he can always be helped when the appeal is rightly made. This was the work of the Initiates in ancient Egypt, as it is of those of to-day. They use the power that made the worlds, the love of God, which is not personal. No one is bound to come forward into occultism, but if he does so he must adopt the motto and attitude of the Brotherhood, which is to live not for himself, but for others, not for personal advancement or satisfaction, but for the work.

He is as a pen in the hand of God, through which His thought may flow, and find for itself an expression down here, which without a pen it could not have.

C.W.L.—It would seem that He must have calculated that at a certain stage of evolution He would have many such pens through which He could write, that God Himself, as a poet puts it, "needs you and me." Our help is part of the plan. That is a grand idea and very logical; we see at once that if we have been able to reach a level of knowledge, of love, of power which is a little higher than the standard about us, we have done it in order that we may be of use in distributing it to others.

Yet at the same time he is also a living plume of fire, raying out upon the world the Divine Love which fills his heart.

C.W.L.—There is a story of two Alexandrian monks who wanted to keep themselves perfectly pure; one did it by making round himself a shell of protective thought, but the other was so full of the love of God that it rayed out from him all the time and kept him pure. There are always the two ways of the occultist, who progresses by work in the world, and the mystic, who retires into himself. In many cases the aim of the mystic is simply to become utterly one with God; yet it is not right to call him selfish, because even in the act of so becoming he must and does shed a tremendous influence on all around him. Our aim, that of the occultist, should be to raise ourselves step by step through all the different stages until at certain high levels of Initiation we can merge our consciousness in the Third Aspect of the Deity, then with the Second Aspect, and finally with the First. The mystic throws himself into the Divine Life here as he stands, but it is a lower manifestation of the Divine Life; then he has to work upwards in order to feel himself one at higher levels also.

The wisdom which enables you to help, the will which directs the wisdom, the love which inspires

the will—these are your qualifications. Will, Wisdom and Love are the Three Aspects of the Logos ; and you, who wish to enrol yourselves to serve Him, must shew forth these aspects in the world.

C.W.L.—That is a beautiful ending, my brothers. As Alcyone achieved, may you attain.

INDEX

INDEX

Printed by C. Subbarayudu, at the Vasanta Press,
The Theosophical Society, Adyar, Madras